This book is due for return by the last date shown above.
To avoid paying fines please renew or return promptly.

Portsmouth
CITY COUNCIL
LEISURE SERVICE

CL-1

D1427202

Bla
Pub

BLACKWELL PUBLISHING
9600 Garsington Road, Oxford OX4 2DQ, UK
350 Main Street, Malden, MA 02148-5018, USA
550 Swanston Street, Carlton, Victoria 3053, Australia

First published 2005 by Blackwell Publishing Ltd as a special issue of *Journal of
Law and Society*

Library of Congress Cataloging-in-Publication Data
The Human Rights Act: a success story? / edited by Luke Clements and Philip A.
  Thomas.
    p.   cm.
  ISBN-13: 978-1-4051-2375-4 (pbk.: alk. paper)
  ISBN-10: 1-4051-2375-3 (pbk.: alk. paper)
    1. Great Britain. Human Rights Act 1998. 2. Human rights–Great Britain.
3. Civil rights–Great Britain. I. Clements, L. J. (Luke J.) II. Thomas, Philip A.
(Philip Aneurin)
  KD4080.H8613   2005
  342.4108'5–dc22   2004029752

A catalogue record for this title is available from the British Library.

Set in the United Kingdom
by Godiva Publishing Services Limited
Printed and bound in the United Kingdom
by J W Arrowsmiths

The publisher's policy is to use permanent paper from mills that operate a
sustainable forestry policy, and which has been manufactured from pulp processed
using acid-free and elementary chlorine-free practices. Furthermore, the publisher
ensures that the text paper and cover board used have met acceptable
environmental accreditation standards.

For further information on
Blackwell Publishing visit our website:
www.blackwellpublishing.com

Contents

Contents

JOURNAL OF LAW AND SOCIETY
VOLUME 32, NUMBER 1, MARCH 2005
ISSN: 0263-323X, pp. 1–2

The Human Rights Act: A Success Story? Introduction

LUKE CLEMENTS* AND PHILIP A. THOMAS*

The Human Rights Act 1998 is still an infant: a child whose first five years have been marked by momentous – and potentially damaging – experiences. The papers in this volume seek to assess its health and prospects for a full and well balanced development.

Sir Stephen Sedley introduces the collection with a wide ranging review of the progress and pitfalls that have marked these early years. In his opinion there is much positive to report concerning this 'historic constitutional project' although much inevitably remains to be done.

The Act is but one strand of a constitutional reform programme that includes devolution and the reform of the Lord Chancellor's role. As to devolution, Professors Tom Mullen, Jim Murdoch, and Alan Miller, and Sarah Craig report on their research concerning the use of Convention law in the Scottish courts. Professor Christine Bell and Johanna Keenan then take the analysis across the water to gauge the post-Belfast Agreement Northern Irish experience through a case study on the right to life. The Welsh perspective is provided by Ruth Costigan and Professor Philip Thomas with an account of their research at the 'coal face' in the deprived south Wales valleys' communities. Their conclusions are bleak: that the area is largely an 'HRA-free zone', not least as a consequence of the restructuring of legal aid.

Roger Smith describes the process by which the reform of the Lord Chancellor's role has surfaced as a key constitutional issue. He considers the 'appallingly handled' upheavals that led to the decision to abolish the LCD and the challenges that are yet to be addressed. Foremost amongst these is the establishment of a Commission with power to enforce the fundamental provisions of the Act. The need for such an institution is considered by Anthony Lester (Lord Lester of Herne Hill, a principal architect of the Act) and Lydia Clapinska.

Two issues above all others have dominated the public's perception of the Act: terrorism and asylum. Professor Conor Gearty analyses the extent to which the laudable aims of the Act have been subverted by the government's response to the September 11 attacks. As to the latter, Shami Chakrabarti

* Cardiff Law School, Cardiff University, Museum Avenue, Cardiff CF1 3NX, Wales

describes how the government has sought to create a link between asylum and threats to national security, and used targeted destitution as a means of undermining the protection afforded to asylum seekers.

It is not only in the media-topping fields of terrorism and asylum that the Act's impact falls to be assessed. If global warming is indeed a greater risk to world security than terrorism – then what has been the Act's impact on environmental law? This question is addressed by Professor Robert Lee. Professor Philip Fennell analyses the extent to which the Act has influenced the debate concerning the reform of the Mental Health Act 1983 – and suggests that, in certain key respects, it has been used as a vehicle to undermine rights. This issue is also addressed by Luke Clements in a paper that considers the incongruity between the government's strategies for combating social exclusion and civil justice.

Like any report on a five year old's progress, there is considerable uncertainty as to the future. The insights in these papers, however, provide wise counsel as to the future development of this much admired infant.

JOURNAL OF LAW AND SOCIETY
VOLUME 32, NUMBER 1, MARCH 2005
ISSN: 0263-323X, pp. 3–17

The Rocks or the Open Sea:
Where is the Human Rights Act Heading?[1]

SIR STEPHEN SEDLEY*

This essay attempts a broad appraisal of how the Human Rights Act 1998 has been interpreted and applied by the courts of England and Wales since it came into force in October 2000. These are early days, but its provisional conclusion is that the Act, despite some judicial hesitancy, is proving viable and, at least in some respects, beneficial.

By October 2000, when the Human Rights Act 1998 came into force, so many predictions had been made about the effect it was going to have on British society and on the United Kingdom's law that it seemed inevitable that one of them would be right. But life is always more interesting and complicated than predictions and probabilities allow. If it weren't, judges and lawyers would be out of a job and parliamentary drafters would rule the world. So neither those idealists who hoped to see a new era of respect for individual rights and freedoms, nor those who, like the Scottish judge Lord McCluskey, foresaw 'a field day for crackpots, a pain in the neck for judges and legislators, and a goldmine for lawyers'[2] have turned out to be right. Nor was central government, which – perhaps panicked by much-publicized comments like Lord McCluskey's – had started to plan for a Canadian-style torrent of constitutional litigation.

Nor was I right – not entirely right anyway – in the foreboding I had expressed more than once during the previous decade that these were rights which if enacted into law would be hijacked by the rich and powerful. Through the door pushed open by Michael Douglas and Catherine Zeta-Jones, seeking to protect the commercial value of their wedding reception,[3]

* *Lord Justice of Appeal, England and Wales, The Royal Courts of Justice, Strand, London WC2A 2LL*

First appeared in *Legal Action* magazine, December 2003.

1 This paper was initially delivered as the 2003 Legal Action Group Lecture. It is updated to October 2004. Abhijit Pandiya and Geoff Davies have provided invaluable research assistance.
2 In *Scotland on Sunday*, 6 February 2000.
3 *Douglas* v. *Hello! Ltd (No 1)* [2001] Q.B. 967

came the two young men convicted of killing James Bulger, now approaching release on licence and threatened by the tabloids with exposure of their new identities and whereabouts. The President of the Family Division was able to build on the then recent decision in the *Douglas* case in order to protect the safety and privacy of two youths very much at the bottom of the social pile.[4]

In a paper I gave in 1995,[5] I made a characteristically rash but uncharacteristically accurate prediction that by the turn of the century the United Kingdom would have a bill of rights. I added:

> There are no guarantees that better educated courts will get everything right, but to be sent, as history is sending us, on a voyage without modern navigational aids and supplies is to experience the worst of both worlds, the old and the new.

Even so, I argued that we ought to assemble the equipment and go on.

Today, three years into the new world, there is still a vast amount to be done in creating access, not necessarily to litigation but at least to an awareness that certain rights are now there to be claimed. The indignities which the elderly and the infirm sometimes suffer in institutions are only one of many examples of the shortfall. The treatment of prisoners' families is another. And when it comes to enforcement, we are starting to appreciate that there are large geographical and social gaps in the legal profession's ability to provide advice and representation.

But it's too soon to draw up a balance sheet. A profit and loss account perhaps – though even here there are important arguments to resolve about whether some major items are to go in the debit or the credit column, and I want to look at some of these. Above all, the experience of the past twenty years in Canada has shown us how temporary any evaluation of a bill of rights is likely to be. Pierre Trudeau's Charter of Fundamental Rights and Freedoms, which was enacted in 1982 and came into force three years later, was hailed by political liberals as the Supreme Court reconfigured Canadian law and, to an appreciable degree, Canadian society to their reading of the Charter. Their opponents both on the left and on the right denounced the process as the judicialization of politics. Then, as the Charter entered its second decade, liberals saw the Supreme Court's jurisprudence going backwards and began to ask whether they had been too ready and too fulsome with their support.

Time's whirligig, in other words, keeps turning. The Canadian Supreme Court is not afflicted with the politicized appointments which dog the Supreme Court of the United States, but in both courts majorities ebb and

---

4 *Venables* v. *News Group Newspapers Ltd, Thompson* v. *News Group Newspapers Ltd* [2001] Fam. 430.
5 S. Sedley, 'Human rights – a 21st century agenda' (the 1995 Sieghart Memorial Lecture), published in *Human Rights for the 21st century*, eds. R. Blackburn and J. Busuttil (1997).

4

flow. In the United Kingdom's supreme court – which the Appellate Committee of the House of Lords will soon be – the added random element of a tribunal of five judges drawn from a panel of twelve or more makes the prediction of outcomes still harder. But the bottom line in a common law system is that judicial policy is what comes out of decisions rather than what goes into them. So when I turn to some of the patterns that are starting to be discernible in the human rights decisions of our highest courts (the plural is there to include the Privy Council's present jurisdiction over devolution and some Commonwealth issues), I shall try to do it by deconstructing judgments in search of policy.

But that is not my only objective. If the courts produce the outputs, it is the university law schools which – along with the providers of professional training – produce the inputs, and I am concerned that they are still not, or not all of them, doing justice to human rights. So, alongside the question of what the highest courts are up to, I want to have a look at what the universities are up to.

By the time I found myself chairing the Judicial Studies Board (JSB)'s working group which (as I suppose I have to describe it) was tasked with delivering training on the upcoming law to the whole of the judiciary, full-time and part-time, of England and Wales, the legislation was a reality and the question was whether the courts were going to make it work or reduce it to a dead letter. By the beginning of 2000 we had a carefully crafted day's programme of lectures and case-studies, chaired by either the JSB's director of studies or myself, which over the next nine months was attended by every judge in the country from Lord Justice to Deputy District Judge, and by several of the Law Lords. We stressed that there were as yet no right and wrong answers: only right and wrong approaches to them. It became rapidly apparent that no tranche of the hierarchy had an inside track on the Convention or the Act. It was heartening, too, that we encountered very little resistance of the curmudgeonly kind, and that much of what there was dissipated at those seminars which were attended by judges of the Strasbourg court. British judges saw that the authors of the decisions to which we were now required to have special regard were not swivel-eyed alien ideologues or puppets manipulated by Buchanesque foreign powers (neither image very far from what we were reading in sections of our press), but were capable lawyers dealing with problems that we recognized, using forms of reasoning that we could readily relate to.

The European Convention on Human Rights is a child of its time – the post-war years when the states of western Europe tried set their faces both against the devastation of the recent past and against any new form of totalitarianism. So the Convention says many important things about due process, personal integrity, and free speech and ideas, but nothing directly about the most elementary of all human needs: a right to enough food and shelter to keep body and soul together. Nor does it say anything about something else we would surely today regard as a fundamental human right,

5

a wholesome environment. Even so, it was inevitable, and in many ways practical and desirable too, that the European convention would constitute the substance of Labour's human rights legislation. It was not only ready-made; it was a regime to which the United Kingdom had acceded by treaty and which, uniquely, was administered by a supra-national court to which citizens had individual access.

It is here, I think, that the source lay of our mistaken anticipation of a litigation deluge when the Act came into force. Unlike Canada, the United Kingdom was not embarking on an uncharted sea. By the century's end the European Court of Human Rights had established a solid body of jurisprudence on the meaning and effect of the Convention. Where in Canada, for Charter advocates, the sky was the limit, in Europe the limit was already largely set for us. That is not to say that over-ambitious cases have not been presented, nor that the jurisprudence of the Strasbourg court has not continued to grow, not least in response to cases from the United Kingdom. But in broad terms we have known from the start where the limits were.

If, however, the point of a human rights regime is to protect people from the abuse of power, there is a major problem with the European Convention, which – again for historical reasons – is cast in a mould which counterposes the citizen to the state. In the five decades since it was signed, the foci of power first in western and then in eastern Europe have shifted steadily away from the state and into private and largely corporate hands. There is something out of joint, it seems to many people, in a major news corporation coming before the courts under article 10 as a victim of state oppression. The asymmetry, however, lies less in the reversal of the roles of David and Goliath than in the resultant paradigm of power without responsibility, for nowhere in the armoury of human rights are citizens given a right not to be deceived or lied to by the public or private corporations which control the supply of information, nor even a right to reply publicly to calumny or falsehood. Any such claim is repulsed as a fetter on freedom of expression.

So there is a problem here. Lawyers, rather inaptly, have christened it the problem of horizontality – the enforcement of human rights as between individuals or, more relevantly, between individuals and private corporations. My own sense of it is that there can be no direct translation of individual rights against the state into individual rights against non-state entities. It is Strasbourg's inventive doctrine of the positive obligations of states to protect people from the violation of their fundamental rights by private as well as public actors which offers a principled bridge across that divide. What I think we can legitimately look for, in addition, is a cascade effect by which private law becomes gradually infused with Convention values. As I shall suggest, the Human Rights Act gives a strong and conscious push in this direction. What it is not going to do is change the world.

At the JSB we assumed without any serious inquiry that the universities and law schools would already be realigning their syllabuses to take account

6

of an innovative Act which was explicitly designed to permeate the whole of our legal system and much of our law. It was to the next generation of lawyers that we looked with some confidence to complete the education of the judiciary for, in a system which still prizes oral advocacy, judges do listen and learn.

But an enterprising survey conducted by Professor Philip Thomas of Cardiff University among the 88 institutes of higher education in England and Wales with law schools, shortly after October 2000 when the Act came into force, showed alarmingly uneven responses.[6] Of the 66 universities which replied (statistically a very good return, though one wonders about the 22 who failed to respond at all), something like a fifth were still not offering any human rights teaching. In most of the others, human rights was only an optional module. Only one in five had done what we at the JSB had assumed all universities would do – bring human rights into all their courses. A more recent research paper from the United Kingdom Centre for Legal Education[7] suggests continuing goodwill but little change in practice in our universities.

It has to be said that this is not good enough. I would not have thought such a comment particularly controversial; but an article I put in the *JSB Journal* about the pedagogic shortfall produced an unnervingly defensive response from a leading legal academic. 'It is the behaviour of the judges in their judgments,' he wrote, 'that will tell teachers how much of their courses need to be rewritten in the light of the Act. Research,' he went on, 'can lead the development of the law. Teaching must, to some extent, follow its development.'[8]

Of course – but to *what* extent? It may well be true of traditional areas of substantive law that they have to be taught with a primary regard to what the judiciary say the law is – though not, I hope, without considering whether the judiciary are getting it right. But the Human Rights Act is designed to generate a new approach to law: a requirement that all public bodies act with due regard for individual rights, and a requirement that all statutes – even those governing private law relationships – be construed so far as possible in ways which respect these rights. I do not understand how the law of evidence, for example, can now be responsibly taught without incorporating the jurisprudence of the Convention into it. The same is true, though perhaps less dramatically so, of tax and property law, of consumer and tort law, and so forth.

I do not accept that academic freedom is a sufficient answer. How subjects are taught is of course a matter of professional judgement. But law schools are teaching a real subject in a real world, and universities are there

---

6 See S. Sedley, 'Learning human rights' in *Human Rights Protection: methods and effectiveness*, ed. F. Butler (2002). P.A. Thomas, 'The Human Rights Act: Ready, Steady, Go?' (2001) 35 *Law Teacher* 360.

7 N. Whitty et al., *Teaching Human Rights* (2002).

8 A. Bradney, 'Another legal revolution' (2002) 15 *JSB J.* 14.

above all to teach people to think. How lawyers and others think affects the progress of the law, and what happens in the law affects people's lives.

A better excuse may well be the lack of resources. Law teachers who themselves know little or nothing of the Convention cannot be expected to start teaching it unaided. So far as I know, no resources have gone, either locally or regionally, into the retraining that many law teachers require. But the case for obtaining these resources is holed below the waterline if at the same time it is suggested that the teaching of human rights need only be elective and reactive. Apart from anything else, wait-and-see law teaching is self-defeating. The moment at which it freezes the frame will tomorrow be history: the first instance judgment which has just been overturned by the Court of Appeal will have been restored by the House of Lords; the definitive decision of the House of Lords will have been held by the European Court of Human Rights to put the United Kingdom in breach of the Convention. Only by thinking critically about what they are reading – which means understanding and applying human rights law – will students become the good and creative lawyers we need in the courts.

It would be wrong, even so, to suggest that the judiciary are having to find their own way. We have a sizeable and growing body of practitioners who have a thorough knowledge and understanding of the Convention and its jurisprudence, and we depend on them for informed arguments. But the outcomes are our responsibility, and it is at some of these that I now want to look.

When, in the run-up to the implementation of the Human Rights Act, I wrote the foreword to the Legal Action Group (LAG)'s still invaluable handbook on European human rights law,[9] I noted a series of issues which at that stage were unresolved: the relation between the supranational and domestic margins of appreciation; the status of commercial speech under Article 10; the relevance of the Convention to environmental protection; the horizontal applicability of rights; the positive obligations of states; the role of the courts as themselves public authorities; improperly obtained evidence – the fruit of the poisoned tree; equality as a freestanding right; the impact of Article 8 on immigration and asylum, and on child protection.

Three years on, and perhaps not surprisingly, pretty well all but the last of these issues remain unresolved: some because they have not come up in useful form before the courts; some – like the margin of appreciation – because they have become muddled rather than clarified; some – like the use of unlawfully obtained evidence – because there probably is no single principled answer; some – like the question of horizonality – because they are in the process of being resolved, but quietly and in slow stages.

I'll explain what I mean about the margin of appreciation when I look at the issue of deference. Horizontality – the application of Convention rights

9 K. Starmer, *European Human Rights Law* (1999).

8

between citizens rather than against the state – is still sharply contested in theory but developing incrementally in practice. Early in the Court of Appeal's decision in the Gary Flitcroft privacy case, you find this:

> ... under s. 6 of the 1998 Act the court, as a public authority, is required not to act 'in a way which is incompatible with a Convention right'. The court is able to achieve this by absorbing the rights which articles 8 and 10 protect into the long established action for breach of confidence. This involves giving a new strength and breadth to the action so that it accommodates the requirement of those articles.[10]

The outcome of the Flitcroft case was, even so, that publication of a highly invasive story amounting to little more than soft pornography was allowed to go ahead. But the principle is there now, and different facts will perhaps generate different outcomes.[11]

More generally, too, it seems inescapable from the terms of s.3 of the Act that even the considerable body of statutes which regulate private law relationships is to be reinterpreted wherever possible so as to give effect to the Convention rights. Without fuss this has been absorbed into – for instance – housing law practice so that, wherever it has to be decided whether it is reasonable to make a possession order against a residential occupier, the court will take it as an Article 8 exercise and – if it is doing its job properly – will go carefully through the elements of proportionality in order to decide whether the interference is justified.[12] The outcome will in most cases be no different from that produced by the blunter test of reasonableness; but it will now be transparently reasoned out – itself a requirement of a fair trial under Article 6 – making it possible on appeal to see whether or not there has been an error of approach.

This kind of change in the modes of legal reasoning does not make headlines but may well turn out to be one of the most fundamental changes worked by the Act. To it we almost certainly owe the decision of the House of Lords in *Daly*[13] to consign the rigidities of *Wednesbury* reasoning to history, and to recognize, at least where fundamental rights are in issue, an obligation on the courts to look considerably harder at the proportionality of what the state does.

The margin of appreciation was always going to be a headache. To start with, it's a meaningless expression in English. It entered our vocabulary as a piece of translationese in the *Handyside* case in 1976,[14] where the bizarre conviction of the publisher of the Little Red Schoolbook for obscene libel was upheld by the Court of Human Rights by a process of deference to the

---

10 *A* v. *B and C* [2002] 3 W.L.R. 542, para. 4.
11 See, also, *Naomi Campbell* v. *Mirror Group Newspapers* [2004] U.K.H.L. 22.
12 *Qazi* v. *Harrow LBC* [2003] U.K.H.L. 43 limited the application of proportionality but only where there is an absolute right to possession.
13 *R (Daly)* v. *Secretary of State for the Home Department* [2001] U.K.H.L. 26.
14 *Handyside* v. *United Kingdom* (1976) 1 E.H.R.R. 737.

9

domestic courts whose decisions, in theory, the Strasbourg court was there to invigilate. The French phrase *marge d'appréciation* in fact signifies a margin of judgment, a defined area within which legitimate differences are possible. But the literal rendering of the phrase has enabled it to acquire a protean significance roughly equivalent to a doctrine of simple deference. In spite of efforts on all hands to stop it happening, it continues to be used in relation to domestic acts and omissions under scrutiny in our own courts. One result has been that the overdue demise of the *Wednesbury* doctrine has been to an extent rolled back by the loose use of a supposed margin of appreciation – sometimes in those words, sometimes using the phrase 'the discretionary area of judgment' – in gauging the legality and Convention-compatibility of governmental measures.

What, like many others, I consider to be the true analysis has now been stated by Lord Hoffmann in the *Pro-Life* case:

> Although the word 'deference' is now very popular in describing the relationship between the judicial and other branches of government, I do not think that its overtones of servility, or perhaps gracious concession, are appropriate to describe what is happening. In a society based upon the rule of law and the separation of powers, it is necessary to decide which branch of government has in any particular instance the decision-making power and what the legal limits of that power are. That is a question of law and must therefore be decided by the courts.
> ... When a court decides that a decision is within the proper competence of the legislature or executive, it is not showing deference. It is deciding the law.[15]

One of the big questions which remains is whether, in applying the Human Rights Act, the highest courts have in fact been more deferential to Parliament than Parliament itself, by enacting section 3, intended them to be. The issue has arisen most sharply in relation to declarations that primary legislation is incompatible with the Convention; but it arises too where primary legislation could be reshaped to accommodate Convention rights and the courts have to decide whether to do so.

I do not find the relative rarity of declarations of incompatibility problematical – not, at least, in itself. The policy of the Act is that they should be a last resort, and the unwillingness of the House of Lords to make or uphold such declarations, save where the legislation is plainly out of proportion to the problem, reflects that intent. Where a real problem is perhaps arising is in relation to what Parliament intended to be the courts' *first* resort – the reading and implementation of legislation, whenever it was passed, so as to make these as far as possible compatible with the Convention rights. The process is, at least in theory, uncomplicated: if the courts can read legislation compatibly with the Convention, they must do so – s. 3 says so; only if that is not possible should they pass the buck back to Parliament by making a declaration of incompatibility under s. 4. But if a

---

15 *R* v. *BBC, ex parte Prolife Alliance* [2003] U.K.H.L. 23, para. 75-6.

conservative use of the s. 4 power is harnessed to an equally conservative use of the s. 3 power, Parliament's great scheme of permeating the statute book with human rights values may start to falter.[16] I should add in self-defence that my remark in a mental health case[17] that s. 3 is nothing like as revolutionary as strict constructionists have suggested was not, as I think has been suggested,[18] a call for retrenchment: it was intended only as a sideswipe at those who think that a Parliamentary intent can anyway be read off the face of any but the clearest legislation.

Let me take a single case to illustrate what I mean. The Children Act 1989, one of the great reforming statutes of our generation, makes provision in broad and relatively unspecific terms for courts to place children who are at risk in the care of the local authority. The necessary practice is for the local authority to formulate a care plan so that the court can see whether a care order is appropriate. But local authority social service departments are chronically overstretched and under-resourced, and if a care plan then falls apart – the grandmother who was going to look after the child dies, for instance – there is nothing in the Children Act which requires social services to return to court for a fresh order. The death of a small girl named Tyra Henry, into which I chaired an inquiry in 1986,[19] was a far from unique illustration of what can happen when the basis of the care order has collapsed and social services have lost track of the child, but the court has no further role in supervising the order. My panel of experts unanimously called for the court to be given such a role; and although, predictably, nothing was then done, the coming of the Human Rights Act seemed to many people to afford a tailor-made occasion for the courts, now with Parliament's express authority, to protect a vulnerable child's right to life and to recognize their own responsibility for doing so by reading into the Children Act an obligation on the local authority to return to the court if a significant part of the foundation of its care order collapses.

In 2001 a Court of Appeal which contained two of the four most senior family law judges in the country held that this could and should be done.[20] Their decision was overset by the House of Lords.[21] The House took the view that what the Court of Appeal had done went beyond interpretation and amounted to amendment of the Children Act. Was the Children Act as it

---

16 In *Ghaidan* v. *Godin-Mendoza* [2004] U.K.H.L. 30, Lord Nicholls suggested that the courts were still 'cautiously feeling their way forward' in their application of s. 3. He confirmed that the application of s. 3 does not depend upon legislative ambiguity and that the court may be required to depart from the legislative intention of Parliament and change the meaning of enacted legislation so as to make it Convention-compliant.
17 *R (Wooder)* v. *Fegetter* [2002] E.W.C.A. Civ. 554.
18 K. Starmer, 'Two years of the HRA' [2002] E.H.R.L.R. 14.
19 *Whose Child? The Report of the Panel of Inquiry into the Death of Tyra Henry 1987* (1987).
20 *Re S (Care Order: Implementation of a Care Plan)* [2001] E.W.C.A. Civ. 757.
21 *Re S (Care Order: Implementation of a Care Plan)* [2002] U.K.H.L. 10.

11

stood therefore incompatible with the Convention? To this too the House said no. In its judgment neither Article 8 nor Article 6 was sufficient to require the state to make some provision for bringing the care order back to the court if the care plan collapsed, even if its collapse put the local authority in breach of the Convention. As to Article 8, it was reasoned that the real problem, if there was one, was the lack of a remedy for a local authority's failure, an issue which arises if at all under Article 13, which is not one of the Convention rights scheduled to the Act. I will say something in a moment about this gap, as I now think it is, in the HRA. As to Article 6, while the House was prepared to accept that the United Kingdom could find itself in breach through the lack of provision for court oversight, this would at most be a lacuna in the Children Act and not an incompatibility. The case is on its way to Strasbourg. For the present I simply draw attention to it as an indicator of an arguably restrictive approach at the highest level of our judiciary to these all-important provisions of the HRA.

The intellectual fascinations of the still problematical can, if one is not careful, eclipse the importance of some of the relatively unproblematical and entirely positive developments there have been under the Human Rights Act. There is not space to give a full account of them, but the progress made over these three years in the protection of patients detained under the mental health legislation, and in establishing the right of prisoners to a judicial determination of questions affecting their prospective release, has been solid and creditable. Its solidity derives from two things. One is the judgments of the European Court of Human Rights, holding the Home Office's grip on the release of prisoners and the medical profession's grip on the liberties of mental patients to be contrary to the guarantee in Article 5 of a judicial decision if liberty is to be curtailed. The other is a series of decisions of the Court of Appeal and House of Lords giving this jurisprudence domestic effect. It is creditable because it represents a principled stance against the populist throw-away-the-key revanchism from which judges are not insulated and which (I deliberately use a strong word) jeopardizes the separation of executive and judicial power.

There is an argument – incapable of resolution but still important – as to whether all or most of these reforms would have come without a Human Rights Act. Perhaps, therefore, the most signal decision of all, because the issue is a freestanding human rights issue which before October 2000 could not have got through the door of the court, is the decision of the House of Lords that the state's positive obligation under Article 2 towards the life of persons in its custody requires government to set up an independent public inquiry into the placing of 19-year-old Zahid Mubarak in a cell in Feltham Young Offenders' Institute with a known racist bully who killed him.[22] The leading speech of Lord Bingham, restoring the pioneering decision of Mr

22 R v. *Home Secretary ex parte Amin* [2003] U.K.H.L. 51.

12

Justice Hooper, is not only in itself a vindication of Parliament's decision to put the Human Rights Act on the statute book; it demonstrates the coherence of the jurisprudence of the Strasbourg court, out of which the decision of the House logically and organically grew. Perhaps, too, the decision will give a necessary impetus to the proposals in the Luce Report[23] for making our creaking coroners' system something closer to an instrument of justice and closer to our obligations under the Convention.

Where arguably Strasbourg has lost the plot is in relation to self-incrimination. So it's encouraging that the Privy Council, exercising its jurisdiction over Scotland's devolved criminal justice powers, has declined to follow suit. The European Court of Human Rights, you may recall, declined to make any distinction between what you could call ordinary crime and regulatory offences.[24] There's no doubt that compelling people to answer random police questions even if the answer incriminates them is deeply distasteful to most of us, though Jeremy Bentham could see nothing wrong with it. But that simply is not the same thing as society offering people a deal, whether it be in order to let them run a public limited company or drive a car. The deal is that in return for a licence to do something advantageous to them but potentially harmful to the public they may have to answer for what they do, and that if their answers show them to have committed offences they may find the answers used in evidence against them. The Privy Council has declined to follow the path taken by the Strasbourg court in holding that Ernest Saunders's answers to departmental inspectors should not have been used against him at the Old Bailey.[25] It has held that there is nothing contrary to the Convention in the law which requires the owner of a car to say whether she has been driving it, even if admitting it means admitting a crime. I would regard the decision as a welcome illustration of the policy of s. 2 that, while we must always take the Strasbourg jurisprudence into account, we are at liberty to improve on it.

On the debit side stands what is probably the result of a structural weakness in the Act itself, but one which has been compounded by a pair of decisions of the House of Lords[26] which the House itself has recognized as – to use a moderate word – unsatisfactory. This is the seemingly dry but in reality important issue of retrospectivity. Section 3 of the Act is explicit in requiring the rereading of legislation whenever this was passed. Section 27(4), in uncharacteristically oblique language (for this is a beautifully simple and generally lucid piece of legislation), aims to do the same wherever proceedings are brought against someone in reliance on a measure or step which would not have been Convention-compliant had the Act been

23 Home Office, *Death Certification and Investigation in England, Wales and Northern Ireland* (2003; Cm. 5831; Chair T. Luce).
24 *Saunders* v. *United Kingdom* (1996) 23 E.H.R.R. 313.
25 *Brown* v. *Stott* [2001] 2 W.L.R. 817.
26 *R* v. *Kansal (No 2)* [2002] U.K.H.L. 62; *R* v. *Lambert* [2001] U.K.H.L. 37.

in force when it was taken. For the rest, the subsection makes it clear that the Act is not retroactive.

There is a plain enough policy here: that, legislation apart, old measures are not to be unpicked on grounds which did not even exist when they were enacted, except where to apply this rule would make somebody the continuing victim of a measure which was but no longer is acceptable. That makes eminent sense in relation, say, to a prosecution in 2001 under a by-law made in 1999 which unreasonably suppresses free speech. If it were not for s. 27(4), such undead measures would haunt us for generations to come. But what the drafter and Parliament seem to have overlooked is the possible effect of carrying this principle into the criminal justice system at large. Does it make sense to consider oversetting a criminal conviction from the 1980s or 1990s because the law stated in the judge's summing-up was not Convention-compliant – not only because it did not have to be, but perhaps too because it could not lawfully be? Because of what now looks like an oversight in the drafting of the Act, the House of Lords has found itself in an avowedly unsatisfactory, perhaps untenable, position on this issue. But presented with the possibility of starting again, the House chose instead to leave things where they were.[27] Quite where that is, we shall have to see.

Of other structural problems which have emerged, the worst may turn out to be one I've already flagged up: the legislature's (or more realistically the government's) decision not to enact Article 13, the right to a remedy. In principle this was because the Act itself was intended to provide a comprehensive set of remedies. But the predictive powers of legislators are still imperfect, as the great Scots jurist Stair pointed out they were over three hundred years ago, and those who argued at the start that this was a significant gap in the Act seem to have been right. To take one example, the failure of the Coroners Rules to allow a verdict to apportion blame for a death would be justiciable under the Human Rights Act if Article 13 had been included among the scheduled Convention rights. Instead the rules must await ministerial attention.[28] If the House of Lords is right, the childcare case I mentioned earlier affords another example.

In at least one other respect, however, the policy of the Act has been seen in effective operation. I am thinking of s. 19, which requires ministers to inform Parliament whether Bills are Convention-compliant. To have to tell Parliament that a Bill is not compliant is to take a serious political risk; it has become correspondingly important for ministers to able to state that their legislation will respect Convention rights. This, in turn, makes it necessary for the promoting department of state and the drafter to make reasonably sure that it is so. It is thanks to this imperative that the Nationality, Immigration and Asylum Act 2002 included in s. 55 a provision that the

---

27 *Wainwright* v. *Secretary of State for the Home Department* [2003] U.K.H.L. 53.
28 This has proved wrong: see the important decision of the H.L. in *R* v. *Home Secretary ex parte Amin* [2003] U.K.H.L. 51.

14

denial of benefits to asylum-seekers who did not claim asylum as soon as reasonably practicable was not to operate so as to breach their human rights.

Presented with cases of utter destitution brought about by the principal provision, the courts in the course of 2003 held that to deny individuals both the opportunity to work and any public assistance while they await a decision on their asylum claim amounts to treatment by the state which therefore breaches Article 3 if it is or becomes inhuman or degrading. The consequence was a major flow into the courts of asylum-seekers denied benefit or housing under the new system and now hungry, homeless, and frequently ill. To rescue them, judges of the Administrative Court made over 1,000 emergency orders for interim payment of benefit. In barely any of these cases did the Home Office return to court to get the order discharged. It is thanks to the safety net which s. 19 of the Human Rights Act required to be placed under this drastic legislation, and perhaps also to the judiciary's unwillingness to pass by on the other side, that these people are not starving in the streets.[29]

This said, there remains and will remain for, I suspect, a long time the issue of the human rights of people who are neither lawful entrants nor refugees. What if, although they have no legal right to stay here, they face return to a country where their human rights are likely to be violated? There is no point in pretending that the courts' decisions here have been taken in a vacuum. We have had to draw practical lines. We cannot know, though we can often guess, whether the restrictions in those states on the qualified Convention rights – private and family life, freedom of thought and religion, freedom of expression and freedom of assembly – will be capable of justification. But if everyone at risk of such violations were proof against removal, the entire system of immigration control *and* of asylum would collapse. No claim need be anything but a human rights claim. So we have steadily fallen back, without pleasure but perhaps inevitably, upon a limited set of risks within the unqualified provisions of Articles 2 and 3 – the right to life and the right not to face torture or inhuman or degrading treatment.[30]

Even here we face huge problems. Many AIDS sufferers whose asylum claims have failed are now receiving treatment under the NHS which they could not find, much less afford, in their home countries. To return them will almost certainly be to shorten their lives, sometimes dramatically, and to condemn them to a wretched end. Is it inhuman to return them? The courts

---

29 The Home Office abandoned the entire system following the decision of the Court of Appeal in *R (Limbuela and others)* v. *Secretary of State for the Home Department* [2004] E.W.C.A. Civ. 540.

30 But see, now, the House of Lords decisions in *R (Razgar)* v. *Secretary of State for the Home Department* [2004] U.K.H.L. 27 and in *R (Ullah)* v. *Special Adjudicator* U.K.H.L. 26, which have shown that a person may rely not only on Articles 2 and 3 but also 5, 6, 8 and possibly 9 to resist a decision to remove them to a state where anticipated ill treatment would or might result in a flagrant denial of these Convention rights.

with growing frequency are saying no. I am not here to say whether the decisions given so far should go into the debit or the credit column. I simply point out that the Human Rights Act sets us a series of new and sometimes dramatic problems to which it furnishes no ready answers.

I am conscious of not yet having said anything about privacy. It's quite true that the right to respect for an individual's private and family life is enshrined in Article 8, subject to necessary exceptions. It's true, too, that the secret policeman whom the framers of the Convention had in mind in 1950 has in significant part been supplanted by the tabloid journalist, who is not – or not yet – a state official for Article 8 purposes, and who enjoys rights of free expression which are protected by Article 10. Without doubt the Convention rights could have been developed in the handful of high-profile privacy cases which have come before the courts in the last three years so as to create the kind of balance between the rights of celebrities to a little peace and the right of journalists to tell all which the German courts have long since elaborated under the German constitution and which the French courts had been striking for some years before the right to privacy was formally enacted in their Civil Code. That has not happened here. But the weakness – and I believe it to be a serious weakness – has not lain in our understanding or use of the Convention. The decision of the House of Lords in the *Wainwright* case[31] manifests a reasoned hesitancy, but a hesitancy nonetheless, to do anything in this fraught area for the first time. There a mother and brother visiting a prisoner who were subjected, in the pre-Human Rights Act era, to a degrading and unnecessary body search were denied any remedy for the invasion of their privacy. This was almost certainly the last opportunity for the courts to hold, as I suggested in the interlocutory appeal in the *Douglas and Zeta-Jones* case[32] it was open to us to hold, that the common law itself had matured to a point where the action for breach of confidence – essentially a means of defending intellectual property interests – would also protect the autonomy of individuals in the face of unjustified invasions of their privacy. That moment has now gone. Some will see it as a wise policy of leaving the complex issue of privacy to Parliament. Others will see both Parliament and the courts as rabbits in the headlights of the press. The argument will roll on.[33]

The House of Lords did, however, recognize that in similar cases arising in and after October 2000, Article 8 will enter the picture; it certainly does not follow from what has happened in cases against the media in these years that an abuse by state officials of the power of search will continue to go unredressed. But there remains the discouraging possibility that if the courts again allow salacious revelations to be published about a minor celebrity

31 [2003] U.K.H.L. 53.
32 [2001] Q.B. 967.
33 See, now, *Naomi Campbell*, op. cit., n. 11, applying the doctrine of breach of confidence to issues of private life.

16

without any apparent regard, for example, to the effect of the publicity on his young family, the United Kingdom may once more find itself coming second in Strasbourg.

There also remains a series of questions about a subject I didn't mention in my original list of unresolved issues – the award of damages for violations of Convention rights. The first claims are being heard amid a degree of unease that litigants are joining lawyers on the trail to Lord MacCluskey's goldmine. But Parliament was quite clear, when it enacted s. 8, that damages were to be available to victims of violations, and the courts are going to have to work out an approach which has rather more consistency than the awards to be found in Strasbourg.[34]

The passing of the Human Rights Act 1998 was a historic constitutional project. It set out to do two chief things: to supplant the received method of statutory interpretation – the divining of Parliament's intention through the drafter's words – by a purposive reading which would reconfigure legislation wherever possible to give effect to Convention rights; and to compel all public authorities, the courts included, to respect those rights in everything they did and decided. In these two fundamental respects it may be said that the courts are not yet fulfilling the mandate which Parliament has given them. Where they are succeeding is in two particular fields. One is the reshaping of important areas of substantive law affecting vulnerable minorities to give effect to Convention rights. The other is a gradual realignment of the processes of legal reasoning, and it is this which in the long term may turn out to be the more significant – whether for better or for worse, future commentators will have to say.

So are we heading for the rocks or the open sea? I do not want to make that stark choice. Perhaps it's enough that, though the weather is uncertain and the course not clearly charted, we are making headway.

---

34 See, now. *Anufrijeva and Another* v. *Southwark LBC* [2003] E.C.W.A. Civ. 1406: damages for infringement of Article 8 rights must afford just satisfaction, and the approach in this jurisdiction should be no less liberal than that of the European Court of Human Rights.

JOURNAL OF LAW AND SOCIETY
VOLUME 32, NUMBER 1, MARCH 2005
ISSN: 0263-323X, pp. 18–33

11 September 2001, Counter-terrorism, and the Human Rights Act

Conor Gearty*

The attacks of 11 September 2001 and the reaction to them has been the gravest challenge to date to the Human Rights Act 1998. The Anti-terrorism, Crime and Security Act 2001 has expanded the remit of the Terrorism Act 2000 and there has been a new concentration on anti-terrorism by government. This article assesses the impact of human rights law on the debate about liberty and security following 11 September. It considers how the provisions of the Human Rights Act have influenced the formulation and interpretation of anti-terrorism laws, and examines the role of the judiciary in adjudicating on disputes between the individual and the state. It ends with some general discussion about the security-driven challenges to human rights that lie ahead.

INTRODUCTION

It is clear that the events of 11 September 2001 have posed a major challenge to the philosophical and political integrity of the Human Rights Act. The basic premise behind the concept of human rights, which is said to be encapsulated in legal form in the 1998 Act,[1] is that of the equality of esteem in which each and every one of us is held in view of our humanity. September 11 has exposed this idea to attack on two fronts by a pair of very different ideological enemies.[2] First there has been the challenge of politicized religious faith. In its initial manifestation, a highly particular

* Centre for the Study of Human Rights, London School of Economics and Political Science, Houghton Street, London WC2A 2AE, England

1 See, for the debates on the Bill in Parliament where its rationale is discussed and explained, J. Cooper and A. Marshall-Williams (eds.), *Legislating for Human Rights. The Parliamentary Debates on the Human Rights Bill* (2000).
2 For an anticipation of the kind of problems that human rights was likely to encounter as a result of these structural weaknesses, see M. Koskenniemi, 'The Effect of Rights on Political Culture' in *The EU and Human Rights*, ed. P. Alston (1999) ch. 2.

reading of Islam[3] has made possible the use of thousands of innocent people as instruments in an attempt to ignite world-wide Islamic revolution, a denial of the victims' esteem so gross as to amount to as grave an abuse of human rights as has been witnessed in the recent past.[4] Reacting to these atrocities, and opportunistically drawing strength from them, there has emerged into the international open a different brand of fundamentalism, this time connected to Christianity, which preaches the moral validity of a war against an open-ended category of evildoers, whose humanity matters less than their perfidy.[5] Joining with the latter sentiment and greatly exacerbating it is a strong collective instinct, beginning in the United States of America but spreading across the world, for national survival, a patriotic devotion to a piece of land that leaves the cosmopolitan citizen first puzzled and then lost for words.[6] This prioritization of territory over people amounts to a second front in the 'War on Human Rights' that (it is now evident) the inflated language of the 'War on Terror' inevitably entails.

It is with one smallish theatre in this global conflict, the interrelationship between the Human Rights Act and United Kingdom counter-terrorism law and practice, that this chapter is concerned. Has the existence of the Human Rights Act made any difference to the content and enforcement of Britain's terrorism law? Would the human rights situation be worse without the Act, or could it – just conceivably – actually be better? Though in its initial justification not rooted in the demands of anti-terrorism, the invasion and occupation of Iraq, in which this country has been deeply involved, have greatly increased international tension and our alleged vulnerability to terrorism. So it is also relevant to ask here what has been the effect on human rights law – indeed on the very language of human rights itself – of this unpopular military adventure. The meta-question behind these various interrogatives is how, if at all, our concern for the equal dignity of all – of which the Human Rights Act is our clearest legal symbol – can survive in a contemporary political and legal culture that has become so deeply preoccupied with matters of war, politicized religious belief, and national security. It is possible that historians writing just a few years from now will regard the idea of human rights as little more than a quaint reminder of a brief liberal interregnum between two kinds of world conflict, the first ending in 1989, the second starting in 2001.[7] If this does prove to be the case, what kind of future lies in store for the Human Rights Act? More to the point, what can be done to prevent the emergence of such a dismal narrative?

3 See G. Kepel, *The War for Muslim Minds. Islam and the West* (2004).
4 For an excellent survey, see G. Oberleitner, 'Human Security: A Challenge to International Law?' (2005) 11 *Global Governance*.
5 Kepel, op. cit., n. 3, ch. 2.
6 Epitomized by the Uniting and Strengthening America by Providing Appropriate Tools Required to Intercept and Obstruct Terrorism Act 2001 (the USA Patriot Act).
7 With more despairingly critical articles like that of K.D. Ewing, 'The Futility of the Human Rights Act' [2004] *Public Law* 829.

19

It is important to acknowledge that the tension between anti-terrorism law and human rights in the United Kingdom long predates the attacks on the Pentagon and the Twin Towers. The problem of political violence arising out of the conflict in Northern Ireland had produced a large body of anti-terrorism legislation during the preceding thirty years,[8] with the European Court of Human Rights in Strasbourg having been frequently called upon to adjudicate in conflicts between terrorist suspects and the state,[9] and on one celebrated occasion between two states, the United Kingdom and the Republic of Ireland.[10] The power of the Human Rights Act 1998 should not blind us to the importance of human rights standards prior to its enactment; international treaty obligations may not have been enforceable directly by court order but they were treaty obligations nonetheless, and in the case of the European Convention on Human Rights, furthermore, they were duties whose true meaning could be fleshed out by a regional court and whose implementation once subject to such adjudication was (as it still is) overseen by a specialist committee.[11] The problem of human rights standards being used to legitimate restrictions on political freedom and on civil liberties generally was also clearly in evidence in this early period.[12]

The Human Rights Act 1998 itself had an active engagement with terrorism law prior to the events of 11 September. Published in the same year as the measure was enacted was the government's White Paper on terrorism,[13] building on a report into this brand of political violence which had been published two years before.[14] These were early days in the reception of the language of human rights into the domestic legal culture, and it is therefore perhaps not entirely surprising that this White Paper should have made only scant reference to the implications for its subject of a piece of

---

8 See L.K. Donohue, *Counter-terrorist Law and Emergency Powers in the United Kingdom, 1922–2000* (2000); C. Walker, *The Prevention of Terrorism in British Law* (1992, 2nd edn.). For a current survey, see C. Walker, *Blackstone's Guide to the Anti-terrorism Legislation* (2002).

9 For example, *Brannigan and McBride* v. *United Kingdom* (1993) 17 E.H.R.R. 539.

10 *Ireland* v. *United Kingdom* (1978) 2 E.H.R.R. 25.

11 See C.A. Gearty, 'The United Kingdom' in *European Civil Liberties and the European Convention on Human Rights. A Comparative Study*, ed. C.A. Gearty (1997). A. Tomkins, 'Civil Liberties in the Council of Europe: A Critical Survey' in the same volume contains much useful historical information on the role of the Committee of Ministers.

12 See K.D. Ewing and C.A. Gearty, *Freedom under Thatcher. Civil Liberties in Modern Britain* (1990); C.A. Gearty, 'The Cost of Human Rights: English Judges and the Northern Irish Troubles' (1994) 37 *Current Legal Problems* 19.

13 Home Office and Northern Ireland Office, *Legislation against Terrorism. A Consultation Paper* (1998; Cm. 4178).

14 *Inquiry into Legislation Against Terrorism* (1996; Cm. 3420; Chair, Lord Lloyd of Berwick).

legislation which had emanated from the same department just one month before. The document opened up for discussion the introduction of an executive power of proscription for organizations deemed by the Secretary of State to be involved with 'domestic or international terrorist activities',[15] with the proposed definition of terrorism being wide enough to extend beyond violence to the person to encompass 'serious disruption' of various sorts.[16] This sat uneasily with the guaranteed right to peaceful assembly and association that Parliament had just included in the other measure as a core human right,[17] a right that had in turn been the subject of robust interpretation in two, then very recent, Strasbourg cases.[18] This latter jurisprudence was one, moreover, to which Parliament had just explicitly directed the executive and judiciary to have regard when interpreting the breadth of the rights it had enacted.[19]

In the period of further reflection that followed the White Paper and preceded publication of the Bill, the human rights dimension to the proposals was digested and the end result, the Terrorism Act 2000, showed the impact of human rights thinking in several important respects. First, and this was anticipated in the White Paper,[20] the statutory power to detain terrorist suspects for seven days without charge was abolished and replaced by a system which involved judicial oversight from an earlier stage, not later than the end of the fourth day in detention.[21] Second, the thrust of human rights law, which is to assert the primacy of the ordinary criminal process over exceptional police powers, was manifested in the increase in the variety and jurisdictional range of criminal offences related to terrorism.[22] Thirdly, the system of proscription eventually set out in the new Act contained various procedural mechanisms which greatly diluted the potential for arbitrariness in the exercise of the power, provided the organizations proscribed with effective opportunities for appeal, and as a result almost certainly brought the whole scheme well within the framework of the Human Rights Act, with the right to freedom of association set out in that Act allowing exceptions where these could be shown to be 'necessary in a democratic society'.[23] It is noteworthy that none of these concessions to human rights law involved the bald elimination (as opposed to mere

---

15 Home Office, op. cit., n. 13, para. 4.17.
16 id., para. 3.17.
17 Human Rights Act 1998 (HRA), sched. 1, art. 11.
18 *United Communist Party of Turkey* v. *Turkey* (1998) 26 E.H.R.R. 121; *Socialist Party* v. *Turkey* (1998) 27 E.H.R.R. 51.
19 HRA, s. 2.
20 Home Office, op. cit., n. 13, ch. 8.
21 Terrorism Act 2000, ss. 40 and 41, reacting to *Brogan* v. *United Kingdom* (1988) 11 E.H.R.R. 117.
22 id., ss. 54–64.
23 HRA, sched. 1, art. 11(2). So in *R* v. *Hundal and Dhaliwal* [2004] E.W.C.A. Crim. 389 the unsuccessful challenge to convictions under s. 11 that was mounted in the Court of Appeal did not even seek to rely on art. 11.

21

procedural elaboration) of powers desired by the executive;[24] right from the start the human rights standard set by the Act in the field of anti-terrorism law has been a relatively low one, with the consequence that only a rather undemanding jump by the executive brings its repressive practices within the zone of human rights compliance.

11 SEPTEMBER 2001

In considering why it was that the legislature proved sensitive to the demands of an Act that was not yet fully in force, with the Terrorism Act 2000 having received the Royal Assent before the date of full implementation of the Human Rights Act, the significance of section 19 of the latter Act should not be underestimated. This provision came into effect as early as 24 November 1998.[25] It required the Minister responsible for a Bill to make, in relation to any such proposed measure, 'a statement of compatibility' or of incompatibility between it and the Convention rights set out in schedule 1 to the Human Rights Act. The effect of this provision has been to internalize within the executive branch the need to assess the human rights implications of its legislative initiatives; as such it is 'an important provision in balancing the role of the executive, Parliament, and the courts'.[26]

Helpful in relation to the Terrorism Bill, section 19 became an even more important pointer towards the importance of human rights law in the difficult months that followed the atrocities of 11 September 2001. During this period, the Anti-terrorism, Crime and Security Bill was conceived and placed before Parliament, receiving the Royal Assent as early as 14 December 2001 after a speedy and highly controversial passage through both Houses of Parliament.[27] In its final form, the measure contains provisions on the disclosure of information,[28] the policing of the nuclear[29] and aviation industries,[30] the retention of communications data,[31] and general anti-terrorism police powers[32] which may with some justification be legitimately considered obnoxious when viewed from a civil libertarian perspective. The

---

24 Interestingly, the one power entirely removed from the range of terrorism laws by the new Labour Government was the power of exclusion which did not in itself raise human rights problems under the Convention, at least in relation to those provisions to which the United Kingdom was committed in international law.
25 Human Rights Act 1998 (Commencement) Order 1998 (S.I. no. 1998/2882).
26 J. Wadham, H. Mountfield, and A. Edmundson, *Blackstone's Guide to the Human Rights Act 1998* (2003, 3rd edn.) 10.
27 See, generally, P.A. Thomas, 'September 11th and Good Governance' (2002) 53 *N. Ire. Legal Q.* 366.
28 Anti-terrorism, Crime and Security Bill 2001, part 3.
29 id., part 8.
30 id., part 9.
31 id., part 11.
32 id., part 10.

seizing of the opportunity to implement the third pillar of the European Union without adequate democratic scrutiny[33] might also be thought to be wrong in principle. There are plenty of valid concerns as well about the sheer bulk of the legislation (129 clauses and eight schedules) with doubts being raised as to exactly how much of it was 11 September-related and how much it amounted to little more than an opportunistic attempt to enact a range of legislative ideas that had been gathering dust in various Home Office cupboards.

As a result of section 19, and also the probability of legal challenge in the future, much of the discussion of the new Bill was conducted in the language of rights. The human rights case against these powers was put in a couple of powerful reports issued by the Joint Committee on Human Rights, a body that would not have existed had it not been for the political atmosphere created by enactment of the Human Rights Act.[34] Despite this, the executive persevered with many of its more illiberal initiatives, and was indeed able to use the breadth of the exceptions in the Human Rights Act to camouflage its intentions with a veneer of human rights sensitivity. It is the case, however, that some concessions were secured which arguably might not have been obtained without the 1998 legislation. Plans to introduce retrospective criminal legislation on bomb hoaxes were dropped even before the Bill was published, with Article 7 of the European Convention on Human Rights (prohibiting retrospective punishments) playing a part in the critical response.[35] An expansion of the law to include incitement to religious hatred was omitted after a strongly negative report on the proposal from the Home Affairs Committee of the House of Commons.[36]

The criticisms that these bodies and other parliamentarians and commentators made[37] were probably not dependant on the Human Rights Act for their existence, in that they would have been made and might well have been successful without the existence of the Act. But their arguments undoubtedly drew strength and energy from being able to point to a piece of legislation which in theory at least posited an alternative legislative vision of the relationship between the individual and the state. Perhaps the best way to put it would be that the human rights critique was able to bite where there was already strong background unease about government proposals, but that it was not effective where no such concerns existed, and that it was not even

33 id., ss. 111–112.
34 See Joint Committee on Human Rights (JCHR), Second Report, *Anti-terrorism, Crime and Security Bill* HL (2001–2002) 37, HC (2001–2002) 372; JCHR, Fifth Report, *Anti-terrorism, Crime and Security Bill: Further Report* HL (2001–2002) 51, HC (2001–2002) 420.
35 id., Second Report, para. 12.
36 Home Affairs Committee, First Report, *The Anti-terrorism, Crime and Security Bill 2001* HC (2001–2002) 351, paras. 56–61.
37 H. Fenwick, 'The Anti-terrorism, Crime and Security Act 2001: A Proportionate Response to 11th September?' (2002) 65 *Modern Law Rev.* 724.

guaranteed to affect outcomes in cases of pre-existing high controversy where the government showed itself determined to act. It needs at this point to be repeated that because the human rights hurdle is set so low in the Human Rights Act – with caveats and exceptions galore, particularly in the national security field – powers that ought to have attracted controversy were more easily secured than would have been the case had the measure been a strongly principled human rights document rather than the rather watery measure that (in this area) it undoubtedly is.[38]

The most controversial part of the new Act was and remains the detention powers in Part 4. These provisions allow for the holding for an indefinite period and without any need to press criminal charges of a person certified by the Secretary of State (on the basis of a reasonable belief or suspicion) to be either 'a terrorist' or someone whose 'presence in the United Kingdom is a risk to national security'.[39] The word 'terrorist' is then further defined in a way which broadens the phrase enormously to encompass far more than is popularly understood to be within the meaning of the term.[40] The power is not one of internment in the strict sense since only those who are subject to immigration control are subject to it, and they are all theoretically free to depart the country if they choose,[41] but for most of those who have been incarcerated under the provision, it has not been possible to leave, either because no country will take them or those that will are run by regimes into the hands of which the suspects have no inclination to fall.

This set of powers has been the subject of immense (and ongoing[42]) dispute in the United Kingdom, despite the relatively small numbers of suspects held (seventeen according to a recent government paper[43]) and the fairly elaborate procedural safeguards that have sought to apply some due process standards to the ongoing detention – the latter are nothing like those to be found in a normal criminal process but even in their truncated form they are far more extensive than anything upon which victims of American authority in Guantánamo, Abu Ghraib, and elsewhere around the world have

---

38 Space does not permit a close textual analysis of the Convention by way of support for the assertions in the text: see arts. 8(2), 10(2), and 11(2) and also the case law on art. 14. See, further, Fenwick, id.

39 Anti-terrorism, Crime and Security Act 2001, s. 21(1).

40 id., s. 21(2)–(5). There is a good critique of the definition in Walker, op. cit. (2002), n. 8, pp. 20–30.

41 2001 Act, id., ss. 22, 23.

42 The powers have been renewed: The Anti-terrorism, Crime and Security Act 2001 (Continuance in Force of Sections 21–23) Order 2004 (S.I. no. 2004/751).

43 Home Office, *Counter-Terrorism Powers: Reconciling Security and Liberty in an Open Society: A Discussion Paper* (2004; Cm. 6147). Table One sets out the details. Two of the seventeen have chosen to leave the country and one of the group has been certified but is being held under other powers. Note that bail is available and that conditional bail has been granted to one detainee: *G v. Secretary of State for the Home Department* [2004] E.W.C.A. Civ. 265.

24

been able to rely.[44] To the ordinary observer unversed in the layers of complexity in the apparently simple phrase 'human rights law', it must seem quite amazing that such laws can even exist in a country that is also and apparently at the same time ostensibly devoted to the protection of human rights. The difficult matter to gauge is an important one from the perspective of this essay: how, if at all, has the Human Rights Act affected the nature of this power, in relation to its conceptualization, its framing, and its subsequent deployment by the state?

The first answer to this question is the counter-intuitive and, at initial glance, unsettling one that the power is explicitly a consequence of human rights law. As the Secretary of State for Home Affairs has made clear on numerous occasions,[45] Part 4 of the 2001 Act was introduced to fill a perceived gap in the law which had resulted from Britain's inability to remove non-nationals where sending them to their home countries would endanger their human rights, in particular their entitlements to life and to be free from torture. This 'gap' flows from clear case-law in the European Court of Human Rights, supported in the United Kingdom courts, that the safeguards in the European Convention on Human Rights have this kind of extra-jurisdictional reach.[46] It had been opened prior to the Human Rights Act and would have applied even if that Act had not been passed. This is also true of the need to deal with the clear infringement of the right to liberty, set out in Article 5 of the European Convention on Human Rights, which likewise was binding on the United Kingdom under international law before its incorporation into domestic law in the Human Rights Act. The problem was addressed by means of a derogation, a withdrawal from the full extent of human rights law which is itself permitted by the European Convention on Human Rights, with Article 15 authorizing such action where the executive judges this 'strictly required' on account of a 'public emergency 'threatening the life of the nation'.[47]

---

44 See, generally, 2001 Act, ss. 24–29. It follows that to describe the situation in Britain as amounting to a mini-Guantánamo is a reckless misuse of language, making it impossible – were such a system to be introduced here – to call it by its proper name. For the very different position in the United States, see D. Rose, *Guantánamo: America's War on Human Rights* (2004); 'How US Rewrote Terror Law in Secrecy' *International Herald Tribune*, 25 October 2004, 1, 4, and 26 October 2004, 2. For a good summary of the legal position in both United Kingdom and United States, see P. Thomas, 'Emergency and Anti-Terrorist Powers: 9/11: USA and UK' (2003) 26 *Fordham International Law J.* 1193.

45 See, most recently, Home Office, op. cit., n. 43, paras. 21–41.

46 *Soering* v. *United Kingdom* (1989) 11 E.H.R.R. 439; *Chahal* v. *United Kingdom* (1996) 23 E.H.R.R. 413. In the United Kingdom, the leading authority is now *R (Ullah)* v. *Special Adjudicator: Thi Lien Do* v. *Secretary of State for the Home Department* [2004] U.K.H.L. 26; [2004] 3 All E.R. 785. The 'gap' only arises where it is not possible to detain such individuals by pressing charges under domestic criminal law.

47 Human Rights Act 1998 (Designated Derogation) Order 2001 (S.I. no. 2001/3644). United Kingdom anti-terrorism law had led to earlier derogations despite the then

25

The question that is impossible conclusively to answer is whether the very existence of this self-destruct button made such an explicit erosion of liberty *more* rather than *less* likely. On balance this would not seem to be the case. Parliament has had no difficulty in the past in agreeing draconian infringements of individual liberty at the behest of the executive,[48] and it seems unlikely that the derogation power tempted the authorities to act in a way that they would otherwise not have done. Relevant here is the apocalyptic language that the Prime Minister in particular has used; his anxieties about the threat of global terrorism[49] would surely have been likely, if given the free legislative rein that existed in pre-Convention days, to have resulted in more rather than less invasions of liberty. It needs also to be remembered (as the government has recently found, to its cost) that the derogation provision does not amount to a blank cheque, and judges are empowered to assess the legitimacy of what is asserted to be required under its head.[50] Maybe those who see the derogation procedure as a constraint on government rather than a cue for illiberal action, if not a red then an amber rather than a green light,[51] have the better of the argument. This is particularly the case in light of the recent House of Lords judgment on the issue.[52]

What the language of human rights has undoubtedly done has been to provide a focus for the unease felt by parliamentarians at being asked to vote for so explicit an invasion of a right to liberty that just three years before they had been invited by the same government to agree was fundamental. This is evident from the legislative debates,[53] the parliamentary committee

---

absence of any domestically enforceable rights' instrument: see Donohue, op. cit., n. 8, pp. 345–52. See, also, C.A. Gearty and J.A. Kimbell, *Terrorism and the Rule of Law. A Report on the Laws Relating to Political Violence in Great Britain and Northern Ireland* (1995).

48 For the record during the First and Second World Wars, see K.D. Ewing and C.A. Gearty, *The Struggle for Civil Liberties. Political Freedom and the Rule of Law in Britain, 1914–1945* (2000) chs. 2 and 8.

49 See T. Blair, 'The Threat of Global Terrorism', speech in Sedgefield, 5 March 2004. For a revealing insight into the Prime Minister's approach to the implications of the extra-territorial reach of the European Convention where the removal of non-nationals to other countries is concerned, see *Youssef* v. *Home Office* [2004] E.W.H.C. 1884 (Q.B.).

50 The lead Strasbourg authority is *Brannigan and McBride*, op. cit., n. 9; see, generally, C. Warbrick, 'The Principles of the European Convention on Human Rights and the Response of States to Terrorism' [2002] E.H.R.L.R. 287. It is true that the judicial oversight may be deferential, but that is not the same as saying it is non-existent. For how the British judges have actually approached this task, see *A (FC) and others (FC)* v. *Secretary of State for the Home Department* ; *X (FC) and another (FC)* v. *Secretary of State for the Home Department* [2004] U.K.H.L. 56, overturning (in part) *A* v. *Secretary of State for the Home Department* SIAC 30 July 2002; [2002] E.W.C.A. Civ. 1502, [2003] 1 All E.R. 816.

51 C. Harlow and R. Rawlings, *Law and Administration* (1984).

52 *A (FC) and others (FC)*, op. cit., n. 50.

53 D. Nicol, 'The Human Rights Act and the Politicians' (2004) 24 *Legal Studies* 451.

26

reports,[54] and the general engagement of civil society in the proposals.[55] It is clear also in the report of the committee of privy counsellors that was so trenchantly critical of the need for the detention power when it published its review in December 2003,[56] and in the subsequent treatment of the subject by the Joint Committee[57] and the statutory reviewer Lord Carlile.[58] Once again it is hard to say whether or not all this would all have happened even without a Human Rights Act, but at very least, the rights formulation proved helpful in framing the discussion as one in which it was necessary to seek to balance freedom and security, rather than to allow an entirely blank cheque to the latter. Liberal thinkers may baulk at even permitting such a balancing exercise to take place,[59] but a tenuous hold on public discourse is surely better than no hold at all.

In contrast, the traditional language of civil liberties – the term that would have needed to have done all the work had there been no Human Rights Act – has many of the definitional vulnerabilities of which human rights are often accused,[60] and its exposure to the demands of a sovereign parliament is greater than that of human rights, there being no equivalent of the Human Rights Act's insistence on compatibility with its requirements.[61] On the other hand, the legitimizing effect of presenting human rights violations as in compliance with human rights does not apply to traditional civil liberties, where no such repressive sleight-of-hand is available. In the final analysis, much probably depends on the public mood of the day, and in this, government plays a very important role. Speculating on hypotheticals plays an honourable part in human rights studies,[62] and in the present context tempts us to ask how a Conservative government led by Michael Howard with as large a majority as Labour but without the Human Rights Act would have acted. Any credible answer to this surely suggests that, from a civil libertarian/human rights perspective, the Human Rights Act (and the government that introduced it) must have done some good.

54 See nn. 34 and 36 above.
55 See E. Metcalfe, 'Necessity and Detention: Internment under the Anti-terrorism, Crime and Security Act 2001' (2004) 1 *Justice J.* 36; Liberty, *Recognising Security and Liberty in an Open Society* (2004); Fenwick, op. cit., n. 37.
56 Privy Counsellor Review Committee, *Anti-Terrorism, Crime and Security Act 2001 Review: Report* HC (2003–2004) 100.
57 JCHR, Sixth Report, *Anti-terrorism, Crime and Security Act 2001: Statutory Review and Continuance of Part 4* HL (2003–2004) 38, HC (2003–2004) 381.
58 Lord Carlile of Berriew QC, *Anti-terrorism, Crime and Security Act 2001, Part IV Section 28 Review 2003* (2004).
59 J. Waldron, 'Security and Liberty: The Image of Balance' (2003) 11 *J. of Political Philosophy* 191.
60 C.A. Gearty, 'Reflections on Civil Liberties in an Age of Counter-Terrorism' (2003) 41 *Osgoode Hall Law J.* 185
61 HRA, s. 3(1).
62 J. Rawls, *A Theory of Justice* (1999, revised edn.); S. Lukes, 'Five Fables about Human Rights' in *On Human Rights*, eds. S. Shute and S. Hurley (1993).

27

RECONCILING TERRORISM LAW WITH HUMAN RIGHTS: THE ROLE OF THE COURTS

As a matter of historical record, it has generally been wrong to expect much from the British courts in their capacity as defenders of civil liberties and political freedom, and, until the House of Lords' remarkable decision in December 2004, the judges' interpretation of the anti-terrorism law outlined above has proved no exception to this general proposition.[63] What had been surprising up to that point had been the extent to which the senior judiciary had been willing to justify egregious attacks on civil liberties as *sanctioned* by, rather than *an affront to*, the Human Rights Act. There had not been conflict, with declarations of incompatibility aplenty and ongoing tension over judicial efforts to rein in executive excess. Instead, there had been the quiet of a code of human rights always anxious not only to see but also to lie down before the other point of view. While even before the Lords' ruling there had been one or two examples of principled judicial decision-making[64] or at least outcomes that even a most civil libertarian judge would have found hard to avoid,[65] the overall picture had been bleak indeed.

This early tone was set in a case in the House of Lords decided shortly after 11 September 2001, when Lord Hoffmann remarked by way of a 'postscript' to his judgment that the events of that day were a reminder that 'in matters of national security, the cost of failure can be high' and that this 'underline[s] the need for the judicial arm of government to respect the decisions of ministers of the Crown'.[66] His lordship noted that such decisions, 'with serious potential results for the community, require a legitimacy which can be conferred only by entrusting them to persons responsible to the community through the democratic process'.[67] There is at

---

63 Ewing, op. cit., n. 7 goes into the record in great detail, and sets it in its political and legal context. For the Lords' decision, see op. cit., n. 50.

64 *Attorney General's Reference (No 4 of 2002)* [2004] U.K.H.L. 44 [burden of proof in Terrorism Act 2000 s. 11 prosecutions]; *M* v. *Secretary of State for the Home Department* [2004] E.W.C.A. Civ. 324 [Special Immigration Appeals Commission (SIAC) correct not to regard suspicious circumstances as the same as reasonable suspicion for the purposes of the exercise of the detention power under Part 4 of the Anti-terrorism, Crime and Security Act 2001]; *G,* op. cit., n. 43. Note, however, that the first case is a rather traditional one on the burden of proof, a topic on which judges have always taken a keen interest, and that each of the latter two cases involved the court of appeal in supporting judgments in favour of detainees which had already been made by SIAC.

65 *Rankin* v. *Prosecutor Fiscal, Ayr* High Court of Justiciary, 1 June 2004, involving a prosecution for wearing items indicative of support for a proscribed organization. No human rights point appears to have been made in the case.

66 *Secretary of State for the Home Department* v. *Rehman* [2001] U.K.H.L. 47, [2002] 1 A.C. 153, para. [62]. The specific question before the lords related to whether support for terrorist activities in a foreign country constituted a threat to national security, but Lord Hoffmann's remarks can clearly be read more generally than this.

67 id.

28

the core of these remarks an important truth about the need for accountability in this area in particular; Lord Hoffmann is surely right to observe that '[i]f the people are to accept the consequences of such decisions, they must be made by persons whom the people have elected and whom they can remove'.[68] But his lordship's willingness to recognize executive responsibility here is uncomfortably close to a judicial posture of de facto total acquiescence, and this is a line to which the senior judiciary pretty rigidly stuck until the House of Lords took a radically different turn, with Lord Hoffmann now in the vanguard of liberalism, in December 2004.

The derogation which permits the detention provision has been subject to one of the earliest and most sustained of challenges.[69] The Lord Chief Justice Lord Woolf remarked, in upholding the government line when the matter came before him:

> [w]hile the courts must carefully scrutinise the explanations given by the executive for its actions, the courts must extend the appropriate degree of deference when it comes to judging those actions.[70]

The House of Lords agreed by the overwhelming margin of 8-1 when the case came before it that not even the deference rightly given in the field of national security could permit the indefinite detention of suspected non-national (but not national) terrorists. Their lordships ruled that the derogation was not valid and, at the same time, made a declaration of incompatibility in relation to the detention provisions of the 2001 Act, on the ground that these breached both Articles 5 and 14 of the Convention.[71] In making these rulings, the Lords have gone some way towards redeeming the reputation of the courts in the field of civil liberties. It remains to be seen whether the decision initiates a pattern of judicial activism, or whether it is merely a reflection both of the huge opprobrium that was heaped on these provisions in particular and of the government's ham-fisted response to that criticism.

A particularly welcome aspect of the Lords' decision is the way in which it approaches the Human Rights Act in a more principled way than had Lord Woolf and his colleagues[72] in the court below. That decision had met with much criticism.[73] Perhaps the most depressing feature of the case in the Court of Appeal had been the way in which the judges seem to have misunderstood the structure of the Human Rights Act: its careful preservation of

---

68 id.
69 See n. 50 above. This is one of the cases that has been argued on appeal to the House of Lords.
70 [2002] E.W.C.A. Civ. 1502, para. [44].
71 Note that SIAC had originally also ruled the detention power to be in breach of Article 14 viewed with Article 5, but that this decision had been overruled by the Court of Appeal: op. cit., n. 50.
72 Brooke and Chadwick LJJ.
73 See, for example, Ewing, op. cit., n. 7.

29

parliamentary sovereignty should have given them the confidence to rule on human rights violations when they saw them, with the declaration of incompatibility procedure in section 4 being designed to ensure that no immediately (and from the executive's point of view) disruptive results should flow from any such intervention. Instead, in this case, the Court of Appeal seemed to have treated itself as though it had the final say and, having made this false assumption, then built in a whole fresh layer of deference to prevent itself from producing a difficult or unsettling (but not legally obligatory) outcome for government.[74] The House of Lords has now gone a long way towards rectifying this error.

It has come too late for *R (Gillan)* v. *Metropolitan Police Commissioner*, decided on 29 July 2004.[75] Here random stop-and-search powers, supposedly provided by way of special authorization under the Terrorism Act 2000 to assist in police action against the threat of terrorism, were being constantly renewed, without any careful consideration of their specific and ongoing necessity. Under these powers, a man on his way to demonstrate outside an arms fair at the Excel Centre in Docklands was stopped and searched. Papers relating to the protest – which had absolutely nothing to do with terrorism – were seized. Another person, a journalist, was also stopped and searched and ordered to stop filming. The Court of Appeal found all this compatible with the human rights to freedom of assembly and expression that it was agreed each individual enjoyed. Because the law was limited to searching for evidence of terrorism, there was nothing in these powers that threatened either the right to freedom of expression or the right to assembly. The judges took the view that:

> the courts will not readily interfere with the judgment of the authorities as to the action that is necessary. They will usually therefore not interfere with the authorities' assessment of the risk and the action that should be taken to counter the risk.[76]

According to the Court of Appeal, the stop and search of the two did not even amount to a technical breach of their right to liberty.[77] Nor was the rolling programme of constantly renewing these powers at all objectionable from a human rights point of view.[78] It is true, but little consolation, that a close reading of the judgment reveals occasional flickers of anxiety on the part of the judges, a mounting concern about the implications of their reasoning, almost as though they were in the centre of a repressive maelstrom but unable to do anything about it.[79]

---

74 On this point see, generally, C.A. Gearty, *Principles of Human Rights Adjudication* (2004) ch. 5.
75 [2004] E.W.C.A. Civ. 1067.
76 id., para. [33] *per* Woolf LCJ giving the judgment of the Court.
77 id., paras. [37]–[46].
78 id., para. [51].
79 See id., paras. [54] and [56].

The final case in this brief overview is the most antagonistic of all to human rights, *A* v. *Secretary of State for the Home Department (no 2)*,[80] a decision that is at the time of writing also coming up for a definitive ruling in the House of Lords. Here we learn that in considering evidence certified by the Secretary of State for the Home Department as to why he had detained a person as a suspected terrorist, the Special Immigration Appeals Commission could take into account material produced in interviews of third parties allegedly obtained by torture. This decision has deserved the opprobrium that has been heaped upon it.[81] There are no weasel words available to dilute the impact of what the court is saying: we live in a human rights culture so will not torture ourselves, but where others bring us the benefits of such torture (or more accurately the alleged benefits: torture is not a particularly efficient means of obtaining information), we will gratefully accept them. This is the anti-terrorism logic brought right into the core of our supposedly human-rights-sensitive system of laws: unless the Lords rule otherwise, a man or woman can be detained here, on the basis of evidence procured by the torture of some-body else – and not only is this not unlawful, it is entirely lawful. It is hard to see how this can be compatible with any version of human rights, and hopefully the House of Lords speaking with its new liberal voice will say so unequivocally.

CONCLUSION

The re-election of George W. Bush in the United States presidential election of November 2004 makes it probable that the 'Global War on Terror' will continue, that it might even up a number of gears and become a legitimating basis for aggression around the world. The American electorate – albeit by a small majority – seems to have given its verdict on the place of human rights in this new discourse, namely, that it has little or no place at all: we can expect the officials and administration members responsible for formulating and executing policies of torture and indefinite detention without trial to be promoted, and it is perfectly possible that the chief legal apologists of such practices will shortly be elevated to the post of US Attorney General.[82] The language of human rights is not yet merely

---

80 The full citation is *A, B, C, D, E, F, G, H, Abu Rideh and Ajouaou v Secretary of State for the Home Department* [2004] E.W.C.A. Civ. 1123.
81 See the leading article, 'Tortured Logic', in the *Guardian*, 12 August 2004; M. Evans, 'The Blind Eye of the Law' *Guardian*, 14 August 2004. Note that the Court was divided on the point, with Pill and Laws LJJ forming the majority and Neuberger LJ dissenting. An excellent but more general critique is J. Jowell, 'Beware the tools of tyranny' *Guardian*, 28 October 2004.
82 See A. Lewis, 'Making Torture Legal' *New York Review of Books*, 15 July 2004, 4–8.

31

'quaint'[83] on this side of the Atlantic, and there remains here a robust debate not about whether human rights has a place in the new security-sensitive paradigm but what that place should properly be.[84]

It is vital that human rights advocates and civil libertarians enter into this discussion with gusto and determination. The door is not yet closed here though unrealistic and uncompromising assertions of supposedly pure principle might lead it to being slammed shut. For example, the recent trend towards the criminal prosecution of suspected terrorists within the jurisdiction is greatly to be welcomed as a paradigm of how things should be done.[85] Likewise the various legislative and executive initiatives, such as proposals for the admissibility of intercept evidence in court, the tagging of suspects, the use of curfew powers, and the like need to be given serious consideration if they are presented as part of a range of measures designed to replace the detention power: the issue in such cases is surely one not of principle but of proper implementation (with accountability and adequate control of discretion). In this regard, Liberty's response to the government White Paper on counter-terrorism powers repays careful reading.[86] Even the subject of identity cards is surely not beyond the pale of rational debate, and the human rights problems with such documents are not obvious, at least at the level of principle.

The House of Lords decision aside, probably the most significant contribution of the Human Rights Act in this particular field has been to create new mechanisms for civil libertarian input and a fresh language for the articulation of traditional liberal concerns. The most recent report of the Joint Committee on Human Rights[87] is a reminder of how much important work that committee continues to do in this important field, and the role of individual members of Parliament should also not be underestimated. At the European level, a very good set of guidelines on the role of human rights in counter-terrorism has been published by the Council of Europe[88] and the EU has also been active in engaging with the human rights strand to its action on

---

83 The word used by White House counsel Alberto Gonzales to describe the Geneva Conventions which ought to regulate the treatment of prisoners in wartime: see Lewis, id., p. 4. For critical perspectives on the United States position, see M. Welch, 'Trampling Human Rights in the War on Terror: Implications to the Sociology of Denial' (2003) 12 *Critical Criminology* 1; P. Chevigny, 'Repression in the United States after the September 11 Attack' (2004) 1 *SUR − International J. on Human Rights* 143.
84 Home Office, op. cit., n. 43.
85 See (all from the *Guardian*) 'Surveillance led to terror arrests', 5 August 2004; 'Terror plot suspects face charges', 18 August 2004; 'Terror suspects in court', 26 August 2004; 'Abu Hamza charged with inciting murder', 20 October 2004.
86 Liberty, op. cit., n. 55, especially ch. 7.
87 JCHR, op. cit., n. 57.
88 Guidelines on Human Rights and the Fight against Terrorism (Council of Europe, 11 July 2002) (2002) 57 *Human Rights Information Bull.* 40; <http://humanrights.coe.int>.

anti-terrorism.[89] The basic building blocks of human rights – equality of esteem; a respect for law; a commitment to the democratic process – remain in place in Europe and the United Kingdom, but the price that needs to be paid every day to ensure the survival of these ideals in these difficult times takes the form of constant vigilance, endless community energy, and ongoing civil libertarian solidarity. If it were to depend on litigation alone, then the human rights spirit would quickly wither on the vine, as would the civil libertarian impetus of past generations. And if those who care about human rights let their attention wander, even for a short while, then they might return from their daydreaming to find a radically different society. The challenges are likely to get even tougher in the future, with the savage stupidity of the war on terror producing more of that which it was supposedly designed to end.[90]

---

89 See D. Bonner, 'Managing Terrorism while Respecting Human Rights? European Aspects of the Anti-terrorism, Crime and Security Act' (2002) 8 *European Public Law* 497. See, for update of EU developments, <http://www.europa.eu.int/comm/justice_home/news/intro/news_intro_en.htm>.
90 'Anti-terror measures "alienate Muslims"' *Guardian*, 21 September 2004.

JOURNAL OF LAW AND SOCIETY
VOLUME 32, NUMBER 1, MARCH 2005
ISSN: 0263-323X, pp. 34–50

Winners and Losers

LUKE CLEMENTS*

This paper considers whether the Human Rights Act 1998 is, in itself, capable of materially improving the lives of those who experience social exclusion – or whether it is likely to exacerbate their difficulties. It draws on the relevant post-2000 research concerning the Act's impact on socially excluded groups which suggests that the response of the statutory agencies has been disappointing – that 'not being proactive' has proved to be the most attractive option. It then addresses the incongruity between the government's strategies for combating social exclusion and civil justice.

INTRODUCTION

Writing before the introduction of the Human Rights Act 1998, a number of authors warned that the Act might make little or no difference to the injustices experienced by socially excluded people: that, in this context, the much vaunted cultural content of the Act might come to be seen as rhetorical. Sir Stephen Sedley expressed this view succinctly when he warned of the risk that society's existing 'losers and winners' would merely become the same losers and winners under a Human Rights Act.[1]

In this short paper I seek to assess the evidence as to whether the Human Rights Act 1998 is, in itself, capable of materially improving the lives of those who experience social exclusion – by which I mean (amongst others) people with profound physical or mental disabilities, unpopular minorities (such as Gypsies), homeless people, chronically poor people, children in care or permanently excluded from school, and recently released prisoners. A group that could be described as 'stranded victims', in the sense that they have become isolated from any effective process for remedying the wrongs they experience.

* Cardiff Law School, Cardiff University, Museum Avenue, Cardiff CF1 3NX, Wales

1 S. Sedley, 'First Steps Towards a Constitutional Bill of Rights' [1997] E.H.R.L.R. 458.

34

To consider this question is not to rerun the socio-economic versus civil and political rights debate, not least because the clearer articulation of the positive obligations within the Convention has, in theory at least, softened the boundaries between these two artificial classifications.[2] The backdrop to this debate is more about whether a process-focused rights system (as opposed to needs-sensitive system) can deliver substantive benefits for such people. New rights may be open to all – like the doors of the Savoy hotel – but in practice they prove more accommodating to the rich than the poor.

A recent case, *HL* v. *UK* (2004),[3] illustrates the point. HL has profound autism associated with frequent episodes of very challenging behaviour. He lacks capacity to decide where to live. He had lived in a psychiatric hospital for almost all his life; however, in 1994 he went to live with two dedicated carers. Three years later, when temporarily away from these carers, he was taken to a psychiatric unit. Despite having the intention to keep him at the unit and despite denying him contact with his carers for over three months, it was argued that he was not deprived of his liberty because he was 'compliant'. He accordingly had none of the protection afforded to such patients under the Mental Health Act 1983 (restricting treatment and enabling the detention to be challenged).

The European Court of Human Rights held that he was detained; that any suggestion to the contrary was a 'fairy tale'. It followed that his rights under article 5(1) had been violated. HL's case was only taken because of the commitment of his carers. One is left to ask what would have happened if there were no such concerned friends or carers? Despite this ruling, there are today most probably tens of thousands of people in a similar situation to HL (particularly elderly people with dementia) but without concerned advocates and for whom this judgment will have no benefit.

THE ASPIRATION

The sales pitch accompanying the Human Rights Act 1998 was impressive: from the Labour Party's briefing paper in 1996[4] to the Lord Chancellor's flourishes during its second reading we were told that it would 'nurture a culture of understanding of rights and responsibilities at all levels in our society'[5] and result in a human rights culture developing across the country.[6]

---

2 See, for instance, Lord Lester of Herne Hill and C. O'Cinneide, 'The Effective Protection of Socio-Economic Rights' in *Economic, Social & Cultural Rights in Practice*, eds. Y. Ghai and J. Cottrell (2004).
3 45508/99; 5 October 2004.
4 Labour Party, *Bringing Rights Home* (1996).
5 id.
6 Lord Irvine of Lairg LC, 582 *H.L. Debs.*, at cols. 1228, 1234 (3 Nov 1997).

In the opinion of the Joint Committee on Human Rights,[7] the government's case was that the Act would 'help to inaugurate a gradual transformation of civil society'; it would, create 'a more humane society' and would 'deepen and widen democracy by increasing the sense amongst individual men and women that they have a stake in the way in which they are governed'. As the committee itself noted, these messages caused concern even to the Act's many 'champions' – who believed that 'the dissemination of such a culture would not [without more] follow the passing of legislation'[8].

There is little of substance to be gained by debating whether the government really expected or intended the Act to materially redress social inequalities. Undoubtedly it did at times overdo the rhetoric, and its choice of the term 'culture' provided comfortable scope for ambiguity – as the research report accompanying the Joint Committee's sixth report noted,[9] 'no public official (outside LCD) interviewed in the course of this research ... could describe what was meant by a "human rights culture".' The phrase is admirably imprecise.

Even if it were not central to the constitutional enterprise, addressing social inequalities by empowering excluded people is a noble and important aim. Constitutional change of the order contemplated by the Human Rights Act 1998 is usually justified in terms of its impact on minorities and the dispossessed. A vibrant civil society requires that society's losers – its marginalized and unpopular minorities and its unassertive members – are provided with a degree of entrenched protection, independent of the vagaries of the electoral process. In the language of the Convention, there is a positive obligation on the state to ensure that the rights of these groups are respected – not merely by providing constitutional safeguards against the so-called dictatorship of the majority, but more importantly by ensuring that concrete, and accessible mechanisms exist which enable these rights to be enforced. As the Strasbourg Court regularly intones, the Convention is intended to guarantee for all 'not rights that are theoretical or illusory but rights that are practical and effective'.[10]

7 Joint Committee on Human Rights (JCHR), Sixth Report, *The Case for a Human Rights Commission*, HL (2002–03) 67, HC (2002–03) 489, para. 9 at <www.publications. parliament.uk/pa/jt200203/jtselect/jtrights/67/67.pdf>.
8 id., para. 10.
9 JCHR, op. cit., n. 7, Appendices, at para 4.1 <www.publications.parliament.uk/pa/jt200203/jtselect/jtrights/67/67ap01.htm>.
10 *Airey* v. *Ireland* (1979) 2 E.H.R.R. 305. *Golder* v. *UK (1975)* (1975) 1 E.H.R.R. 524.

Although the reason for the existence of new rights-based legislation may not be to redress social inequalities, it is legitimate to ask whether such new rights do benefit socially excluded groups or, indeed, whether they actually exacerbate their problems. This question is not relativist or semantic in the sense it might be if predicated on a notion of exclusion defined solely in terms of 'relative deprivation',[11] in the sense that any improvement could be challenged because the benefits are not enjoyed by all simultaneously, such that, in relative (but not in absolute) terms, certain sections fall further behind. The issue here is that the introduction of rights may result in a deterioration in the lot of certain groups – without the promise of improvement. For example, the primary purpose underlying Kenneth Baker's 1980s educational reforms, providing parental right to choose a state school,[12] may not have been the removal of social inequalities in education but, nevertheless, any attempt to assess the success of this initiative would need to consider, amongst other things, its impact on socially excluded groups. Such an evaluation might note that the new right was commandeered by the middle classes, creating ghetto schools in poor neighbourhoods. Likewise the people who take advantage of a right to challenge social services care provision (introduced by Virginia Bottomley as a result of the 1990 Community Care Act reforms[13]) may be the articulate, assertive, and well informed, with the consequence that this group receives a greater share of these resource-limited services, inevitably at the expense of the inarticulate, unassertive, and poorly informed.[14] Rights-based legislation does not, therefore, in itself advance the interests of all sections of society: indeed, without other positive action by the state, such legislation not infrequently makes matters worse. Abusers have rights too – and they are almost invariably better at asserting these rights than their victims.

The problems that are likely to be encountered in any attempt to deliver rights to stranded victims can be characterized as either problems of access or problems associated with the law itself. The following section briefly considers the nature of these barriers: why the system may be seen as inaccessible or unattractive or irrelevant by socially excluded people. In the subsequent section, I review the evidence of the last five years, as to whether these barriers have in fact prevented such people from benefiting from the more humane society that the Act promised to deliver.

11 P. Townsend, *Poverty in the United Kingdom* (1979).
12 The Education Act 1987; see, however, Nick Davies, 'Crisis, Crisis, Crisis: the State of Our Schools' *Guardian*, 14 September 1999.
13 s. 50 NHS and Community Care Act 1990.
14 See, in this respect, K. Simons, *I'm Not Complaining, but ...* (1995).

37

Although socially excluded people are frequently the objects of the 'justice system' they are seldom its customer. The problem is one of access: the system is simply inaccessible. The difficulties experienced by disabled people in this respect have been expressed in terms of the relevant remedies not being:

> sensitive to the needs of people who may be exhausted, in pain or overwhelmed, who frequently have an ingrained feeling of powerlessness, who may be very short of information and who may also fear the repercussions of making a complaint.[15]

Evidence of this problem can be found in dearth of cases taken to the Strasbourg court by people with profound physical disabilities, 'unpopular minorities', homeless people, chronically poor people, children in care or permanently excluded from school or by recently released prisoners.[16] How, for instance, could a person with profound learning disabilities challenge the legal restrictions on his/her sexual freedom? It is an extraordinary fact, that whilst there have been many thousands of complaints concerning age and gender related restrictions on sexual freedom, there have been no reported decisions concerning the proscription of all sexual activity for those with severe learning disabilities (notwithstanding that in 2000 the Home Office accepted that the law in this respect probably violated Article 8).[17]

At the most basic level, there is of course the simple fact that many socially excluded people are simply ignorant of their rights. Rights are never as straightforward as they seem. Since the Human Rights Act 1998 required unprecedented investment in judicial training (over £4 million[18]), it is reasonable to assume that many vulnerable people, especially those with intellectual disabilities or with very limited education, would also need help in understanding or indeed being made aware of the new rights regime. Realistically this would need to take the form of help from others: sympathetic service providers (for instance, local authority or NHS staff), intermediaries such as advocates, families, lawyers, or by patient judges with abundant time at their disposal.

Many socially excluded people – even if aware of their rights – have been so worn down through years of stress, hard physical endurance, and poor

---

15 L. Clements and J. Read, *Disabled People and European Human Rights* (2003); see, also, H. Glenn, *Paths to Justice* (1999).
16 There have of course been many cases concerning children – but it is rare indeed for such cases not also to concern parental grievances. A few such cases, not involving parental rights, are made but see, for instance, *SP, DP & T* v. *UK* (2001) 22 E.H.R.R. CD 148 for the procedural difficulties encountered.
17 Home Office, *Setting the Boundaries: Reforming the law on sex offences* (2000) para. 11, app. H6.
18 Lord Chancellor's Department, News Release, 12 July 2000.

health that they simply not have the energy to assert their rights. For some there is additionally the real fear that to do so would result in negative consequences. In a major research study into the social services complaints process,[19] 'fear of the consequences' was 'by far the most commonly cited reason for not making formal complaints'. The research highlighted the problem of 'implicit threats of retribution' such as one complainant being told by a social work manager that the department was under 'no obligation to care for your son, you know'.

A 2003 Audit Commission investigation into the implementation of the Human Rights Act 1998[20] also noted this factor. Referring to older people, children and to people with disabilities, it found that 'these groups of people were less likely to complain even where they had suffered unfair and/or degrading treatment at the hands of service providers'. Frequently the rights denied to socially excluded people result from administrative or corporate decisions which require collective challenge. Since isolation is a defining characteristic for many stranded victims, it is generally the case that they lack the cohesion and resources to instigate group action.

Of course, it takes no sociological genius to comprehend the reasons why the residents of Richmond and its environs were more likely to initiate public interest litigation concerning night flights into Heathrow[21] than are the Gypsies living on the official caravan site beneath the Westway motorway in central London. The obverse of this reality is that those with skills to coordinate collective action may do so at the expense of those without these skills – thus environmentally malign developments are more likely to occur in the neighbourhoods of those least able to assert their collective rights. Once again, the existence of a right can (in the absence of appropriate administrative safeguards) actually act to the detriment of socially excluded groups.

In similar vein, assertive groups are able to use collective action to influence procedural rules and substantive outcomes in ways that are not open to socially excluded people. Examples span the spectrum from access to land to social security benefits. As to the former, the process which determines the grant or refusal of planning permission depends in large measure upon the content of the Local Development Plan which, although produced by a local authority, is shaped by the consultation and public review process. Inevitably, therefore, the plan will be influenced by those for whom the process is accessible – for instance, the powerful House Builders' Federation – rather than those for whom it is not, such as the homeless Gypsy.

Likewise, an assertive and well informed social security claimant may challenge an adverse benefits decision by appearing in person before an

19 See, in this respect, Simons, op. cit., n. 14.
20 Audit Commission, *Human Rights: Improving Public Service Delivery* (2003) 5.
21 *Hatton* v. *UK* (2003) 8 July 2003; Application 36022/97.

Appeal Tribunal, whereas someone without these skills may not feel able to attend. The evidence is strongly supportive of the fact that claimants who opt to be present at their social security appeal tribunal hearings are more successful than those who do not appear. Stein suggests that representation is the key factor in explaining this disparity.[22] Anecdotally, however, it has been suggested[23] that this may not be the explanation, that merely seeing the claimant and hearing his or her testimony is what makes the difference. The argument advanced is that, in general, claimants are apprehensive about appearing before a tribunal, alone, and the value of representation lies not in the advocate's eloquence, but his or her mere presence emboldening the claimant to attend.

In both these examples, the rights of the Gypsy and the non-appearing appellant will in consequence depend in large measure upon the attitude and human rights awareness of the street-level bureaucrats[24] with whom they have contact: the officer that prepares the social security case papers; the officer that determines the content of the development plan.

The civil justice system, its rules of court, its court fees, the adversarial process, the architecture of court buildings, the sensitivity of the judiciary to the handicaps faced by disabled people, and so on, are all factors that may militate against socially excluded people accessing their rights. For many there is little or no possibility of direct access. For reasons of intellectual or communication disabilities, the need for third-party assistance is essential – be that from a friend, an informal or a professional advocate[25] or lawyer. Well before one reaches the issue of the state funding for advocacy support or legal aid[26] there is the issue of how stranded victims are likely to find someone to help enforce their rights. HL was fortunate to have two dedicated 'befrienders' – but for the 44 years before he met them, he was (we now learn) unlawfully detained.

Even where there is a motivated person involved, procedural rules, such as the rules on 'standing' may see off any opportunity for assistance. In Sweden,[27] for example, a psychologist visited a care home for people with learning disabilities and found a number of them unlawfully locked in their rooms. Following his internal complaint he was denied further access to the

---

22 In this respect, Stein (J.M. Stein, *The Future of Social Justice in Britain: A New Mission for the Community Legal Service* (2001) at 16, see <http://sticerd.lse.ac.uk/dps/case/cp/CASEpaper48.pdf>) cites the DSS *Quarterly Appeal Tribunal Statistics* (June 2000) as showing tribunal success for applicants with a representative as being 62.4 per cent versus 48.9 per cent where there is an appellant present with no representation, versus 16.9 per cent where there is no appellant in attendance. Clearly the significant difference is between those that attend and those who do not.

23 Author's personal communication with a number of Tribunal chairs.

24 See M. Lipsky, *Street-Level Bureaucracy* (1980).

25 For a review of the role of informal advocacy, see R. Henderson and M. Pochin, *A Right Result?* (2001).

26 In this article I refer to 'public funding' as 'legal aid'.

27 *Skjoldager* v. *Sweden* (1995) 22504/93.

40

residents. When he subsequently complained to the European Commission in a representative capacity (in his own name because the municipality had refused to provide him with the names of the residents – who were incapable of lodging the complaint themselves), the case was rejected on the ground that the applicant had no specific authority to make the complaint.

That the United Kingdom's civil justice system has been infused with provisions and principles loaded against the interests of socially excluded people is hardly news. The property-based origins of the common law meant that it was predicated on the model of wealthy people's problems. The interests of the aristocracy may have yielded to the realigned property classes[28] but the capitalist paradigm remains: poor people do not, as Wexler observed,[29] 'have legal problems like those of the private plaintiffs and defendants in law school casebooks'.

The incorporation of a humanitarian-based body of law into this system is likely to be frustrated (in so far as it relates to the needs of socially excluded people) if the 'law is not for the poor' mindset simply migrates. In this respect, it is not only traditional common law principles that need scrutiny.[30] The businessification of the law has also considerable potential to operate against their interests. Externally this is seen in the 'increasing exposure of judicial administration to the budgetary and other disciplines of the "New Public Management"':[31] the running of the civil justice system as a quasi-commercial enterprise; and of judges aligning themselves with the target-setting agenda, expressing grave disquiet about the volume of administrative cases, about case costs, and so on. Internally, this is exampled in the increased focus of courts on due process analysis at the expense of discretion: the application of logic rather than judgment; law rather than justice. In the context of poor peoples' access to justice Adler,[32] for instance, has referred to the absence of a causal relationship between substantive justice and procedural fairness, observing that 'scrupulously fair procedures can result in manifestly unjust outcomes' and that 'low levels of entitlement can be given a high degree of procedural protection whereas high levels of entitlement can receive very little protection at all'.

THE EVIDENCE – POST-2000

If ignorance of the new rights regime (or fear of asserting these rights) is a particular problem for stranded victims, then the remedy must involve help

28 C. Hill, *Liberty against the Law* (1996) 332.
29 S. Wexler, 'Practising Law for Poor People' (1970) 79 *Yale Law J.* 1049.
30 But see, in this context, L. Clements, 'Dirty Gypsies – ex turpi causa and Human Rights' *Human Rights*, December 2002, 204–12.
31 'Comment' [1998] *Public Law* 1–7.
32 M. Adler, 'Substantive Justice and Procedural Fairness in Social Security: The UK Experience'in *Poverty and the Law*, eds. P. Robson and A. Kjønstad (2001) 126.

41

from others particularly the statutory authorities with whom they may come into contact, either as service providers or as enforcement agencies (the 'sharp legal things that poor people are always bumping into'[33]).

For many such people therefore, the benefits of the 1998 Act will only be experienced if public bodies proactively review their policies and procedures to remedy any non-compliant practices. The government in its Human Rights Act 1998 implementation advice stressed the importance of this process and asked councils to 'think about how, and the extent to which, the laws underpinning your policies and procedures could help you do more to build a culture of rights and responsibilities'.[34]

An Economic and Social Research Council (ESRC)-funded research study, undertaken by Cardiff Law School, on the extent of local authority preparations for the implementation of the 1998 Act[35] contrasted the general responses (for all council activities) with those relating to a specific subject area: namely, their responsibilities in relation to Gypsies and other Travelling people.[36] The research found that 61 per cent of local authorities surveyed had undertaken a general, across-the-board 'Strasbourg compliance' review of their policies. However, it found a marked disparity in relation the extent of review of Travelling-people-related policies (in the function areas of education, eviction, planning, and site management). In every case the review rate was materially less, averaging only 36 per cent. Only 25 per cent of councils had undertaken a policy review in relation to the issue of planning and Travelling people, despite it being generally predicted to have been one of the key risk areas. It was only in relation to the issue of evictions that review rate (54 per cent) approached the general figure of 61 per cent.

The conclusion drawn was that in relation to this socially excluded group 'not being proactive' was the most attractive local authority option; that there were 'few votes to be gained by elected members actively promoting policies on behalf of unpopular causes'. This factor was also highlighted in a 2002 District Audit Report,[37] which stated that:

---

33 Wexler, op. cit., n. 29.
34 Home Office, *Putting Rights into Public Service: The Human Rights Act 1998: An Introduction for Public Authorities* (1999) 12.
35 ESRC-funded research, ref. R000239238; see L. Clements and R. Morris, 'The Millennium blip: local authority responses to the Human Rights Act 1998' in *Human Rights Brought Home: Socio-Legal Studies of Human Rights in the National Context*, eds. S. Halliday and P. Schmidt (2004).
36 Gypsies and Travellers constitute the single largest category of people (numerically) deemed to be 'at very high risk of social exclusion': Office of the Deputy Prime Minister, *Breaking the Cycle: Taking stock of progress and priorities for the future. A report by the Social Exclusion Unit* (2004) para. 1.61.
37 District Audit, *The Human Rights Act: a Bulletin for Public Bodies* (2002) 3.

42

within local government, an obstacle to adopting a corporate approach for [a human rights review of] policies has been a lack of member interest and engagement. This has resulted in a lack of support for front-line staff and inertia as far as taking the human rights agenda forward was concerned.

The Cardiff Law School study also sought to explain why 'eviction policies' were an exception to the disparate review rate. In the researchers opinion, unlike the other areas (education, planning, and site management) which could be viewed as providing potential benefits to the Travelling minority, robust eviction policies tended to command majority support and so their continued vigour was of direct relevance and importance to elected members.

On this basis it appeared that local authorities were only likely to undertake human rights reviews of policies that were seen to be of benefit to the interests of the majority (or an influential minority). The report theorized that the nature of a review might vary, depending upon whether a review might result in positive benefits to the majority or negative impact on an unpopular minority, and suggested that in the former there would be a likelihood of a 'full' human rights review whereas in the latter, the review would be more of a Strasbourg proofing exercise (that is, to ensure that the policy could withstand challenge).

If 'fear of the consequences' constitutes a significant barrier for stranded victims then, again, institutional resistance to embracing the cultural agenda would perpetuate this problem. In relation to officer attitudes towards Gypsies, the Cardiff Law School research found little evidence to suggest that cultural attitudes within local government had changed; the authors concluding that reform agenda had been:

> frustrated, or at the very least been distorted, to conform with the pre-existing organisational norms of local authority work. Although the survey encountered a number of officers who were endeavouring to bring about a 'rights based cultural' change – these could perhaps be characterised as those engaged in 'subversive decision making' that in effect undermines their authority's dominant agendas.[38]

It could reasonably be argued that Gypsies are an exception – that deep-seated prejudice against this group presents particular problems. However the Cardiff research findings have been reinforced by research undertaken by the British Institute of Human Rights (BIHR) in 2002.[39] This considered the Act's impact on 'those who are particularly disadvantaged' who 'often do not know, or understand the significance of, the Human Rights Act and how it could positively affect their lives' including 'people that are, or can at certain times in their lives, be considered vulnerable: children, disabled people, older

---

38 S. Halliday, 'The Influence of Judicial Review on Bureaucratic Decision-Making' [2000] *Public Law* 110–22, at 118.
39 J. Watson, *Something for Everyone: The impact of the Human Rights Act and the need for a Human Rights Commission* (2002).

people and refugees and asylum seekers'.[40] It found that the Act had 'simply not had an impact in the sectors that this project considered', that:

> little serious attempt by any organisation – whether in government or in the voluntary sector – to use the Human Rights Act to create a human rights culture that could in turn lead to systemic change in the provision of services by public authorities.[41]

More recently, a 2003 Audit Commission investigation[42] also expressed concern about the needs of vulnerable individuals being addressed by local authorities. It again emphasized the importance of policy reviews and audits to ensure human rights compliance – but found that these reviews had 'stalled' in almost half of all local authorities (44 per cent) and in most (60 per cent) of the health sector.

Research undertaken by the Public Law Project in 2002–03 concerning the impact of the Act on judicial review also came to a similar conclusion, that 'decision makers in public bodies have yet to absorb and incorporate in their decision making processes that values inherent in the Human Rights Act 1998'.[43]

THE COMMERCIALIZATION OF THE LAW

Court fees are an important indicator of the extent to which the civil justice process has become businessified. The dramatic fee increases under New Labour would have made the system inaccessible to poor people, without an enhanced means-testing 'dispensation' system. Whilst the expansion of means testing appears antipathetic to a government pledged to combat social inequalities, Stepney, Lynch, and Jordan[44] suggest that this is not the case. In their view the social exclusion agenda is based upon two broad assumptions:

> First, that the benefits of largely unregulated markets outweigh their social costs. Second, the significance of a growing underclass in society is that it poses a threat to economic recovery and stability, and that therefore the government is morally justified to use coercive means to get people off benefits and into work.

Emphasis of the communitarian nature of Convention rights could therefore be interpreted as one such coercive response.

Means testing has made a significant contribution towards entrenching social exclusion,[45] with many unassertive, poorly informed or otherwise

40 id., at p. 5.
41 id., at p. 8.
42 Audit Commission, op. cit., n. 20.
43 V. Bondy, *The Impact of the Human Rights Act on Judicial Review* (2003) 32.
44 P. Stepney, R. Lynch, and B. Jordan, 'Poverty, exclusion and New Labour Critical Social Policy' (1999) 19 *Critical Social Policy* 109–27, at 112.
45 See, for example, R. Lister, *The Exclusive Society: Citizenship and the Poor* (1990).

44

vulnerable people being deterred and thereby excluded from the benefit in question. Court fees are part of that system, and although the worst excesses of the regime may have been trimmed in *R* v. *Lord Chancellor, ex p. Whitham* (1997),[46] it remains government policy that the cost of providing the civil justice service is funded entirely out of court fees.[47] The Lord Chancellor's announcement[48] of this radical policy shift preceded the introduction Human Rights Bill in 1997. By April 1998 a very satisfied Parliamentary Secretary to the Lord Chancellor's Department, Mr Hoon, was able to announce that (due to fee increases) there had been a hike of over 20 per cent in the court services income – such that it now covered 99 per cent of its costs this way (as opposed to 81 per cent in the previous year).[49]

Given the extent to which the government has sought to introduce business practices into the justice system, it is perhaps unsurprising how rarely impaired access to justice is mentioned in official pronouncements as a factor in the measure (or cause) of social exclusion. In contrast to the frequent references to health, education, and social services, the Social Exclusion Unit's publications are silent on the question of impaired access to the civil justice. An exception to this official silence is to be found in the 1998 *Modernising Justice* White Paper[50] which listed in the categories to be accorded 'greatest priority' for legal aid funding 'social welfare cases which help people to avoid, or climb out of, social exclusion'. The only other post-1997 government publication which addressed this issue is a 2001 joint Lord Chancellor's Department and Law Centres Federation publication[51] which accepted that 'lack of access to reliable legal advice can be a contributing factor in creating and maintaining social exclusion'. The report relied heavily on a 1999 research report,[52] and cited its finding that an estimated 2 million adults in England and Wales failed to take any kind of action to deal with their legal problems. People in this group generally lacked educational qualifications; had money, employment or injury/ill-health problems; were on a low income and lived in rented accommodation; and were isolated in the sense that they had not previously accessed outside advice.

46 [1997] 2 All E.R. 779.
47 Court Service, *Consultation Paper on Fee Changes Code No CP 10/04* (2004) para. 4, accessible at <www.courtservice.gov.uk/using_courts/fees/civil_court_fees_2004/court_fees.htm#4>.
48 Lord Irvine LC, 581 *H.L. Debs.*, col. 881 (14 Jul 1997): 'the present principle is to recover the full cost of providing the civil courts, less an amount equivalent to the sum of exemptions and remissions'.
49 G. Hoon, 309 *H.C. Debs.*, col. 515 (1 April 1998): Written Answers to Questions, Lord Chancellor's Department. Civil Courts; and see, also, 'Civil Court fees pay their way, says Hoon' *Law Society's Gazette* 8 April 1998, 10.
50 Lord Chancellor's Department, *Modernising Justice. The Government's plans for reforming legal servies and the courts* (1998; Cm. 4155) at para. 3.7.
51 Lord Chancellor's Department, *Legal & Advice Services: A pathway out of social exclusion* (2001) accessible at <www.dca.gov.uk/laid/socex/index.htm>.
52 H. Glenn, *Paths to Justice* (1999).

Stein[53] explores the government's perplexing silence on this question. He highlights the lack of a strategic social justice mission within the Community Legal Service and the contradiction this creates with the New Labour's 'joined up government' approach to achieving policy objectives.[54] He argues[55] that access to legal assistance must form a central pillar of any programme designed to address social exclusion, stating:

> Informed, holistic and proactive legal services advocacy and advice should be viewed as a prime instrument of the Government in remedying social exclusion, as the interplay of law, policy and administration often form the web of the structures that keep especially low income people from participating in the norms of economic, social and civic life ... advocacy that gives practical voice to the aspirations and 'participative' needs of dispossessed people, can be a most effective engine of social inclusion and should stand as a critical component of a national strategy on poverty and social exclusion.

In his view a reinvigorated role for the Legal Services Commission is (or ought to be) a fundamental component in any strategy to 'seize the opportunities for rights enforcement and development under the Human Rights Act' as a mechanism for advancing the 'anti-poverty, social inclusion and community regeneration initiatives of the Government'. This has not however come to pass. Indeed, he argues[56] that, instead of safeguarding (or expanding) access to legal assistance, there has (since the 1998 Act came into force) been 'a diminution of spending in this area'.[57]

As noted above, there also exist within the substance of the law and judicial preconceptions material barriers to poor people who seek to advance a human rights argument. One aspect of this problem is evidenced by the satisfaction that senior judiciary have expressed with the way that they have digested this new body of law – contrasted with their relentless expressions of concern about the number of cases coming before them.

Lord Woolf, for instance has expressed pleasure at the 'great success' and the 'extremely smooth implementation'[58] of the Convention into domestic case law. His explanation for this is that the 'values to which the European Convention on Human Rights gives effect are very much the same values that have been recognised by the common law for hundreds of years' – a

---

53 Stein, op. cit., n. 22, p. 12.
54 id., at p. 5.
55 id., pp. 4–5.
56 id., at p. 15
57 Stein supports this assertion by (amongst other things) citing the Legal Services Commission's Corporate Plan 2001/02–2003/04, which, at p. 14, states that 'Legal Help (i.e. advice) in the contract category of social welfare law will be reduced from £76.1 million in 2000/01 to £64.3 in 2001/02'.
58 Lord Woolf LCJ, 'On the occasion of the opening of the judicial year at the European Court of Human Rights', speech on 23 January 2003, at <www.dca.gov.uk/judicial/speeches/lcj230103.htm>.

common law whose primary purpose was 'to protect property',[59] that failed to provide equal protection of the law and effective protection against discrimination, that long refused to acknowledge a right of privacy, that detained HL without procedural protection, and so on.

This smooth transition was achieved with no significant increase in the use of judicial review attributable to the Human Rights Act 1998.[60] Nevertheless, during 2001 Lord Woolf reiterated his concern about the increasing use of judicial review, lambasting the parties in *Cowl* v. *Plymouth City Council* (2001)[61] for not pursing 'Alternative Dispute Resolution', stating that 'in disputes between public authorities and the members of the public ... the paramount importance [is to avoid] litigation whenever this is possible'.[62] *Cowl* concerned eight elderly claimants, all frail and in poor health, who had lived in a care home (that was to be closed) for differing periods, the longest being nine years. Cases of this type concern issues of enormous substance: not merely the loss of a home (within the protection of article 8) but, in many cases, the likelihood of premature death, since research suggests that relocating institutionalized elderly people may have a dramatic effect on their mental health and life expectancy.[63] Some studies suggest that the increase in mortality rates might be as high as 35 per cent.[64]

Lord Woolf expressed this concern in a year when the total number of cases issued in the Administrative Court amounted to 6006.[65] Many commentators have observed how infinitesimally small this number is, when compared to the immense number of decisions that must be made by public officials/bodies every day[66] and questioned the appropriateness of shunting off for ADR issues that concern such fundamental questions as those in *Cowl*.[67] Could it be that the courts do not in fact regard issues of this type as within the substance of human rights law?

---

59 *Malins VC in Springhead-Spinning Co* v. *Riley* (1868) L.R. 6 Eq. 551.

60 Bondy, op. cit., n. 43, p. 31.

61 [2001] E.W.C.A. Civ. 1935 [2002] 1 W.L.R. 803.

62 See, also, Woolf LCJ, *Access to Justice: Final Report* (1996) ch. 18, para. 7, at <http://www.dca.gov.uk/civil/final/> where he referred to judial review as the 'remedy of last resort'.

63 See, for instance, C. Robertson, J. Warrington, J.M. Eagles, 'Relocation mortality in dementia: The effects of a new hospital' (1993) 8 *International J. of Geriatric Psychiatry* 521–5; see, also, 'Elderly patients die within weeks of transfer' *Times*, 7 July 1994.

64 C. Aldrich and E. Mendkoff, 'Relocation of the aged and disabled: A mortality study' (1963) 11 *J. of Am. Geriatrics Society* 185.

65 Bondy, op. cit., n. 43.

66 See, for instance, M. Sunkin, 'Trends in the use of judicial review and the Human Rights Act' (2001) 21(3) *Public Money & Management* 9–12; L. Bridges, G. Mesazaros, and M. Sunkin, *Judicial Review in Perspective* (1995, 2nd edn.); and C. Harlow and R. Rawlings, *Law and Administration* (1997) 537.

67 See, for instance, Public Law Project, *Is ADR here to Stay: Conference briefing* (2004), accessible at <www.publiclawproject.org.uk/policyres.html>.

In its 2002 research project, the BIHR considered the impact of Act on people who in many respects were not dissimilar to the applicants in the *Cowl* proceedings. The research revealed that many social care staff were routinely abusing their power in relation to such vulnerable people without even appearing to realize that they were doing so. Baroness Hale of Richmond, in the annual Paul Sieghart Memorial Lecture (2004),[68] referred to two graphic examples detailed in the research. One concerned older residents of a care home who were fed their breakfast whilst sitting on the toilet so that staff could get their work done within an allotted timeframe, and the second, an elderly man who was made to sit naked in a double room for a prolonged period whilst five male and female staff 'took turns to do the bits that they needed to do with the door wide open leading into the corridor'. As the report noted 'he was just left sitting with absolutely no clothes on whatsoever in the middle of this congregation taking place around him, with people walking past the door'.

In relation to these examples, Baroness Hale observed, 'I sometimes wonder whether we can recognise a real human rights abuse when we see one' and additionally whether the obvious rights abuses these residents experienced would indeed 'seem obvious to the law?' In view of the courts rebuff in *Cowl*, Baroness Hale's hesitancy is well placed.

Vulnerable people like those described in the BIHR report will generally have no contact with people sensitive to the abuses they are experiencing. Just as HL spent most of his life unlawfully detained before he encountered people prepared to challenge his treatment, so too is it probable that tens of thousands of elderly and vulnerable people experience abuse of the kind described by the BIHR study without hope of respite. Indeed it appears to be the case that:

> one in three elderly people suffer from psychological abuse, one in five are physically abused, the same number are conned out of their savings and more than 10 per cent are neglected and 2.4 per cent are abused sexually.[69]

The barriers to such stranded victims accessing the courts are self evidently immense and since *Cowl* are even greater: legal aid is now generally refused for such cases as the Legal Services Commission have taken Lord Woolf's robust comments to heart.

The vulnerable people of the type described in the BIHR report were institutionalized or reliant upon social care packages and of this group the vast majority now receive their services from independent organizations (albeit arranged by local authorities or the NHS). In *Heather* v. *Leonard*

---

68 Baroness Hale, 'What can the human rights act do for my mental health?', at <www.bihr.org/sieghart.html>.
69 Master of the Court of Protection in evidence to the Joint Committee on the Draft Mental Incapacity Bill – *Minutes of Evidence* 14 October 2003, Q505, *Volume II, Oral & Written Evidence* HL 189-II.

Cheshire Foundation (2002),[70] the Court of Appeal held that LCF was not a public authority and did not exercise any public function within the meaning of s. 6 Human Rights Act 1998. In so deciding, the Court gave a highly restricted interpretation to the meaning of 'public authority' and failed 'to give effect to the intention of Parliament that the protection offered by the Act should be comprehensive'.[71] In this respect the Joint Committee on Human Rights commented:

> As a result of the combined effects of a restrictive judicial interpretation of one particular subsection of the Act on the one hand, and the changing nature of private and voluntary sector involvement in public services on the other, a central provision of the Act has been compromised in a way which reduces the protection it was intended to give to people at some of the most vulnerable moments in their lives.[72]

CONCLUSION

In September 2004 the Social Exclusion Unit published a 'taking stock' report[73] which sought to assess the progress that the government had made in tackling social exclusion. There were many positives in the report, but it was also noted that the policy had failed in relation to three general categories of people, namely, people with physical or mental disabilities or chronic health problems, together with their carers; people with poor skills and no qualifications; and people from some ethnic minority groups (most notably Gypsies and other Travelling people). This paper suggests that these groups have also been excluded from the benefits of the Human Rights Act.

The research findings concerning the implementation of the Act are virtually unanimous in two respects; first, that the promised rights revolution cannot take hold without a cultural shift in the way public service organizations operate; and secondly, that no such cultural shift in attitudes has as yet occurred. This paper has not considered potential solutions. Undoubtedly a Human Rights Commission could make a significant impact, provided its resources were adequate and directed at this largely overlooked sector. Undoubtedly, however, a Commission alone cannot be the whole answer.

Charles Epp[74] suggests that there are four key factors that have to be in place for a 'rights revolution' to take hold in any particular country. The first

---

70 *Times*, 8 April 2002; [2002] 2 All E.R. 936.
71 Joint Committee on Human Rights, Seventh Report *The Meaning of Public Authority under the Human Rights Act* HL (2002–03) 39, HC (2002–03) 382.
72 id.
73 Office of the Deputy Prime Minister, *Breaking the Cycle: Taking stock of progress and priorities for the future. A report by the Social Exclusion Unit* (2004) para. 1.61.
74 C. Epp, *The Rights Revolution* (1998).

three of these are traditional and unsurprising, namely: constitutional guarantees, judicial leadership, and a 'rights consciousness'.[75] To these, he adds an 'essential' fourth factor, namely, the existence of a cadre of radical lawyers, who have adequate support mechanisms to mobilize their commitment. The evidence suggests that in the United Kingdom there is much that remains to be done to address all four of Epp's factors, most particularly – in relation to the rights of stranded victims – the fourth.

We live in a country where winners are vaunted and losers are excluded: in a system where the prevalent dogma is that 'the benefits of largely unregulated markets outweigh their social costs'.[76] For a true conception of communitarian rights to take root, we must create a system where the winners see that it is in their interests not always to win – or at least not to win so fabulously.

---

75 Which Epp considers as having at its core the '"Lockian creed" of liberal individualism which encourages complainants to frame their political ideals in terms of individual rights, to take their concerns to courts, and to expect courts to make policies on such questions'
76 Stepney, Lynch, and Jordan, op. cit., n. 44.

JOURNAL OF LAW AND SOCIETY
VOLUME 32, NUMBER 1, MARCH 2005
ISSN: 0263-323X, pp. 51–67

The Human Rights Act: A View from Below

RUTH COSTIGAN* AND PHILIP A.THOMAS**

The paper is based on survey work undertaken in the Cynon valley, south Wales, an area of high social deprivation. We interviewed local solicitors to establish their understanding and usage of the Human Rights Act (HRA). Outside of south Wales there is evidence of growing awareness and involvement of specialist practitioners in human rights actions. This we call a top-down process. Our work starts at the other end: a bottom-up account of high-street, small-practice solicitors.

The United Kingdom has moved from liberties to rights.[1] The Human Rights Act was described as having 'the potential for being one of the most fundamental constitutional enactments since the Bill of Rights over 300 years ago'.[2] Other lawyers were even more exuberant. For example, Helena Kennedy declared: 'something is happening: a different *Zeitgeist,* a shift in the legal tectonic plates'.[3] Professor Wade stated that the Act is a 'quantum leap into a new legal culture'.[4] On the other hand, Professor Allott observed, 'The Minima Carta, known as the Human Rights Act, is the misbegotten product of an alliance between shallow liberal rationalism and executive branch cynicism.'[5]

* *Law Department, Swansea University, Singleton Park, Swansea SA2 8PP, Wales*
** *Cardiff Law School, Cardiff University, Museum Avenue, Cardiff CF10 3XJ, Wales*

1 T. Campbell, *The Left and Rights: A Conceptual Analysis of the Idea of Socialist Rights* (1983); T. Campbell, 'Human Rights: A Culture of Controversy' (1999) 26 *J. of Law and Society* 6. See, also, L. Clements, 'The Human Rights Act – A New Equity or a New Opiate: Reinventing Justice or Repackaging State Control?' (1999) 26 *J. of Law and Society* 72.
2 L. Clements and J. Young, 'Human Rights: Changing the Culture' (1999) 26 *J. of Law and Society* 1.
3 F. Klug, *Values for a Godless Age: the story of the United Kingdom's new Bill of Rights* (2000) 11.
4 W. Wade, 'Human Rights and the Judiciary' (1998) E.H.R.R. 532.
5 *Times,* 2 January 1999.

The early years after the Act's commencement saw mixed messages in terms of appreciation, training, and acceptance by politicians,[6] the judiciary,[7] and law teachers.[8] Today, the Act continues to bed in but its usage also continues to grow as specialist solicitors and barristers, in niche practices and chambers, explore the jurisprudential possibilities of the legislation.[9] There is a developing internalization of legal norms within the judiciary, the bar, and senior practitioners, though the litigation process is slow.[10] But a feature of this development is that it appears to be a top-down process. The effectiveness of the trickle-down exercise of normative change is widely reviewed.[11] The mechanistic, hierarchical programme of international human rights treaties being adopted into domestic law, thereby producing change at the highest levels which in turn affect and alter court and legal practice, has a certain ordered appeal based on precedent, despite the limitations, uncertainties and reinterpretations during the exercise of this process. The 'gap' between the law in the books and the law in practice, as powerfully exposed by McBarnet, demonstrates how cautious we must be about these two elements and also, indeed, how we must see the reality of the law which in itself presents major opportunities for improper exploitation.[12]

The legal profession in the United Kingdom continues to constitute the principal gatekeeper to the courts. However, the solicitors and barristers in England and Wales do not constitute a homogenous work-practice group. Matrix chambers, London, does very different work from that undertaken in Do-It-All chambers in Cardiff. Clifford Chance, London, has a client base of national and international companies which expects protection and safety concerning the movement of its money, credit, goods, and intellectual property around the world. On the other hand, Grabit and Run, Abertuff, operates with clients on social security benefits who are anxiously waiting for increasingly hard-to-obtain legal aid certificates in order to stay out of

---

6 D. Nicol, 'The Human Rights Act and Politicians' (2004) 24 *Legal Studies* 451. John Bercow MP stated in the House of Commons: 'We are creating a collision course between the courts and the House of Commons', 306 *H.C. Debs.*, col. 842 (16 February 1998). The position of the Conservative Party in the House of Commons regarding the need for the Act was one of great scepticism and very limited support.

7 C. Guarniere and P. Pederzoli, *The Power of Judges* (2002) 185.

8 See P.A. Thomas, 'The Human Rights Act 1998: Ready, Steady, Go?' (2001) 35 *Law Teacher* 360.

9 There is a plethora of literature on the Human Rights Act. Web sites and data bases allow greater access to the literature, legislation, and case law concerning human rights.

10 J. Raine and C. Walker, 'Implementing the Human Rights Act into the Courts in England and Wales: Culture Shift or Damp Squib?' in *Human Rights Brought Home*, eds. S. Halliday and P. Schmidt (2004) 111.

11 For example, see S. Silbey, 'Cultural Analysis of Law' (1992) 17 *Law and Social Enquiry* 39; D. Englel and F. Munger, *Rights of Inclusion: Law and Identity in the Life Stories of Americans with Disabilities* (2003).

12 D.J. McBarnet, *Conviction: Law, the State and the Construction of Justice* (1981).

© Cardiff University Law School 2005

jail or to keep a violent partner away from the family home. One practice deals with governments and global wealth, the other deals with consequences of bad government and immediate poverty. Thus, the top-down process follows different, discrete routes as the legal expertise is applied on behalf of the clientele. Both sets of lawyers and their clients are strangers to the concerns, needs, and expectations of the alternative practices and their clients. J.K. Galbraith stated that the top-down theory produced the same results as putting quality oats into the nose bag of the horse. What came out the other end was not quality oats![13]

Jack Straw in the parliamentary debates on the Human Rights Bill isolated the principal and innovative jurisprudential feature when he advanced the Bill as seeking to create a pervasive rights culture throughout society.[14] With these words of the then Home Secretary clearly stating the position of the government[15] we move to focus on a 'bottom-up' account of access to justice for those who are socially excluded.[16] Despite Tony Bair's acknowledgment that 'legally enforceable rights and duties underpin a democratic society, and access to justice is essential in order to make these rights and duties real',[17] the reality is that justice remains a commodity subject to state direction, public and personal financial constraints and client social status. Our research,[18] undertaken in a south Wales valley, provides the backbone of this paper. It focused on a socially deprived community, examining the experiences, knowledge, and expectations of solicitors who practice in the valley. We examine the working lives of local solicitors who seek to provide bottom-up access to justice and we review their appreciation and usage of the HRA.

The research methodology involved structured interviews conducted with twenty-one of the twenty-five solicitors who practice within the Cynon valley.[19] These practices are small, being largely sole or two-person practitioners, though one practice has seven fee earners. The interviews took

---

13 Personal communication, 1992.

14 J. Straw, 306 *H.C. Debs.*, cols. 768–70 (16 February 1998).

15 There is an argument that these rights were never intended to be exercised in full. For example, see N. Ardill, 'Justice for All?', *LAG Journal*, September 2002, 6, which identified the Access to Justice Act 1999 as major limiting legislation in terms of obtaining public funding for HRA cases. This point is taken up again regarding the latest Legal Services Commission code on funding of public law cases (Editorial, *LAG Journal*, October 2004, 3). It is suggested that these limitations make the provision of an 'effective remedy' under the Convention an impossible dream.

16 G. Room, *Beyond the Threshold: the Measurement and Analysis of Social Exclusion* (2005).

17 'Foreword' in *Law Reform for All*, ed. D. Bean (1996) xiii.

18 R. Costigan, J. Sheehan, and P.A. Thomas, *The Human Rights Act 1998: An Impact Study in South Wales* (2004). A limited number of free copies of this book remain available from P.A.Thomas.

19 One solicitor refused an interview on the grounds that it would be a waste of our time, and more importantly of his time, as it was about legislation of which he is ignorant and he anticipates remaining in that state of grace.

place in their offices and were semi-structured and recorded. The interviewees were guaranteed anonymity.

THE CYNON VALLEY

The Cynon valley is a major sector of the Rhondda Cynon Taff (RCT) local authority.[20] Eight per cent of the population of Wales lives in RCT, of whom 90 per cent were born in Wales. The population of the Cynon valley is 63,512 with a non-white ethnic group of 1.1 per cent. Despite the authority's close proximity to Cardiff, to those who visit or live there it might as well be a world away. Historically the area was heavily dependent upon coal mining, which effectively ceased in the 1980s with the enforced closure of the mining industry. Economic regeneration within the former mono-economy has met with limited success.

The Cynon valley has a disproportionate number of people who suffer from ill health,[21] with 29 per cent of the population identified as suffering from limiting, long-term illness. Of the people who fall into this category 84 per cent are of working age. Individuals making up 17 per cent of the population describe their general health as 'not good';[22] 53 per cent of households have one or more persons who self-classify as having a 'limiting long-term illness'. Although the percentage of home ownership stands at 73 per cent, one in nine houses is unfit for human habitation.[23] Nine per cent of houses are occupied by a single parent with dependent children. Six out of ten people are classified as obese, and less than half the population takes any form of exercise on a weekly basis. Working and living conditions have contributed to the ill health of older people in the valley, particularly in relation to men, where there are recorded high rates of death from chronic obstructive pulmonary disease, including emphysema and chronic bronchitis.[24]

The level of economic activity amongst men has declined since the last census; that in relation to women has increased by 2.8 per cent; 51 per cent of the authority's residents are in employment. Of the unemployed, 28 per cent have been unemployed for at least ten years. For employment rates, RCT ranks 362 out of 376 local and unitary authorities in England and Wales.

---

20 Much of the data that follows applies to the Rhondda Cynon Taff area. Cynon valley is typical of the area and the figures that apply to RCT can be extrapolated to give a social account of life in the Cynon valley. The principal source of the data is the National Census of 2001.

21 These figures are taken from '2001 Census of Population: Cynon Valley' (Members' Research Service, Research Paper 03/030, April 2003).

22 This figure compares unfavourably with Guildford, a sample town in the south of England, where 6 per cent of the population place themselves in the same category.

23 Bro Taf Health Authority, *Improving the Health of Older People* (2001).

24 id.

54

Thirty-five per cent of households in the Cynon valley have no car. Forty-three per cent of those aged 16–74 have no educational qualifications, compared with 26 per cent in Cardiff. RCT ranks 364 (of 376) in England and Wales qualification statistics. Twelve per cent of the population has an initial degree or higher qualification, compared with 25 per cent in Cardiff. Cardiff is approximately fifteen miles from the Cynon valley, but is much further away in terms of work opportunities, life styles, housing conditions, educational and community facilities, support systems, and ultimately, access to justice.

SOLICITORS' AWARENESS OF THE HRA

All solicitors interviewed for the study had some awareness of the HRA. Those working in family and criminal law demonstrated the greatest knowledge of the Act. Solicitors outside these areas were commonly of the view that the HRA was of little relevance to their work. The pervasive nature of the HRA was not widely recognized. For example, whilst Article 6 was the most recognized right, there was little awareness of the relevance of the Article to civil matters.

Practitioners were asked to speculate about the level of knowledge of the HRA amongst their local colleagues. These individual responses are typical:

> No one has ever mentioned to me that they intend to make an argument using the HRA. No one has ever discussed it with me, I haven't heard it mentioned by another solicitor in any application I've made, so I think the awareness of other people in this area is minimal.

> Very low awareness, I suspect. It is not a topic that rises to the fore when I am talking with my colleagues.

> I think it's something that people have not attached sufficient importance to; some people have attached no importance at all. So, I think it's a patchy response ...

The valley solicitors are high-street, general practitioners who deal with issues as presented across the desk by local people. Thus, their practices are made up of cases frequently supported by the Legal Services Commission, and reflect criminal and family matters, along with conveyancing, personal injury, probate, and some commercial work. They do what they have traditionally done and do it to the best of their ability. The pressures to maintain their practices were described as 'constantly increasing'.[25] For example, one solicitor was described as 'possibly making £14,000 a year'. A senior partner in another firm stated that he is 'looking forward to the day he makes £50,000 a year'.[26]

---

25 One practitioner has taken early retirement since the publication of the report.
26 Contrast with B. Cole, *Trends in the Solicitors Profession* (2002) 46, where it is stated that 25 per cent of solicitors in sole practice earn less than £19,000 as compared with the median profits per partner, in the 26–80 partner firms, of £154,000. Partners in the largest firms earn considerably more.

The valley solicitors are themselves local people. Sixty-three per cent studied for their degree in Wales and 74 per cent were trainees in their current practice. Sixty-three per cent were born in the Cynon valley and a further 21 per cent were born within twenty miles of the valley. There was virtually no movement to other firms upon completion of the training contract. Indeed, no solicitor has worked as a fee earner in more than one practice. The growing number of specialists on Law Society panels and specialist niche practices is not reflected in the small practices that operate in this valley. Within this close, and possibly closed, legal community opportunities for movement, introduction of new ideas, and innovative change appear limited. For those who serve as legal generalists for a deprived community, the knowledge, usefulness, and income generating potential of the Human Rights Act has yet to be realized.

By way of sharp contrast, there is some early evidence that elsewhere the field of human rights has attracted specialists. For example, a survey conducted on behalf of the Law Society of England and Wales in 1998 demonstrated that of the solicitors interviewed who dealt with human rights cases, 31 per cent had been educated at private schools; 20 per cent had postgraduate qualifications, of whom 40 per cent had studied the European Convention on Human Rights. Indeed, 33 per cent had delivered courses on the ECHR and 20 per cent were fluent, to a legal usage level, in French. Twenty per cent described themselves as human rights specialists and 60 per cent were members of human rights organizations such as Amnesty International and Liberty. The top-down process has its adherents and supporters whilst the bottom up-process, according to our survey, remains relatively quiescent.

USE OF THE HRA

Under half of the solicitors interviewed had used the HRA. What is more revealing is *how* the Act was used. It had not been used as a cause of action. Only one solicitor had used it as a primary argument (in a successful judicial review on an employment matter). As might be expected, the rights most commonly invoked were those contained in Articles 6 and 8.

The solicitor who used Article 6 as a primary argument in a successful judicial review had received no training on the HRA. This practitioner referred to keeping up to date in a 'roundabout way' through reading newspapers. But the solicitor's on-going awareness of human rights was vital to the recognition that an Article 6 principle was at stake:

> It just stuck out in my mind that I'd read quite a bit about the fact that people have a right to a fair hearing. It just occurred to me that this chappie hasn't been given the right to put his case, or to have his say. Even though it was a relatively informal meeting, he should have been given the opportunity to have his say. They just got rid of him without even hearing from him.

The solicitor then bought a guide to the HRA. This person was the only one to have in the office a specific text on human rights. Indeed, firms' stocks of law books were, in general, limited.

Article 6 was employed by criminal law practitioners in relation to incorrect procedure, abuse of process, the right against self-incrimination, and the right to be heard. But, even here, practitioners observe that the HRA has had limited impact:

> It comes up occasionally, but in the criminal courts, certainly locally, it doesn't seem to be a live issue ... It's 'tweaked up the system' and it's put people on their toes but it hasn't made a terrific impact.

> The courts do without fail ask, 'are there any Human Rights Act matters or arguments?' So it is there, it is in the forefront of their minds, and it is brought to everybody's attention. At the moment I have to say I can't remember the last time that I argued it, nor indeed while I have been in court heard anybody else argue it: where they have said 'yes, there is a human rights argument on this particular case'. When I first did some training, and when the Human Rights Act matters were being looked into and before it came into force around the 2000 mark, I can remember a solicitor saying 'this is what we are going to be arguing about day in day out, every single case is going to be human rights this, human rights that'. [But] that's not transpired, it hasn't happened.

A variety of reasons emerged for the apparently limited impact of Article 6 on criminal law practice. The courts' receptiveness, which is considered below, was the single most prominent factor. Another element was defence solicitors' apparent preference for more familiar legislative provisions (such as s. 78 of the Police and Criminal Evidence Act 1984) and common law authorities to support challenges based on procedural propriety and fairness. In cases involving clear irregularity, the HRA was not pivotal to the outcome. In one case, a police witness had, contrary to explicit instruction from the District Judge, talked with other officers (who had earlier testified in the trial) during an adjournment. The Judge concluded that the circumstances endangered a fair trial. Commenting on the role of the HRA in that case, the defence solicitor said:

> I tend to think that the court would have come to the same conclusion shall we say two or three years ago, prior to the Act, because what had happened simply, quite clearly, had been wrong. Everybody saw it as being wrong, as being unfair. But the Human Rights Act helped to bolster everybody's views in that case.

Solicitors working in family law had some knowledge and experience of Article 8, but the HRA has not had a significant impact on their work. The commonly held view was that the Act did not add much to existing legislation and common law in family law. There was, however, some expectation that the Act's relevance would be revealed through future domestic jurisprudence. These are typical descriptions of practitioners' experiences:

> The only time I have come across any reference to the HRA at all, since the HRA came into effect, is in care proceedings, where social workers now lodge

57

statements with the court. There is a little paragraph, either at the beginning or at the end, that says it has been prepared in conjunction with 'Article' something – I can't even remember what it is now, but the HRA – and that they've taken the HRA into account when preparing care plans in respect of children. Other than that, I've not ever come across it mentioned in court, or in court documentation in the work that I do.

I'm aware of [the HRA] but I can't say that it's made any real difference to what I do at the moment. There are cases that have sort of crept into it, but at the moment I haven't actually done anything substantial on it, although I could be just starting to be doing something substantial on it.

It hasn't had, in my view, a huge impact on private family law which is what I mainly do, because it's all a balancing exercise anyway. The reason that the courts come to a decision is because they are weighing up conflicting interests and everybody has got human rights, and so you have to look at everyone's human rights: it's a balancing exercise.

I think it is very difficult from a care point of view because there are usually very good reasons why the children have been removed, and so you have to pick your case where you can argue it, and they are limited situations.

Many solicitors referred to an unfulfilled expectation that the Act would have a profound impact on their practice. Prominent and widespread predictions that the Act would generate a considerable amount of work were confounded, in general to the disappointment, and some relief, of practitioners. There was initial enthusiasm for the HRA: most of the solicitors in the study who had used the Act did so soon after it entered into force. But unfulfilled predictions and disappointing responses have contributed to a significant marginalization of the HRA in solicitors' thinking. This having happened, there is unlikely to be rejuvenation, as solicitors' knowledge becomes more dated and the weight of unfamiliar jurisprudence appears more daunting. The experience of the valley practitioners is not unique. Indeed, it might be symptomatic of a growing malaise. For example, an editorial in a leading practitioners' journal declared:

> Most people have retreated into a state of bafflement about what the Human Rights Act means to them in practice ... Public awareness of the Human Rights Act seems to have been diminishing rather than increasing.[27]

EXPLAINING THE LIMITED USE OF THE HRA

Exploring knowledge and use of the HRA is not about seeking to 'blame' professionals or the courts for a lack of expertise or receptiveness. Rather, understanding the experience and practices of those delivering legal services helps identify needs, which represent opportunities to contribute to the effectiveness of the HRA. The interviewees identified a wide range of

27 Editorial, *LAG Journal*, October 2004, 3.

reasons for the limited impact of the HRA on their work, which are considered in this section.

A key explanation for the relatively low impact of the HRA on the interviewees' work was uncertainty about how to access the rights contained in the HRA. The interviewees knew of at least one of the routes through which the rights can be enforced, but no solicitor demonstrated awareness of more than two paths. Exceptionally, one solicitor, in whose field of work the HRA has particular relevance, was under the misapprehension that using the HRA would necessitate a hearing in the European Court of Human Rights.

A related explanation for the apparent under-use of the HRA was a lack of recent, targeted, and practical training. Fifty-eight percent of the interviewees had participated in HRA training, in most instances prior to the Act's implementation. Subsequent training events typically took the form of updates on specific areas of law, with HRA jurisprudence referred to in the course of presentations, rather than the Act's mechanisms being addressed. There were some positive experiences of training, with one solicitor being enabled to offer guidance to colleagues after attending an event six months prior to implementation:

> It was a good course: I had plenty of information and details and all the rest of it, which gave some foundation to the Act. Then I did some research myself. Then I put it all together to present a course to the staff.

But the overwhelming assessment of those who had participated in training was that it was insufficiently practical in orientation:

> It was too general. It was teaching us: it was like a university lecture, rather than [giving] a procedural [context], saying 'well look this is how it affects ...'. There was nobody giving us examples. Nobody asked, 'has any one of you ever used it?'

> I would be more inclined to go to local barristers' chambers, or perhaps if there was a reasonably well known local solicitor who would put the emphasis on practical exercises and practical case discussion as opposed to the theoretical and the academic side of it. We work in an entirely practical environment and it would be great if somebody came along and said 'I used this argument in a bail application case', or 'I used this argument is a such and such case'. I think that might help to grab the attention some of the local practitioners.

Another common criticism was the accessibility of training events, in terms of cost and location:

> I would have to put myself down as pretty much self-taught, I suppose. In terms of training I can tell you straight away what the deciding factor would be amongst local defence solicitors (by which I mean probably throughout South Wales): it's a cost issue. If you did us a course cheaply on it, we would flock to your door ... I think a number of organisations have simply 'jumped on the band wagon'. We have to do compulsory training, and they charge the earth for it, on top of which we don't have many courses run locally to South Wales: frequently we have to trot off to Birmingham, Bristol, Manchester, London, at vast expense.

59

Some solicitors referred to being cautioned, at training events, against being too ready to use the HRA:

> I remember that there was a big point when it first came out: be very, very careful about arguing human rights points before the courts, because if you are just arguing frivolously that would be frowned upon by the District Judge, or whoever you are before. I think that may have had the effect of lessening the applications made using the Human Rights Act.

A significant barrier to solicitors in the Cynon valley keeping pace with human rights developments is the prohibitive cost of many subscription-based electronic legal resources. Solicitors relied instead on free internet sites. Use of the internet varied quite widely, with the age of the practitioner generally being a factor in the level of comfort with the internet as a resource. Nearly all firms referred to a need to update their IT resources and skills.[28]

Solicitors observed that many (potential) clients in the Cynon valley would have difficulty funding legal challenges:

> There's not much point in saying 'access to justice', 'human rights', unless you have the means to fund it. The majority of people in this valley either cannot afford it, or they're working: not earning a great deal, but because of the income they have, they're probably going to have to pay a large contribution to get legal aid. People just can't afford it. So, this phraseology, 'access to justice', doesn't cut with people who really know, and are sort of the 'coal face' in areas like this, where people have got major problems in litigating. 'Access to justice' is okay for people who can get legal aid for nothing and it's okay for people who are wealthy. If legal aid isn't available, there's no access to justice for a lot of people.

The issue of public funding was, unsurprisingly, of great significance to the interviewees. In a deprived community, the monies controlled by the Legal Services Commission are of particular relevance. The following comments are representative of solicitors throughout the country.

> There is a serious risk that if legally aid work is associated with low fees, this may have a serious impact on the quality of people who undertake legally aided work.[29]

> Legal aid contracting has left vulnerable people combating domestic violence and homelessness without legal advice because solicitors have left the system.[30]

> A fragmented, under-funded and patchy legal aid scheme is leaving single parent families without decent legal advice.[31]

---

28 One practice continues to use manual typewriters.
29 *Parliamentary Constitutional Affairs Select Committee Report*, July 2004.
30 News section, *Law Society Gazette*, 10 June 2004, 4.
31 R. Moorhead et al., *The Advice Needs of Lone Parents* (2004). R. Moorhead, 'Advice Needs of Lone Parents' *Family Law*, September 2004, 667.

The pages of the professional press are full of such claims. However, some solicitors have gone further than picking up their pens. In Cardiff, forty firms undertook a token strike against legal aid cutbacks. The editorial of the Law Society Gazette, when commenting on this unusual action, declared 'Their claim is undeniably valid'.[32]

Responses to questions about awareness and use of the HRA were often candid and reflective. Some solicitors saw potential for making more use of the HRA:

> I think if we were quite frankly a little bit more imaginative, and did a little bit more digging and even a bit more thinking, I'm sure we could apply human rights issues with a lot more cases than we do at the moment.

But pressure of time is a major obstacle to research and creative thinking:

> Most practitioners would tell you that they were overworked and under permanent pressure. The amount of stuff that has to be shifted is close to overwhelming.

> A successful criminal practice depends on you doing the work you do, in bulk. You've got to 'stack it high and sell it cheap', you've got to do it in bulk or you'll just 'wither on the vine'. So there are time issues: the more you can do, and the more quickly you can do it, the more successful at it you're going to be.

> If you're in a specialised law firm that deals with immigration and criminal law, then you would be more aware of it. The non-contentious lawyer is under an ever burgeoning workload. It's practicalities: you've got clients hassling you and ringing up about ... this, that and the other, as well as the financial advisors, the estate agents, other parties, the other side's solicitors. There's too much going on, too many interruptions, too much to worry about.

HUMAN RIGHTS AND THE LOCAL COURTS

There was an expectation prior to the commencement of the Act that the workload of courts in the United Kingdom would increase considerably.[33] Extensive training involving all branches of the legal profession and judiciary was offered and in some cases was obligatory.[34] Statistical evidence of workloads is provided by Raine and Walker[35] whose review of selected Crown courts, County and magistrates' courts leads them to the conclusion that:

---

32 Editorial, *Law Society Gazette*, 30 September, 2004.
33 'The lawyers will dominate all the debates'. K. Ewing, 'The Human Rights Act and Parliamentary Democracy' 62 *Modern Law Rev.* (1999) 79.
34 See Thomas, op. cit., n. 8, and Raine and Walker, op. cit., n. 10.
35 Raine and Walker, id.

One year after enactment at least, the clear message from the research was that the Human Rights Act had *not* had the impact that many anticipated in relation to the number or complexity of challenges. The consensus experience to date has been that relevant court business has been fairly tranquil.[36]

Our study sought to establish why 'tranquillity' was the order of the day in those courts where the valley solicitors practice on a daily basis. What were the barriers to developing a pervasive legal rights culture in the lower courts? There is a firm perception among Cynon valley solicitors that local courts are unreceptive to human rights arguments. Negative experiences were common among those who had used the HRA. This raises the prospect that solicitors' preparedness to use human rights arguments will be stifled. It was commonly felt that courts pay 'lip service' to the HRA:

> ... it is brushed aside. They get it in there somewhere: 'we've considered the Human Rights Act', or they'll say, 'you are right to bring up the Human Rights Act and I have considered it but it's not right, here'. But you know damn well that they haven't really considered the Human Rights Act. It's a stock answer ... so you can't appeal on a human rights issue.

Interviewees were of the view that Crown and County courts were much more willing to entertain human rights arguments than were magistrates' courts. A lack of receptiveness on the part of magistrates' courts was a persistent observation:

> The Human Rights Act tends to perhaps not bother the magistrates' court. I don't think that it is used terribly frequently by the practitioners in the magistrates' court. I think it is used more often in the Crown Court ... [T]he magistrates' court isn't by and large interested in much law; it isn't interested in much legal argument, either. It is far better founded to deal with factual issues ... [Magistrates] are familiar and at ease with resolving factual issues: they can simply apply common sense, that's territory that they are familiar with. Once the practitioner starts to embark upon a legal argument, they begin to lose their attention. I actually find they're against you: you know, 'we'll decide what the facts here are, we will decide who is guilty and who is not, and don't you go telling us about this, that and the other'.

> There may be, amongst some solicitors in some courts, and with certain magistrates, a sense of cynicism about them being pro-prosecution. Certainly, some magistrates will almost make the defence solicitors 'vicariously liable' for their clients' actions! That's how certain magistrates make us feel. That type of magistrate – where you know s/he is pro-prosecution in their outlook (and you can tell after practising in the local courts) – any type of defence gets up their nose, and that includes the Human Rights Act. [This happens] particularly on adjournments, because I think magistrates, probably quite rightly, don't like cases hanging about on the list. They have their print out and they see how many times it's been adjourned and they want to make progress: they've got targets as well.

Solicitors tailor their arguments according to the status of the court in which they are appearing, and, in the case of magistrates' courts, the particular bench they are addressing. Arguments without merit should not, of course,

36 id., at p. 133.

be encouraged. But human rights law is necessarily creative. Furthermore, it is early days in the settling of the HRA's parameters. If courts (which are, after all, under a legal duty to observe the Convention rights in the HRA) do not receive arguable human rights claims in a knowledgeable and considered manner, an opportunity for lawyers to develop human rights jurisprudence becomes a burden without reward.

The reported resistance of some lower courts to human rights arguments is attributable to a complex interplay of factors and pressures. But whatever the causes, there is some evidence that lower courts are signalling that the HRA has, for the most part, a symbolic role to play. Many solicitors shared this perception:

> It doesn't seem relevant to us here. I read a lot about it in the press and it seems to be the big thing; however, in practice, I think 'well, where is it?' I don't see it and it doesn't seem to be relevant to us here.

> We all thought it was going to be great and revolutionary. [But] the European Court decisions seem to apply really as common sense things: 'yes there is a human rights issue here, it does apply but it doesn't apply sufficiently for it to overturn this decision', and so it didn't appear to have any teeth.

> I've never had any counsel or barrister involved on it, or mention anything on human rights either. They sort of go 'full on' with English law and then they are using ... [the HRA] as a helper ... You can just go with that and chuck a bit of human rights in.

> I have heard it mentioned before the courts. [But] it was being just thrown at the court, to see if they could deflect away from the actual real issue of the matter ... I have never, when I have been in court, seen it argued properly at all.

A number of solicitors referred to using the HRA to add weight, rather than as an argument of substance:

> I have used [the HRA] but I think I have been somewhat guilty of what we were told on the initial course on the Human Rights Act not to do: 'don't just raise the Human Rights Act, get the specific Article'. But sometimes if you're not sure of what Article would apply, you can still just throw it in ... It has worked now and again, but you've got to know the cases to use it for.

There was some perception of human rights issues as dramatic and exceptional, excluding relatively commonplace matters:

> I can understand how it works to stop people being tortured, and degrading behaviour. I can imagine it being applied to international matters, but not in domestic matters. I can't see how it can apply. It's difficult to say what is sufficient, what's so bad as to be treated as a breach of human rights. It's all very ambiguous and vague, it's all very interesting but I don't think it's got any practical application.

> You know, a lot of it is groundbreaking work, and groundbreaking work is expensive work and we're a small practice. It would be difficult for us to fund groundbreaking litigation *pro bono*. The bigger firms can possibly stand that. The amount of *pro bono* work has to be limited and obviously legal aid is not easy to get.

Another, fairly common perception was that the HRA works to the benefit of criminals or others identified as 'undesirable':

> I think many people, even society if you like, tend to think that the Human Rights Act is only really going to be used for the benefit of the defendant, and it really goes against the rights of the poor complainant, the poor victim. There is a big problem, I think, with the law that society has got at the moment ... I do think the Human Rights Act is seen really to bolster the rights of the criminal as opposed to doing anything at all to try and bolster the rights of the victim ... That happens to be an argument that I agree with. I think poor victims are cast to the four winds.

> That's my perception of the Human Rights Act, and certainly I think [that of] a lot of people in the street ... They do read an awful lot of negative things about it ... [People have] got a real perception of crime and what's fair. [They] see people coming in who have supposedly been given huge amounts of benefits as income, for example to asylum seekers, or economic migrants. Then you have others who can't understand why their own elderly relatives have to pay for their care, having to dwindle away all their resources ... With the Human Rights Act, it would be for example, Myra Hindley – are this person's human rights being violated? Is this prisoner in solitary confinement being deprived of his right to family life or association with his wife? I think this is probably why a lot of ordinary people think 'it doesn't apply to me'. I think you rarely get much in the media where people say 'oh good old Human Rights Act, it's a good job we've got that legislation.' I think you would be hard pushed to say 'that was well worth bringing in: we wouldn't have had this protection unless it had been incorporated'.

A common theme in the interviews was reluctance to use the HRA for fear that it would give the impression of a weak case. And, indeed, many lawyers would themselves see recourse to the HRA as somewhat of a 'desperate measure':

> When this all came out, you could guarantee that you would hear submissions on human rights. Now, you very rarely hear submissions on human rights. It's as if it was used as 'the new thing in' and now you don't often hear submissions on human rights. It seems to me, it's a kind of last resort argument. If all else fails, my last resort is to 'flag this up' and say, 'don't forget that my client has got human rights'. And you will argue whatever Article, or, you know, 'this provision in this legislation is not compliant with the Human Rights Act' ... If you've got a strong argument, you wouldn't put that in. If you were in difficulties, you'd grab anything you can to bolster up your case as much as you can, and you would put that in.

> I suspect that there are very few people who would say to you 'look this human rights stuff is a complete load of nonsense.' It isn't, but it has been shouted about far more than it should be. I perceive it really as a safety net. It's sort of the last refuge: 'we haven't got a statutory remedy, or we haven't got a remedy on standard principles of tort or contract or whatever, so can we make a human rights argument as a last resort?'

> My view of it is, in principle, it is the proverbial good thing. We never argue against another piece of legislation, or another avenue for litigation. [The HRA] opens out the possibilities for an alternative means of attack, or making an issue out of something when there is no immediately obvious remedy.

64

Other than that, I think that the general response to human rights is that if you put it in a pleading, or you raise it in correspondence with the other side in a litigation context, the response is somewhat sceptical: 'if you're pleading human rights it's because you haven't got a case'. It is the last refuge for a lawyer who hasn't got a case.

Yet, as Sir Stephen Sedley observes:

> the Human Rights Act should represent not an end but a beginning: not the last resort of a lawyer without an argument, but the first port of call for lawyers and courts alike.[37]

The HRA is essentially designed to be self-enforcing, by means of the section 6 duty on 'core' and 'functional' authorities to observe the Convention rights. But the Audit Commission has consistently found a lack of preparedness on the part of public bodies in terms of this obligation. In a recent study of 175 public bodies in local government, health, and criminal justice services, the Commission warned that 'three years on, the impact of the Act is in danger of stalling and the initial flurry of activity surrounding its introduction has waned.'[38] The study revealed that 58 per cent of the bodies reviewed had no human rights strategy. Sixty-one per cent had taken no action to ensure that service providers under contracted out arrangements complied with human rights law. Moreover, of the 175 bodies:

> Most failed to see the benefits of using human rights as a vehicle for service improvement by making the principles of dignity and respect central to their policy agenda, which would place service users at the heart of what they do.[39]

In 44 per cent of bodies, reviews of policies and procedures to ensure compliance with the HRA had 'stalled'. This was in part attributed to pressure of other priorities. But, significantly, it was also ascribed to the adoption of a passive attitude. The Commission observed:

> Reacting to complaints and case law when they happen is not an appropriate response to the Act and will not bring about service improvement, particularly for those who are most vulnerable and heavily dependent upon public services. Unfortunately, in many cases 'wait and see what happens' or 'let's defend a challenge' approaches are common.[40]

This is exacerbated by the fact that 56 per cent of the bodies studied are not monitoring developments in human rights jurisprudence, so are unlikely to learn from others' liability for unlawful practices or procedures.

---

37 Costigan, Sheehan, and Thomas, op. cit., n. 18, p. 12.
38 Audit Commission, *Human Rights: Improving Public Service Delivery* (2003) para. 2.
39 id., para. 20.
40 id.. para. 6.

CONCLUSION

The Audit Commission's research demonstrates that there is a real need for lawyers to be abreast of human rights law if those who are at the receiving end of unlawful practices are to have access to a remedy. The Cynon valley research does not provide grounds to expect that, for everyone, those lawyers will be there to fulfil that need. There is a high level of dedication amongst practitioners to delivering the best possible service to their client communities. But they are not always equipped to provide this service in the human rights field. Seventy-nine per cent of solicitors interviewed said they would welcome (further) training on the HRA. There is a fundamental need, and thus a significant opportunity, for practical and accessible training. If the needs of clients with human rights problems are to be met, and if local practitioners and courts are to make a contribution to the developing human rights culture in the United Kingdom, lawyers must be able to recognize human rights issues and to formulate knowledgeable arguments, and courts at every level must be ready to hear them.

Our research focused on a small group of sole and small-practice solicitors working within a deprived south Wales valley community. However, the findings appear to be symptomatic of a much larger and more widespread shortfall in awareness and usage at the grass-roots level of the HRA. For example, Richard Stein, a London solicitor, stated:

> The hopes that the Human Rights Act would redress the balance of rights for deprived individuals has not been borne out. It has raised new intellectual debates for lawyers but whether it makes much difference is debateable.[41]

The Cynon valley research reveals that the bottom-up strategy is currently failing and that the HRA is not being used to its potential.[42] The reasons for this are complex and varied. There is scope for solicitors to deepen their appreciation of the HRA, but to state this is not to undermine their professionalism and commitment to delivering effective legal services to the community. These sole and small-practice practitioners are operating on tight financial margins with a number of immediate and pressing concerns which push into the background issues of innovative cases via the HRA. For example, they are concerned about the growth of 'Tesco Law'[43] and its

---

41 R. Stein, 'Comment', *Law Society Gazette*, 16 April 2004. See, also, Editorial, 'The Department of Constitutional Affairs, the Human Rights Act's primary custodian, acknowledges that a human rights culture is yet to be created' *LAG Journal*, October 2004, 3.

42 'This important study demonstrates how much needs to be done to help those in an area of significant social deprivation in the UK, who really ought to be the primary beneficiaries of the Human Rights Act. A way must be found for this to be rectified.' Thomas LJ, *Law Society Gazette*, 16 April, 2004, 3.

43 See 'Comment', *Law Society Gazette*, 24 June 2004. <www.tesco.com/legalstore>; Tesco expects a million visitors a year to this site.

66

predicted impact on their traditional services. They describe themselves as being on 'a production line' with legal aid cases, and constantly claimed that the administrative work associated with legal aid franchises is particularly burdensome for small practices.[44] Such concerns are of particular relevance to a community such as those people who live in the Cynon valley, most of whom would be solely dependent on legal aid certificates in order to access justice. It is proving increasingly difficult to attract young practitioners into the valley to undertake legal aid work[45] and solicitors talked about how the solicitors appearing in the local courts are 'ageing'. A consequence is the likely reduction in both the number of solicitors and also solicitors' firms, thereby reducing the range and availability of services to the local community.[46] One result will be the creation of 'advice deserts' amongst communities with the greatest needs.[47] Within such an economic and working environment it is unsurprising that solicitors have little time to consider and work within the new and challenging parameters of the HRA. In Sir Stephen Sedley's words:

> It's easy to criticise practitioners at the foot of the pyramid for lacking the expertise of those near the peak. But lawyers nevertheless have a bedrock of obligations to the people who come through their doors, and a knowledge of the Human Rights Act must surely now be part of this. That's easily said. What is less easy is to see how to make a reality of it. It's one thing for local solicitors to keep up to date with changes in conveyancing or criminal law; it's another for them to acquire a whole new mindset, a new approach to statutory interpretation and public administration, which stands outside anything they themselves were taught. And when you look at the daily tally of drug-related crime, family breakdown and social and economic deprivation, it's not hard to see why local practitioners feel they have enough on their plate without worrying about something as seemingly abstract as human rights.[48]

44 'Some firms are going to think having a franchise is not worth all the hassle. It is quite hard to comply just because of the volumes and volumes of paper.' A Cynon valley solicitor.

45 Law Society of England and Wales Survey (*Law Society Gazette*, 25 March, 2004) states that 90 per cent of new entrants into the profession shun legal aid work because of low pay, poor job prospects, and crippling debt.

46 'The number of solicitors is going to dwindle. It's happening now. There are a lot of other firms in the valley that haven't expanded. People in them are getting older, once they retire there is nobody to take their place. Its beginning to contract.' Another solicitor stated 'It's difficult to attract quality staff because we are not making as much money as we used to, and we can't pay as we used to.'

47 'Legal aid lawyers are providing a service more to the public and the government than for an income for themselves.' C. Sutton, chair, Sole Practitioners Group, *Law Society Gazette*, 22 April 2004, 3.

48 'Foreword' to Costigan, Sheehan, and Thomas, op. cit., n. 18.

JOURNAL OF LAW AND SOCIETY
VOLUME 32, NUMBER 1, MARCH 2005
ISSN: 0263-323X, pp. 68–89

Lost on the Way Home?
The Right to Life in Northern Ireland

CHRISTINE BELL* AND JOHANNA KEENAN*

This article starts from the premise that, through the Belfast Agreement, the Human Rights Act 1998 (HRA) was invested with a 'transitional justice' function in Northern Ireland, unlike in the rest of the United Kingdom. The article evaluates how far the HRA has met this challenge by examining a case study of the right to life. The European Court's development of a procedural aspect to the right to life in the form of a right to an effective investigation, has implicated both institutional reform for the future, and also a need to revisit past state killings with their 'transitional justice' implications. There have been some positive developments, but, despite this, domestic institutions and courts have largely failed to deliver on Article 2's procedural aspect. The article concludes by questioning whether the very design of the HRA has limited the possibilities for a 'transformational constitutionalism' capable of incorporating Article 2's procedural right.

This article examines the impact of the Human Rights Act 1998 (HRA) in Northern Ireland, through a case study on the right to life. Any analysis of the HRA in Northern Ireland, must acknowledge a political context quite distinct from the rest of the United Kingdom. Three main reasons for the HRA were given by the Labour government in 1997: that accessing rights domestically would be speedier and cheaper; that it would enable British judges to make a distinct contribution to human rights jurisprudence; and

* Transitional Justice Institute, University of Ulster, Magee Campus, Londonderry/Derry BT48 7JL, Northern Ireland

This article was in part based on interviews with Paul Mageean, Paul O'Connor, Hugh Orde, Karen Quinlivan, Eric Strain, Jane Winter, and Ritchie McRitchie, all of whom we would like to thank for their time and expertise. We would also like to thank Maggie Beirne, Kathleen Cavanaugh, Murray Hunt, Paul Mageean, Fionnuala Ní Aoláin, Maggie O'Conor, Ursula O'Hare, and Jane Winter, for commenting on earlier drafts. Mistakes which remain are our own.

that it would improve rights protection.[1] Four years in, these justifications can be turned into questions through which to evaluate the HRA. However, consideration of the HRA in the Northern Irish context can add a fourth question: whether the HRA has helped Northern Ireland move from conflict to peace.

This ambitious aim is implicit in the Belfast Agreement, which coincided with enactment of the HRA: the two became inextricably linked. The Labour government's plans for giving domestic effect to the European Convention on Human Rights (ECHR) stood independently of the peace process. However, when the Belfast Agreement came to be signed, 'incorporation' was presented as a central part of what has become known as the human rights and equality agenda. It was one of a number of human rights measures that together went far beyond the constitutional reform/devolution package as conceived of elsewhere in the United Kingdom. Unlike the rest of the United Kingdom, this package included a Human Rights Commission and a single Equality Commission, and contemplated further development into a possible Bill of Rights for Northern Ireland, and an all-Ireland Charter of Rights.[2]

These measures emerged during negotiations as vital to underwriting the 'big constitutional fix' of devolution. Together with power-sharing and cross-border bodies, they aimed to take the sting from the Constitutional question of British versus Irish sovereignty – resolution of this question having been left open – by ensuring that in the interim, society would be fair for everyone. The inclusion of a human rights and equality agenda also responded to the analysis that human rights abuses by the state had contributed to the onset, escalation, and sustenance of conflict and required to be addressed if a lasting peace was to be achieved. This agenda reflected a coincidence of principled human rights arguments with the negotiated search for avenues for on-going conflict resolution that would remove vestigial arguments for paramilitary violence.

Human rights measures, while primarily addressing the vertical relationship between citizen and state, also held some potential for mediating the horizontal relationship between Protestant Unionist and Catholic Nationalist communities and cultures, by providing new fora for dealing with public order disputes, equality, and language rights, through which 'parity of esteem' could grow. Thus, the HRA, already on new Labour's devolution table, took on a new dimension and was invested with a deeper political role with respect to Northern Ireland. This different context has given rise to arguments that the new constitutional order in Northern Ireland does not 'fit' within notions of traditional British constitutionalism, even in their

---

1 Home Office, *Rights Brought Home: The Human Rights Bill* (1997; Cm. 3782).
2 *Agreement reached in the multi-party negotiations, 10 April 1998*, [hereinafter *Belfast Agreement*], 'Rights, Safeguards and Equality of Opportunity'. See, further, P. Mageean and M. O'Brien, 'From the Margins to the Mainstream: Human Rights and the Good Friday Agreement' (1999) 22 *Fordham International Law J.* 1299.

modernized, devolution-friendly guise, but are indicative of a more complicated 'transitional justice' terrain.[3]

It follows that in evaluating the HRA in Northern Ireland, we must begin from a different starting point. In the rest of the United Kingdom such evaluation is classically a critique of the Act's capacity to improve rule of law protections against the worst excesses of government. In Northern Ireland, however, it is being expected to assist a transition from a less liberal-democratic, violent past to a more liberal-democratic, peaceful future, by affecting both vertical (state-citizen), and horizontal communal (Catholic-Protestant) relationships. In its vertical ambition, the HRA and the other human rights measures are being expected to reconstruct and 're-legitimate' a degraded rule of law. Crucial to this was the Belfast Agreement's programme of legal institutional transformation focused around delivering a new accountability, particularly in policing and criminal justice. This more radical goal opens up a rather different series of questions through which to evaluate the HRA in Northern Ireland. In particular, how has the HRA influenced the programme of legal institutional transformation? Has it played a part in buttressing institutional reform? To what extent has it assisted more broadly in drawing a line under Northern Ireland's past, and establishing new institutional practices for the future? To what extent has the HRA capacity to undertake this role?

The role of the HRA can also be examined at a deeper level – one which implicates the horizontal inter-communal relationships. The view of transition articulated thus far remains contested communally, and this contestation affects not only understandings of the Agreement itself, but also understandings of the necessity for legal institutional reform or transformation. Inter-communal differences revolve around the extent to which legal institutions have been complicit in the maintenance and management of conflict, and result in diametrically opposed views on whether reform is necessary or even desirable. This has created not only a vertical dynamic, but also an inter-communal one with relation to key legal institutions. As noted elsewhere, if these institutions are viewed as having 'done a good job in difficult circumstances,' then demands for recon-figuration are seen as charged political assault on the integrity and neutrality of such institutions and law itself.[4] Change can only be countenanced as necessary when couched in managerial language tied to modernization projects in the rest of the United Kingdom. However, if such institutions are viewed as having fundamentally failed, as evidenced by multiple human

---

3 See, for example, C. Campbell, F. Ní Aoláin, and C. Harvey, 'The Frontiers of Legal Analysis: Reframing the Transition in Northern Ireland' (2003) 66 *Modern Law Rev.* 317.

4 C. Bell, C. Campbell, and F. Ní Aoláin, 'Justice Discourses in Transition' (2004) 13 *Social & Legal Studies* 305.

70

rights abuses, then the imperative is for substantial reform articulated in the language of 'transformation'.

This adds a jurisprudential layer to the evaluation of the HRA in Northern Ireland, by inquiring how government, public bodies, and judicial system have positioned themselves with regard to these two competing views, when dealing with the HRA. Have they endorsed either 'traditional' or 'transitional' approach, or have they tried to mediate between the two? To what extent have they tried to maintain law's stability, and to what extent have they tried to acknowledge and address its failings during the conflict? Have they found ways to do both? What has been the significance of their approach in terms of both a jurisprudence of transition, and in terms of the actual transformation of legal institutions? Where has this left inter-communal relationships?

THE RIGHT TO LIFE

The right to life forms a good case study from which to evaluate the impact of the HRA in Northern Ireland. The right to life found in Article 2 ECHR is acknowledged to be one of the most fundamental rights – the right on which all others depend. The state's use of lethal force during the conflict, and attempts to hold state actors accountable, formed a central and controversial place in human rights activism throughout the conflict. These efforts were to result in May 2001 in the consolidation of the so-called 'procedural' aspect to the right to life by the European Court in the cases of *Jordan, McKerr, Kelly, Shanaghan* v. *United Kingdom*, emanating from Northern Ireland.[5] Here the Court found that an effective investigation was a necessary component of the right to life, setting out a critique of domestic institutions which suggested a blueprint for reform. The coincidence of Agreement, HRA and the development of the procedural aspect to Article 2, makes the right to life a test case *par excellence* for evaluating the HRA's impact on institutional reform.

However, the right to life also lies at the heart of more paradigmatic 'transitional justice' debates over how to deal with the abuses of the past, post-peace agreement, and the relationship of justice to peace.[6] From the 1990s onwards, peace processes have increasingly produced mechanisms to address

---

5 *Jordan* v. *United Kingdom* (2003) 37 E.H.R.R. 2; *McKerr* v. *United Kingdom* (2002) 34 E.H.R.R. 20; *Kelly* v. *United Kingdom* (ECHR), *Times*, 18 May 2001; *Shanaghan* v. *United Kingdom* (ECHR) *Times*, 18 May 2001. See, also, *Finucane* v. *United Kingdom* (2003) 37 E.H.R.R. 29.

6 The literature is too extensive to be fully referenced here, but see, in particular, P. Hayner, *Unspeakable Truths* (2001); N. Roht-Arriaza (ed.), *Impunity and Human Rights in International Law and Practice* (1995); S. Cohen, 'State Crimes of Previous Regimes: Knowledge, Accountability and the Policing of the Past' (1995) 20 *Law & Social Enquiry* 7.

71

issues of accountability for human rights abuses, although these have varied in design. Northern Ireland's peace process stands out as one of the few not to have yet produced such a mechanism, dealing with the issues in a piecemeal way.[7] During the conflict in Northern Ireland over three thousand were killed; studies indicate that 367 were killed by security forces, 1050 by loyalist paramilitaries, 2139 by Republican paramilitaries, and 80 killed by civilians or not known.[8] These figures leave open the 'dark figure' of collusion – the number of deaths by paramilitaries in which the state may have colluded in a variety of ways. As the peace process has developed, pressure to 'deal with the past' through some form of accountability or acknowledgement of conflict-related deaths has remained. This is true with relation to all deaths. However, the *Jordan et al.* decisions have injected detailed normative standards into this debate as regards those killed by state forces, and those killed after alleged collusion between state and non-state actors. Here the families are entitled to an accounting of the state's actions, including access to information about planning and decision-making around the use of force. However, underlying the quest for information is a search for a broader acknowledgement of the state's role in the conflict. As Ní Aoláin writes, these:

> Represent a unique class of cases intimately linked with the progress and form of the conflict itself... At this transitional stage of the conflict, these cases represent an enormous accountability gap for the State. The story about these cases is a missing narrative about the role of the State during the conflict itself.[9]

This story is integral not just to future state accountability, but to communal attempts to move to a shared understanding of the conflict that could enable the peace process to move forward. Evaluating the Convention's 'transitional justice' role involves evaluating what the Convention brings to debates about the past, and considering what it should bring.

BRINGING ARTICLE 2 HOME

The development of Article 2's procedural aspect itself stands testimony to the difficulties of holding state actors accountable domestically.[10] Over the years, families, lawyers, and NGOs had cooperated in a wide variety of strategies aimed at holding state actors accountable domestically and internationally. Domestically, these strategies were ineffective with domestic

---

7 C. Bell, 'Dealing with the Past in Northern Ireland' (2003) 26 *Fordham International Law J.* 1095.
8 D. McKittrick, S. Kelters, B. Feeney, C. Thornton, *Lost Lives: The stories of the men, women and children who died as a result of the Northern Ireland Troubles* (1999).
9 See F. Ní Aoláin, 'Truth Telling, Accountability and the Right to Life in Northern Ireland' [2002] E.H.R.L.R. 572.
10 See, further, F. Ní Aoláin, *The Politics of Force* (2000).

72

processes, such as the inquest, becoming ever more closed. Internationally, however, the very impossibility of evaluating the state's arguments that its use of force was always legitimate, logically gave rise to the notion that a 'procedural' aspect to Article 2 was vital to ensuring the substantive protection of life. This procedural aspect began to be developed by the European Court in the case of *McCann* v. *United Kingdom* (1995), where the United Kingdom became the first state found by the Court to have violated the right to life, with respect to three IRA operatives shot dead by British security forces in Gibraltar.[11] While not central to the finding in *McCann*, the Court noted that:

> a general legal prohibition of arbitrary killing by the agents of the State would be ineffective, in practice, if there existed no procedure for reviewing the lawfulness of the use of lethal force by State authorities.[12]

The procedural aspect to the right to life was developed through a series of Turkish cases,[13] and consolidated and elaborated on in the cases of *Jordan* v. *United Kingdom, McKerr* v. *United Kingdom, Kelly and Others* v. *United Kingdom*, and *Shanaghan* v. *United Kingdom*. These cases, analysed elsewhere,[14] involved a finding that the United Kingdom had violated Article 2 because it had not properly investigated the killings of twelve individuals, some of them killed by the police, some by the army, and one killed by loyalist paramilitaries in circumstances suggesting collusion. The United Kingdom had argued that a combination of police investigation, review by the Director of Public Prosecutions, the inquest system, and the possibility of civil proceedings had satisfied the procedural requirement of Article 2. While the Court acknowledged that a combination of remedies indeed could satisfy Article 2, it found that they had not in these cases. The investigation had to be capable of leading to a determination of whether the force used in such circumstances was or was not justified in the circumstances and to the identification and punishment of those responsible. The Court set out the relevant institutional defects, as shown in Table 1.

Bringing the right to life home in Northern Ireland, therefore involves a fascinating 'completing of the circle' with respect to international adjudication and domestic institutional reform. An optimist could have expected two things: first, that adequate investigations would now ensue in these particular cases, and others like them; and second, that the institutional failings identified by the Court would form a blueprint for holistic change

---

11 *McCann* v. *United Kingdom* (1996) 21 E.H.R.R. 97.
12 id., [161].
13 See, for example, *Akdeniz and Others* v. *Turkey* (31 May 2001) App. no. 23954/94; *Avsar* v. *Turkey* (10 July 2001) App. no. 25657/94 [2003] 37 E.H.R.R. 53; *Semse Onen* v. *Turkey* (14 May 2002) App. no. 22876/93; *Ulku Ekinci* v. *Turkey* (16 July 2002) App. no. 27602/95; *Aktas* v. *Turkey* (24 April 2003) App. no. 24351/94 [2004] 38 E.H.R.R. 18.
14 Ní Aoláin, op. cit., n. 9, p. 588.

73

Table 1

Police investigation	Lack of independence of investigating officers from officers implicated
Prosecution process	Lack of public scrutiny, and information to victim's family from Director of Public Prosecution (DPP) regarding non-prosecution
Inquest	Lack of compellability of state actors Lack of verdicts or findings capable of leading to prosecution Absence of legal aid for families Non-disclosure of witness statements to families prior to inquest Public Interest Immunity (PII) certificates preventing examination of central issues Delay Limited scope Lack of prompt or effective investigation into collusion allegations on state's own initiative

relating to police, prosecution, and coroner practices, aimed at ensuring an effective investigation. These were, after all, the institutions also targeted for reform by the Agreement (in part due to a lack of public confidence generated by cases such as *Jordan et al.*). The declaratory nature of the Court's decisions, of course, left the need for either response technically open.

The government made a formal response to the Committee of Ministers regarding the findings of the Court as it is obliged to by virtue of Article 46(1) of the ECHR. This response has been supplemented by processes emanating from peace process pressures and negotiations; by continuing reform of the inquest system; and by the intervening litigation strategy in Article 2 cases.

THE GOVERNMENT RESPONSE

On 19 March 2002 the government produced a 35-point response to the Committee of Ministers in what has proved to be an on-going negotiation.[15]

---

15 Northern Ireland – Article 2 Cases [hereinafter *Government Package*] (Copy on file with Author). The government supplemented its response on 19 May 2003, and 14 June 2004, and (orally) on 20 September 2004. At time of writing a secretariat document became public setting out the full government response, critical comments received from third parties, and a secretariat assessment of the adequacy of the response; 'Cases concerning the action of security forces in Northern Ireland', CM/Inf/DH(2004) 14 Revised (Restricted) 27 September 2004.

The package points firmly only to institutional reform for the future – there are to be no new investigations into the cases in question. As regards institutional reform, however, rather than envisioning what would deliver an effective investigation in the *Jordan* sense, the package adopts a piece-meal and minimalist approach to addressing discrete *Jordan* defects. While the HRA forms a central plank of the response,[16] paradoxically, it is used to displace the onus for holistic institutional reform away from government proper onto the relevant institutions themselves through their Article 6(1) duty to act compatibly with the Convention. Thus, the DPP, the Chief Constable, all coroners, as well as Ministers of the Crown are 'bound to act compatibly with Convention rights'.[17] The DPP's obligation to comply with the HRA in making decisions is stated in a context where very little other change is proffered.[18] The problems with the scope of inquest are largely to be 'cured' by the coroners ensuring compliance with the Convention.[19] A summary of the rest of the government's response is contained in Table 2. Interestingly, where positive changes are proffered these for the most part had predated the judgments owing their existence to peace process human rights reforms.

Criticisms regarding the adequacy of this response can be made.[20] The failure to renew investigations into the actual cases in question has been criticized as violating the judgments. The Police Ombudsman's office while clearly independent of police, does not cover cases where the army was involved – significant given that the ECHR, in *Kelly* v. *United Kingdom* and later *McShane* v. *United Kingdom*,[21] found that police investigators were not sufficiently independent of implicated army personnel. The duty on the Chief Constable to remain 'mindful' of the need for investigation stands at odds with the more stringent HRA requirement of compatibility. Whether the DPP's stated policy will produce further reasons in cases of alleged state-wrongdoing remains to be tested, although early evidence is not encouraging.[22] Reasons have only been forthcoming in one of the cases that were subject to the judgments. The refusal to have verdicts in inquests

---

16 id., para. 2.
17 id., para. 2.
18 id., paras. 2, 10–15.
19 id., paras. 2, 16, 18, 20, 21, 22.
20 See Committee on the Administration of Justice, 'Preliminary Response from the Committee on the Administration of Justice (CAJ) to the "package of measures" submitted by the United Kingdom to the Committee of Ministers', 8 October 2002; Northern Ireland Human Rights Commission, *Comments on the United Kingdom Government's Package of Measures Intended to Address the Issues Raised by the European Court of Human Rights in Its Article 2 Judgments of 4 May 2001* (2002).
21 [2002] 35 E.H.R.R. 23.
22 See *In re John Boyle* (N.I.Q.B.) 29 September 2004 (failure of judicial review of DPP's decision not to prosecute). Reasons have been given in Article 2 cases of Thompson, Brecknell (where families rejected them as inadequate), and McKerr.

Table 2

Problem	Response
Police investigation	
• Independence	– Police Ombudsman's office for dealing with complaints against police
	– Chief constable to remain 'mindful of need to ensure unlawful killings are investigated expeditiously and thoroughly'
	– Police and Police Ombudsman to have family liaison officers
DPP	
• Lack of public scrutiny and information to families (failure of DPP to give reasons)	– Recognition by DPP of need to evolve policy within context of HRA obligations
	– Current policy restated (policy of refraining from giving reasons except in cases of exceptional nature, where a decision on giving reasons will be reached 'having weighed the applicability of public interest considerations material to ... each case').[23]
Inquest	
• Lack of jury verdict	– Verdicts not considered necessary
• Narrow scope of examination	– Coroner to ensure adequate width given his/her HRA duty
• Lack of compellability of state actors	– Coroners rules amended to provide for compellability of witnesses
• Non-disclosure of witness statements	– Chief Constable normally will disclose statements sent to the Coroner in cases involving the state
• Absence of legal aid	– Ex-statutory legal aid scheme established
• PII certificate prevented examination	– Recent case law and policy changes providing that the government will focus on 'damage caused' by disclosure rather than automatic claims based on the class and contents of documents
• Delay	– HRA obligation now applies to coroners
	– Appointment of additional full-time Deputy Coroner for Belfast
	– Additional administrative support to part-time coroners.
	– Northern Ireland Court Service (NICS) to provide statistics and information on outstanding inquests
	– NICS aware of need to minimize delay and are in contact with coroners

23 id., para. 10–15, 631 *H.L. Debs.*, col. WA 260 (1 March 2002); *Adams's, In Re* [2001] NICA 2 (19 January 2001).

76

has been criticized as inadequate to meet the judgments' criticisms, a position now further supported by the House of Lords.[24] While state witnesses are now compellable, protection against self-incrimination still applies, leaving the inquest's scope, in this regard, limited. The provision for disclosure of statements, and the government's PII response, have not always been implemented.[25] Furthermore, the Police Ombudsman's failure to disclose relevant police documents to families has been challenged as violating the Article 2 procedural requirement.[26] Delay is still a practical feature of the system, and indeed has been exacerbated by the wait for litigation to filter through to the House of Lords (as discussed further below).

This package has since been supplemented with regard to coroners' practices and deaths in custody. In the summer of 2001 the government established the 'Luce review' to review and report on 'Death Certification and Investigation in England, Wales and Northern Ireland'. This was established largely in response to the scandals surrounding the Shipman, Alder Hey, and Marchioness cases, which had highlighted deficiencies in the inquest system in England. In response to both Article 2 pressures and peace process pressures (the Criminal Justice Review Group established as a result of the Belfast Agreement having recommended an independent review into the law and practices of inquests in Northern Ireland), it was agreed, after much NGO lobbying, to include a review of coroners' services in Northern Ireland. The Luce review contemplates an overhaul of the inquest system which if implemented would go far to meet Article 2 concerns left unaddressed by the government's response, such as provision for juries in controversial cases, and the lifting of protection from self-incrimination for compellable witnesses.[27] A special chapter in essence extends the recommendations to Northern Ireland, with both it, and the Northern Ireland Court Service response[28] couched in the language of managerial change, rather than transition from a problematic past.

---

24 R. (Middleton) v. Her Majesty's Coroner for the Western District of Somerset [2004] 1 A.C. 182.
25 Committee on the Administration of Justice, op. cit., n. 21, p. 5; N.I. Human Rights Commission, op. cit., n. 21, para. 23. McCaughey & Another, Re Application for Judicial Review [2004] N.I.Q.B. 2 (20 January 2004) later changed the law on PIIs with respect to inquests, finding that Police or Ministry of Defence are under a duty to disclose documents to the coroner to decide on relevance, and ultimately on disclosure if any PII is then presented.
26 O'Brien v. Police Ombudsman (judicial review awaiting judgment).
27 Death Certification and Investigation in England, Wales and Northern Ireland: The Report of a Fundamental Review (2003).
28 Northern Ireland Court Service, The Coroners Service of Northern Ireland Proposals for Administrative Redesign, A Consultation Paper (2004) addresses primarily restructuring and reporting issues, does not address jury verdicts scope, or testimony of implicated witnesses, also proposed by Luce. Compare Home Office, Reforming the Coroner and Death Certification Service: A Position Paper (2004; Cm. 6159), adopting similar managerial approach.

While the government's response rules out further investigations in the cases in question (and, it would seem to follow, in other 'past' cases), political developments have resulted in a commitment to establish public inquiries in a number of other cases involving state use of force, in what has continued to be a 'piecemeal' approach to the lingering question of 'how to deal with the past'. As a confidence-building measure in January 1998, prior to the Belfast Agreement, the government established a judicial inquiry into 'Bloody Sunday', an incident in which security forces killed thirteen people at a civil rights demonstration in Derry on 30 January 1972 (a fourteenth person dying later). The inquiry, now finished and due to report in 2005, already holds some sobering insights as to the effectiveness of public inquiries in delivering truth or accountability, touched on below.[29] Post-agreement, as a result of negotiations aimed at restoring devolution, Canadian Judge Peter Cory was appointed to make 'a thorough investigation of allegations of collusion' in six cases, many of which had been the subject of years of non-governmental organization and family pressure.[30] Cory recommended public inquiries in five of the cases (one in the Republic of Ireland), and the United Kingdom government has now committed to holding inquiries in the four cases in its jurisdiction, although not without caveats and controversy in particular relating to how public they will be.[31]

At the time of writing, the Committee of Ministers' response was still awaited.[32]

LITIGATION STRATEGY

While the government response has focused primarily on institutional reform for the future, the litigation strategy has focused primarily on bringing the judgments home with respect to past cases, in particular the cases of *Jordan* and *McKerr*, which were the subject of the ECHR judgment. Of course, these cases remain important also to sharpening institutional reform. It is worth

29 A. Hegarty, 'The Government of Memory: Public Inquiries and the Limits of Justice in Northern Ireland' (2003) 26 *Fordham International Law J.* 1148.
30 Weston Park Proposals, published by the Northern Ireland Office, and the Republic of Ireland Department of Foreign Affairs, in the form of a letter to the party leaders, 1 August 2001 (available at <www.cain.ulst.ac.uk/events/peace/docs/bi010801.html>).
31 P. Cory, *Cory Collusion Inquiry Reports into Chief Superintendent Breen and Superintended Buchanan; Patrick Finucane; Lord Justice Gibson and Lady Gibson; Robert Hamill; Rosemary Nelson; and Billy Wright* (2004). The Irish government have committed to an inquiry in the fifth case but not yet established terms of reference. See NIO Press Statement, 16 November 2004 (announcing Hamill, Nelson, and Wright Inquiries); and NIO Press Statement, 11 January 2005 (announcing steps towards Finucane inquiry case).
32 The secretariat assessment, op. cit., n. 15, cannot be fully reviewed here. While finding 'significant improvements in existing procedures', it requests further information on a number of points, and identifies matters which are outstanding.

78

noting the extent to which their strategies have exhibited continuity with pre-*Jordan*, pre-HRA strategies, now supplemented by the jurisprudence of *Jordan* and the HRA. The difficulties of implementing the HRA are not, in this case, difficulties of lack of knowledge or capacity of clients or lawyers. In fact families have continued to press their claims, with the teams of lawyers who took the cases to Europe remaining involved afterwards in the struggle to 'bring the judgments home'.

There have been three main planks to the litigation strategy. The first plank focused on the inquest procedure. Cases were taken to push the courts to 'cure' its defects, so that it was capable of fulfilling the procedural aspect of Article 2. Thus, cases focused on pushing inquests to be prompt,[33] for legal aid for families,[34] for an expanded scope of review and jury verdicts,[35] and for adequate document disclosure.[36] The jurisprudence in this regard became intertwined with that from cases emanating from England, focusing for the most part on the scope of the inquest in cases of deaths in custody, and whether it enabled attribution of responsibility for the state's role in those deaths.[37] The second plank of the legal strategy focused on cases where the inquest had finished or run aground, where the Secretary of State was asked to initiate a new investigation, and judicially reviewed in terms of Article 2 where he did not.[38] The third plank of the litigation strategy supplemented these two, by focusing on the DPP process, and judicially reviewing decisions not to prosecute, and/or the failure to give reasons for such decisions.[39]

33 *Jordan, Re Application for Judicial Review* [2002] N.I.C.A. 27 (28 May 2002); *In Re McIlwaine* N.I.Q.B. (18 May 2004).
34 *Hemsworth, Re* [2003] N.I.Q.B. 5 (7 January 2003); *Jordan, Re* [2003] N.I.C.A. 30 (12 September 2003); *Hemsworth, Re an Application for Judicial Review* [2004] N.I.Q.B. 26 (26 April 2004).
35 *Jordan's Application for Judicial Review, Re* [2002] N.I. 151; *Jordan, Re an Application for Judicial Review*, [2002] N.I.Q.B. 20 (8 March 2002); *Jordan, Re Application for Judicial Review*, op. cit., n. 33; *Jordan, Re an Application for Judicial Review* [2004] N.I.Q.B. 27 (12 January 2004).
36 *Jordan, Re Application for Judicial Review* [2001] N.I.Q.B. 32 (4 September 2001); *Wright, Re Application for Judicial Review* [2003] N.I.Q.B. 17 (7 March 2003); *McCaughey & Anor*, op. cit., n. 25; *In Re McIlwaine*, op. cit., n. 33.
37 See, cases culminating in *R.(Amin)* v. *Secretary of State for the Home Department* [2004] 1 A.C. 653; *Middleton*, op. cit., n. 24; *R (Sacker)* v. *HM Coroner for the County of West Yorkshire* [2004] 1 W.L.R. 796; and *R (Kahn)* v. *HM Coroner for West Hertfordshire & Anor* [2002] EWHC 302 (Admin).
38 *In Re McKerr*, Q.B.D. (26 July 2002); *McKerr, Re* [2003] N.I. 117 (10 January 2003); *Jordan, Re Application for Judicial Review* [2004], op. cit., n. 35; *In Re McKerr* (Northern Ireland) [2004] 1 W.L.R. 807.
39 *Jordan, Re* [2003] N.I.Q.B. 1 (6 January 2003); *Jordan, Re Application for Judicial Review* [2003] N.I.C.A. 54 (12 December 2003). *McCaughey & Anor*, op. cit., n. 25. *In re Marie Louise Thompson*, N.I.Q.B. (29 September 2004). This third plank tended to apply only to non-collusion cases, as the state's alleged involvement in such cases generally had not reached the DPP, whose decision to prosecute had revolved around non-state killings.

79

Cases quickly crystallized the matters left open by the European Court's declaratory judgement. Challenges to the inquest system became vulnerable to the argument that the Court had not specified 'in any detail which procedures the authorities should adopt in providing for the proper examination of the circumstances of a killing by State agents.'[40] Therefore, it was argued, the institutional failings identified could not be read as discrete and cumulative – a failure to deliver one did not necessarily amount to an Article 2 violation. Secondly, it was argued that not all the criteria were required to be met in any one forum (for example, the inquest), given the possibility of other routes to investigation remaining open.[41] Thus, an attempt to compel documents failed on the argument that disclosure was not invariably necessary for the satisfaction of Article 2.[42] Challenges to the restrictive scope of the inquests failed on the grounds that the Article 2 duties rested on the state and not the coroner, and so it was up to the state to provide the effective investigation rather than for the coroner to extend the scope of the inquest.[43] This type of argument was also raised in the English 'death in custody' case of *Middleton*, which focused on whether a jury finding of 'neglect' was essential to the inquest being Article 2 compliant. While this case was appealed to the House of Lords, inquests, and challenges to them, ground to a halt in many areas of Northern Ireland as coroners and courts adjourned them for the intervening period (almost two years).[44] Article 2 challenges to the consequent inquest delays on the grounds that these themselves violated *Jordan et al.*, were unsuccessful.[45] If the judgments had provided a step forward, asserting them under the framework of the HRA appeared to result in two backwards.

The domestic courts resolved many of these issues in the House of Lords decisions in *Amin, Sacker*, and *Middleton*. *Amin* made it clear that *Jordan et al.* did have a clear minimum content, which the state had to deliver.[46] As an inquest was no longer possible, a public inquiry was ordered. In *Middleton*, the House of Lords further affirmed that normally 'a coroner should assume that his inquest is the means by which the state will discharge its procedural investigative obligation under Article 2.'[47] This position affirmed judicially the position stated by the government in its response package. In *Middleton* the House further found that the implications of *Jordan* were that the central question of the state's responsibility had to be left to the jury.

---

40 *Jordan* [143], *Kelly* [137], *McKerr* [159], op. cit., n. 5.
41 See, for example, *R (Amin)*, op. cit., n. 37 and *R (Middleton)*, op. cit., n. 24.
42 *Jordan, Re Application for Judicial Review* [2001], op. cit., n. 36; compare *Wright*, op. cit., n. 36.
43 *Jordan, Re Application for Judicial Review* (8 March 2002), op. cit., n. 35.
44 See, *Jordan*, id. (28 May 2002).
45 *Jordan*, id. (12 January 2004).
46 *Amin*, op. cit., n. 37.
47 *R (Middleton)*, op. cit., n. 24, at [47].

However, even as this was clarified, a more devastating derailment of Article 2's journey home reached its culmination, seemingly making these decisions redundant with regards to dealing with the past in Northern Ireland. This was through the success of the 'retrospectivity' challenge to families' HRA claims. With respect to the DPP's failure to give reasons for non-prosecution, the courts in Northern Ireland had persistently found that these involved retroactive application of the HRA. The question of retroactivity was finally dealt with in the House of Lords decision in *In Re McKerr*.[48] The European judgments' declaratory nature had avoided the question of what, if any, investigation should ensue in the cases in question. Litigation sought to require further inquiries, with the McKerr family judicially reviewing the Secretary of State's decision not to order a new investigation. As *McKerr* progressed through the courts, the very applicability of Article 2's procedural aspect was challenged as a retroactive application of the Human Rights Act, on the basis that the death in question took place prior to 2 October 2000.

Despite findings of a continuing violation in the lower courts, in the House of Lords five judges unanimously found that the Human Rights Act did not apply to deaths occurring prior to 2 October 2000.[49] They distinguished between rights arising under the Convention and rights created by the HRA with reference to the Convention. Whereas 'the former existed before the enactment of the HRA and they continue to exist', the latter only 'came into existence for the first time on 2 October 2000'.[50] The court found that the obligation to hold an investigation did not exist in the absence of a violent death, and therefore reasoned that if the death itself was not within the reach of section 6 HRA, because it occurred before the Act came into force, it would be surprising if section 6 applied to an obligation consequential upon the death. As Nicholls LJ stated: 'This interpretation has the effect, for the *transitional* purpose now under consideration, of treating all the obligations arising under Article 2 as parts of a single whole.'[51] The House of Lords further dismissed an attempt to rely on common law grounds.[52]

The *McKerr* judgement therefore, would appear to carve out an extraordinary state of affairs – namely that the HRA incorporates the Convention as regards all public bodies, except those dealing with deaths occurring prior to 2 October 2000. This exception prevails regardless of the on-going nature of these processes, and regardless of what new information comes to light regarding such deaths. The judgment is categorical, it is unanimous, and it appears final.

---

48 *In re McKerr (Northern Ireland)* op. cit., n. 38.
49 id.
50 id., at [26].
51 id., at [23] (emphasis added).
52 id., at [28]–[33], and see, in particular, judgment of Steyn J at [36].

Despite this, it leaves the law in a state of some confusion. It was delivered the same day as a different panel of the House of Lords decided the cases of *Middleton* and *Sacker*, which – like *Amin* before them – had involved deaths prior to October 2000. In all three, the House of Lords found a procedural violation of Article 2 noting in *Middleton* that, as no question has been raised on the retrospective application of the HRA and Convention, it had been assumed to be applicable, and noting in *Sacker*, that there had been no decision on this point.[53] It would, of course, have been open to the House of Lords to consider the retroactivity argument in these cases notwithstanding the failure of the state to argue it. That it did not, has prompted some to question what drives the distinction. It is difficult not to question whether the key distinction is the fact that *McKerr* was a case involving the past in Northern Ireland, indicating the ongoing capacity of the conflict to affect HRA interpretation. However, another related legal distinction between *McKerr* and *Amin, Middleton* and *Sacker* could be found. The latter cases involved inquests which were still ongoing thus limiting their future implications to a finite number of pre-HRA cases, while requiring the investigation in *McKerr* to be reopened would have opened the floodgates to an indefinite number of pre-HRA cases, apparently on a family's request. However, this distinction is belied by the categorical wording of *McKerr*, and in particular its notion that Article 2's procedural aspect only arises in domestic law where the death occurred after 2 October 2000.

Ironically, post-*McKerr* the strategic litigation on Article 2 in Northern Ireland lives on by removing section 6 of the Human Rights Act as a ground of challenge in judicial reviews. With regard to questions of policy, cases now fall back on 'pre-HRA' style judicial reviews based on reviewing public bodies where their practices depart from stated policy. Thus, cases against the DPP continue by striking out any reference to the Human Rights Act and relying on the public commitments that public bodies and the government have made. As regards inquests, the cases rely on the government's response package commitment that inquests will be Article 2 compliant. The Convention here plays an indirect role, providing the reason why public bodies have made public commitments as regards their procedures in right-to-life cases, commitments which can then be used to hold them to account.[54] It also has a pre-HRA-style domestic impact in that it can be used to resolve ambiguities in domestic legislation or practice. However, where legislation is involved, for example, in inquest cases, there is also a 'back-door incorporation' argument that while the HRA may not apply to public bodies

---

53 *R (Middleton)*, op. cit., n. 24, at [50]; *R (Sacker)*, op. cit., n. 37, [29].
54 These arguments had some successes in the cases of *Hemsworth, Re*, op, cit., n. 34 and *McCaughey*, op. cit., n. 25; but compare post-*McKerr* case of *R (Challender) and Another* v. *The Legal Services Commission* [2004] E.W.C.A. 925 (Admin) where court refused to turn a section 6 case into a section 3 one, and followed *McKerr* more strictly.

dealing with pre-HRA deaths under section 6 and 7, it does apply as a *general* tool of statutory construction under section 3 (requiring that legislation be read and given effect in a way which is compatible with the Convention rights), even when public bodies are interpreting the statute with regard to a pre-HRA death.

The recent NICA judgment *In Re Jordan*[55] illustrates how this post-HRA 'twist' to the 'old-style judicial review' is capable of reinserting HRA and Convention in cases where inquests are on-going, and force on *McKerr* the distinction that the House of Lords did not make. This latest *Jordan* case involved a long-running judicial review of the Lord Chancellor's and Coroner's refusal in Pearse Jordan's case to establish an inquest where the jury would able to bring in a verdict such as unlawful killing or an open verdict. Girvan J agreed with Counsel for the applicant that section 3 of the HRA is of *general* application as a tool of statutory construction, and thus applies to on-going inquest proceedings regardless of *McKerr* (which had not involved such on-going proceedings). Any other finding, he reasoned, would have the result of a coroner applying legislation one way for pre-HRA deaths, and another way for post-HRA deaths. The court did not order a legislative change to allow such verdicts, finding that *Middleton*-type jury findings could be accommodated within the existing rules governing verdicts in Northern Ireland (even though these preclude 'short-form' verdicts as were used in *Middleton*). Nevertheless, the capacity of this reasoning to erode the *McKerr* judgment with regards to past cases should not be underestimated. However, as we went to press, the Court of Appeal (NI) overruled itself in *McCaughey & Anor*, finding that due to *McKerr*, 'section 3 [HRA] is not triggered' and there was therefore 'no obligation to hold an article 2 compliant investigation'.[56]

Finally, also of note, Article 2's procedural right has come under attack from another angle, namely Court of Appeal (England) decisions emanating from challenges to Bloody Sunday Tribunal rulings by the security force personnel whose actions are at the centre of the inquiry. These cases posit the 'substantive' aspect of Article 2 against its 'procedural' aspect.[57] Security force personnel have successfully challenged decisions regarding identification (screening and anonymity) and venue, on the basis that their lives are at risk. In these cases, the Court of Appeal (England) has set up a balancing act wherein Article 2's 'substantive' protection (as beefed up from European Court jurisprudence) almost inevitably trumps its 'procedural' aspect (the two appearing as disconnected). Cumulatively the resulting limitations on the

---

55 *In Re Jordan* [2004] N.I.C.A. 29 (10 September 2004).
56 *Police Service of Northern Ireland* v. *McCaughey & Anor*, NICA 14 January 2005 (inquest disclosure case whose possible appeal is likely to lead to further stalling of ongoing inquests).
57 See, for example, *Lord Saville of Newdigate & Ors* v. *Widgery Soldiers & Ors* [2001] E.W.C.A. Civ 2048 (19 December 2001).

83

Tribunal's inquiry has impacted on its ability to 'restore public confidence', and also the capacity of future inquiries to reach 'the truth'.[58]

The litigation strategy itself bears testimony to the lack of comprehensive institutional reform. It provides some evidence that HRA litigation can on occasion supplement and clarify reform, as illustrated by *Amin* and *Middleton*. However, it illustrates the difficulties of using the HRA to deal with Northern Ireland's past, and clear differences between the Northern Irish courts and the House of Lords, which throw light on the transitional justice questions raised in the introduction, as discussed further in the evaluation below.

EVALUATING THE HUMAN RIGHTS ACT

How then, does the HRA fare when evaluated from the perspective of the right-to-life case study? The questions derived from the government's rationale for the HRA, together with those raised by the Northern Irish context, outlined in the introduction, form a framework.

1. *A speedier and cheaper way to enforce rights?*

The right-to-life cases indicate that the HRA does not necessarily provide a speedier and cheaper way to enforce rights. As regards institutional reform for the future, litigation is only clarifying some of the Article 2 implications for investigation procedures, four years post-HRA, and three post-*Jordan et al*. However, even families whose deaths have occurred since 2 October 2000 – and unfortunately conflict related deaths do continue – have encountered many of the same problems of inadequacy of police investigation, and delay and non-disclosure of documents in inquests. Resort to judicial review is still a feature of these cases. For example, in the case of David McIlwaine, involving an ostensible non-state killing apparently in connection with a loyalist feud, the coroner was judicially reviewed for the failure to hold a prompt and effective investigation as required by Article 2 ECHR, due to the failure of the Police Service to furnish written statements relating to the death of David McIlwaine and the failure of the coroner to deal with these statements. The judge made it clear 'that the documents should be released at the earliest possible moment'.[59] Some similar difficulties have continued in death in custody cases in Northern Ireland.

As regards dealing with the past, it now seems that families pushing for remedies in deaths occurring prior to October 2000 are now operating officially in a non-HRA context. As a result, in September 2004, protective

---

58 See Hegarty, op cit., n. 29.
59 *In re McIlwaine*, op. cit., n. 33 (judge refused to make Article 2 breach declaration given coroner's commitment to release statement).

84

letters were sent to the European Court in the cases of *Kelly*, *McKerr*, and *Shanaghan*, given the state's failure to provide new investigations. Whether the families proceed with these cases depends to some extent on the outcome of the Committee of Ministers process. Five other cases have also been lodged in Europe post-*McKerr* on ground of violations of Article 2's procedural right.[60]

2. British contribution to European jurisprudence?

The clear import of *Jordan et al.* is that an effective, publicly transparent investigation is required – capable of either identifying culpability, or of putting allegations of state wrongdoing to rest. While domestic judgments analyse thoughtfully the Article 2 implications, an audit of the cases as a whole reveals a picture which does little to further the underlying rationale of the European Court's decision – the need for an investigation capable of determining whether there was a substantive violation of Article 2 or not. Rather the cases tend to continue a pattern of litigation, forum bouncing, and denial of investigation. A cynic could observe that the clearest thread that runs through cases emanating from the conflict is that Article 2 violations are seldom found - the state tends to win, substantively or by default. Thus, apart from some legal aid decisions, and the Bloody Sunday cases (where the 'victims' are themselves alleged security force 'perpetrators' of Article 2 violations), it would appear that successful cases have resulted in declaratory relief only, and/or have failed to withstand higher challenge.[61]

3. Better protection of rights?

As the discussion thus far indicates, the HRA has not yet ensured a full delivery of Article 2's procedural right. It has not delivered effective investigations in the cases brought to Europe, or in other similar cases; it has not delivered holistic reform of institutional practice; and the House of Lords have effectively excluded the HRA as regards dealing with Northern Ireland's past. However, some positive developments must be noted. Incremental institutional reform is ongoing, and inching towards delivery. Also, the HRA can be seen to be having some impact in what might be termed 'the shadow of the law', where it is affecting the interactions of families with the Police Service and the Director of Public Prosecutions. NGOs report that they increasingly are getting more details from both the police and the DPP regarding murders, even when judicial review is not an option. Police now engage with NGOs as normal practice (although this may have more to do with the style of the new Chief Constable than the HRA),

---

60 Interview, Ritchie McRitchie, Madden and Finucane, Solicitors.
61 The most clearly substantive cases of *McCaughey & Anor*, op. cit., n. 25 and *Jordan*. op. cit., n. 55 are now overruled by the NICA in *McCaughey & Anor*, op. cit., n. 56.

85

and senior officers appear informed about, and influenced by, Article 2.[62] In some cases where the Ombudsman has exposed inadequate investigations, new approaches to reinvigorating the investigation are emerging. In the case of the loyalist killing of Sean Brown, for example, where the Ombudsman revealed a catastrophic failure in the police investigation, the new investigation has established a novel cooperation between police and a local human rights NGO (the Pat Finucane Centre), with support from the family, overseen by a senior officer from Britain and by an Irish government official.[63] Witnesses are being encouraged to give statements either to police or, where unwilling to go to the police, the NGO. Moreover, while the use of Article 2 by the state in the Bloody Sunday cases raises concerns about protection of rights, it could perhaps be argued to provide somewhat positive evidence of former state law enforcers embracing and engaging with the Convention, albeit out of self-interest.

4. How has the HRA impacted on the Northern Ireland's transition to peace?

Incorporation has had little effect in buttressing institutional transformation as regards prosecution and inquest processes. In fact, quite the converse – peace process reforms have formed the core of the government response package and it depends on these deeper reforms for any semblance of adequacy. As noted, the HRA is used to deny the need for a more holistic government response, rather than to develop institutional reform. When litigation is included in the picture, it could be argued that the HRA has slowed reform in some cases, witness the inquest delays, and the potential of *McKerr* to undermine government commitments included in the package. When we turn to the issue of dealing with the past, the *McKerr* decision aims to take the HRA out of the picture, and it remains to be seen whether this will hold or be eaten into by decisions such as those in *Jordan* (September 2004). Domestic Convention jurisprudence in the Bloody Sunday cases has obliterated Article 2's procedural right in its expansion of its substantive component. The right to life, of course, only becomes procedural after a death.

Interestingly, as regards the deeper question of how the Convention has operated as between transitional justice conceptualizations and traditional British conceptualizations of what the HRA can and cannot do, the answer is complicated. The piecemeal approach of the government to institutional reform is consistent with the traditional 'managerial approach' but, as noted, only comes close to being adequate in terms of *Jordan et al.* because of peace process reforms which acknowledge the need for more fundamental transformation. Both the House of Lords and the lower courts in Northern Ireland, acknowledge in small ways that 'something different is going on' in the Northern Ireland cases. However, this recognition of 'something

---

62 Interview, Jane Winter, British Irish Rights Watch, September 2004.
63 Interview, Paul O'Connor, Pat Finucane Centre, September 2004.

different' is used by the courts as an excuse to 'back off' a robust bringing back home of Article 2's procedural aspect. In the House of Lords it is a complete backing off through the *McKerr* 'retroactivity' argument that Article 2 does not require (and is not permitted) to be brought back home in these cases. Interestingly, the House of Lords in *McKerr* refer to the problem of past deaths as a 'transitional' one – albeit not with the meaning invested in the term here. However, in the NICA, a pattern observed during the conflict of a more creative engagement with the complexities of the Northern Ireland conflict can still be seen.[64] Most notable in this regard is the September 2004 decision in *Jordan*, limiting the application of *McKerr*. However, while the NICA has been quicker to find violations of Article 2 in Northern Ireland's past, it tends to 'back off' from robust implementation by refusing to order substantive relief in the form of new investigative measures. This stands in contrast to the English courts in English cases who have been prepared to order a public inquiry as a remedy in *Amin*. The failure to order relief in Northern Ireland is often justified by reference to the very political developments that make Northern Ireland distinctive. Thus, in *In Re Wright*, where Kerr J affirms the application of Article 2, he refuses to order the release of a police file to the family, on the grounds that the Cory inquiry is investigating and determination of disclosure must await any resulting inquiry.[65]

It can be argued that the Convention cannot be expected to deal satisfactorily with transitional justice issues, and was not designed for such a purpose. In rebuttal, it could be noted that the decisions in *Jordan et al.* applied Article 2's procedural aspect to a situation of conflict (although it could be argued that this approach to United Kingdom violations was perhaps emboldened and enabled by the end of the conflict). Yet, to some extent the argument stands. In all these cases litigation only provides a route to an effective investigation being established. Any ensuing information will only be as good as the investigation, which may find itself limited by Article 2 and by the unwillingness of state actors to cooperate, as the Bloody Sunday litigation indicates. Thus, litigation can remain at best a means to an end – that end being an effective and transparent investigation.

However, the HRA and Convention continue to impact on the debate over how to deal with the past. While it has not delivered new investigations, Article 2's procedural aspect has, in cases where state actors have been involved, given families of these victims some leverage on a victims debate which has often relegated them to a low place in a 'hierarchy of victims', and refused to recognize a discrete set of needs as regards information and accountability relating to state involvement. As has been noted elsewhere, Northern Ireland's transition is not a paradigmatic one, but is shaped by the

64 S. Livingstone, 'The House of Lords and the Northern Ireland Conflict' (1994) 57 *Modern Law Rev.* 333, at 351.
65 *In re Wright* [2003] N.I.Q.B. 17, at [21].

fact that the Britain is a Western liberal democracy.[66] In this context, which has not involved regime change or indeed an acknowledgement of the state's role in the conflict, Article 2 remains one of the few pressures on a state whose approach to the conflict has been to present it as inter-communal/horizontal, rather than vertical. This pressure adds to political peace process pressures. That the government want a 'way out' is evidenced by its recently announced consultation on 'how to deal with the past'.[67] However, a paradox remains: Article 2 not only provides the pressure to have a holistic response to the past, but constrains the type of 'trade-offs' which are possible (for example 'truth' in place of 'accountability'), making it more difficult to negotiate a holistic mechanism which would meet the full range of political demands as regards state and non-state actors.

There are also indications of the HRA's capacity to fulfil its horizontal 'intercommunal' ambition, albeit in somewhat negative ways. Although the Article 2 pressures described above have the potential to polarize communities with respect to the HRA in reinforcing the view that human rights are a 'nationalist' tool in the dealing with the past debate, there are counterveiling factors. Continued failings of investigations and obstacles during transition have affected the loyalist community, and this has resulted in the increased use of Article 2 by that community. This has led to an increased human rights skilling of lawyers dealing therein, and novel communal interaction as regards furthering cases, most notably the use of the same barristers to run similar arguments in the joined cases of loyalist Billy Wright and Catholic solicitor Pat Finucane. As well, there is an increasing realization among the Unionist/Protestant community that Article 2's procedural aspect has implications for non-state killings. Police figures indicate that out of 2,788 conflict-related killings between 1969 and 1998, individuals were subsequently charged in only 955 cases.[68] Evidence in relation to some cases has indicated acute investigative failures, calling into question police competence and use of informers, opening up further Article 2 implications.[69] Interestingly, the Police Service has begun a review of 'historical cases' aimed at reopening investigations or giving further

---

66 C. Campbell and F. Ní Aoláin, 'The Paradox of Transition in Conflicted Democracies' (2005) *Human Rights Q.* (forthcoming).
67 In the spring of 2004 the Secretary of State for NI announced a consultation process to examine the means of 'dealing with the past'. To date the consultation has been a private process of consulting experts and opinion formers by invitation only, and has included a trip by the Secretary of State to South Africa. The process may be broadened, see <www.nio.gov.uk/index/key-issues/victims.htm>.
68 *Security Situation Statistics for Northern Ireland*, provided by the Police Service, 22 January 2003, on file with authors. The statistics do not apparently include around 367 deaths caused by state actors.
69 See, for example, Police Ombudsman, *Statement by the Police Ombudsman for Northern Ireland on Her Investigation of Matters Relating to the Omagh Bomb on August 15, 1998* (2001).

information to the families about the state of the investigation.[70] There has been some commitment to introducing outside police officers into the relevant unit, to inject an element of independence. While couched in managerial language of bringing police practice into line with that in England, it clearly also forms a police response to Article 2 pressures.

CONCLUSIONS

As this review demonstrates, the right-to-life case study indicates an approach which often limits Northern Ireland's possibilities for institutional and political transformation by failing to put clear water between past approaches to human rights abuses and present ones. While this article has questioned whether Article 2 has 'got lost on the way home', a different view exists. It can be argued that the very notion of 'bringing rights back home' and the mechanism chosen was aimed at presenting 'incorporation' as unthreatening – a repatriation of the Convention which was deliberately ambiguous as to whether it was intended to radicalize British constitutionalism, or to enable containment of the Convention's domestic reach. The concept of bringing rights back home could be sold to human rights advocates as increased rights protection which would consolidate and extend human rights jurisprudence which was already seeping into domestic courts. But it could also be sold to enemies of increased rights frameworks as adding little in practice, while making it more difficult to get to Europe, and reasserting the primacy of British judges and judgments as against 'European' ones.

The right-to-life case study may illustrate exactly what bringing Article 2 back home looks like, because from this second limiting notion of incorporation there is little room for the Article's procedural right. Implementation of *Jordan et al.* domestically requires a 'transformative constitutionalism' which the very design of the HRA is evidence of ambivalence to. While glimmers of this transformative constitutionalism exist in the judgments relating to English death-in-custody cases, and some Northern Irish decisions relating to the past, the Northern Irish case study indicates the capacity of its conflict to skew and limit the HRA's impact in *both* these areas. The need for a transformative constitutionalism capable of recognizing the differing needs in the different jurisdictions – those of transition in Northern Ireland and those of democratic renewal in the rest of the United Kingdom – remains.

70 <www.policefed-ni.org/uk/chair_conf04.htm>. Interview, Hugh Orde, Sept. 2004.

JOURNAL OF LAW AND SOCIETY
VOLUME 32, NUMBER 1, MARCH 2005
ISSN: 0263-323X, pp. 90–110

Convention Compliance, Public Safety, and the Social Inclusion of Mentally Disordered People

PHIL FENNELL*

The first part of this paper considers the impact of the HRA 1998 in the courts, and the application of Articles 3, 5, and 8 in relation to psychiatric detention, treatment without consent, and seclusion. The second part looks at its effect on the discourse of law reform. Here a key theme is the way Convention compliance has been used by the government to justify measures that will lead to a broadening of the scope of compulsory powers and a reduction in psychiatric service users' rights.

There are three parallel agenda in mental health law and policy: public safety; respect for Convention rights; and social inclusion (protection against discrimination and combating stigma). Since the 1990s successive governments have pursued a public safety agenda in relation to mental health services responding to concerns about homicides by mentally disordered people. Although these fears have been exaggerated, they have had a disproportionate impact on mental health law and policy, and produce tensions between the agendas of public safety and social inclusion.[1] The

---

* Cardiff Law School, Cardiff University, Museum Avenue, Cardiff CF1 3NX, Wales

1 P. Fennell, 'Reforming the Mental Health Act 1983: "Joined Up Compulsion"' (2001) 7 *Journal of Mental Health Law*, 5–20. The social inclusion agenda is reflected in the *National Service Framework for Mental Health: Modern Standards & Service Models* Department of Health; September 1999, accessible at <www.doh.gov.uk/pub/docs/doh/mhmain.pdf>, and the Welsh Assembly Government, *Strategy Document for Adult Mental Health Services in Wales: Equity, Empowerment, Effectiveness, Efficiency* (2001). See, also, the report of the Social Exclusion Unit on *Mental Health and Social Exclusion* (9 June 2004 Office of the Deputy Prime Minister), where the Prime Ministerial foreword notes the need for 'determined action to end the stigma of mental health – a challenge not just for Government, but for all of us.' At the European level the social inclusion agenda is reflected most recently in Recommendation (2004)10 of the Committee of Ministers of the Council of Europe to member states concerning the protection of the human rights and dignity of persons with mental disorder adopted on 22 September 2004.

government has followed its immediate predecessors in pursuing a legislative policy of increased control over mentally disordered people in the community whilst at the same time, through the non-statementing National Service Frameworks for England and Wales, promoting policies of social inclusion, combating stigma, and user and carer involvement. Although Convention compliance has been a major issue in mental health law since at least the 1980s, since October 2000 it has been a direct issue in the courts, and has also come to be a major, if not the dominant focus of ethical debate about law reform.

DETENTION ON GROUNDS OF UNSOUNDNESS OF MIND

Article 5(1)(e) of the Convention reflects the attitudes of the 1950s, authorizing detention on grounds of unsoundness of mind, alcoholism, addiction to drugs, or vagrancy, provided that detention takes place in accordance with a procedure prescribed by law. Although the Convention cannot by any stretch of the imagination be seen as an enlightened statement of the rights of persons of unsound mind, the Strasbourg Court has striven to build additional safeguards through its jurisprudence.

The Council of Europe has issued the Bioethics Convention 1997 and the 2004 Recommendation setting out principles for the treatment of people with mental disorder, although the United Kingdom government has avoided becoming a party to either. In 1979, in *Winterwerp* v. *the Netherlands*,[2] the Court laid down three important substantive and procedural requirements for lawful detentions of persons of unsound mind:

(i) Except in emergencies, the individual must reliably be shown to be suffering from a true mental disorder on the basis of objective expertise.
(ii) The mental disorder must be of a kind or degree justifying confinement.
(iii) Those carrying out the detention must satisfy themselves at intervals that the criteria for detention continue to be met.[3]

Winterwerp established that detention must be a proportionate response to the patient's circumstances.[4]

These requirements are met in the detention procedures under the Mental Health Act (MHA)1983. Admission is by administrative process, based on professional expertise and checks and balances. Only an Approved Social Worker (ASW) (with specialized mental health training) or the patient's nearest relative may apply for detention, supported by two medical recommendations, one from a person with psychiatric expertise. The ASW

2 *Winterwerp* (1979–80) 2 E.H.R.R. 387.
3 id.; *X* v. *UK* (1981) 4 E.H.R.R. 188, and *Van der Leer* v. *The Netherlands* (1990) 12 E.H.R.R. 567.
4 *Litwa* v. *Poland* (2000) 63 B.M.L.R. 199, (2001) E.H.R.R. 53.

presents objective medical evidence of a true mental disorder of a kind or degree warranting detention to a competent authority, the hospital managers. The competent authority has the duty to review the detention at reasonable intervals and to discharge if the criteria are not met. An application may only be made if the treatment cannot be provided without detention, reflecting the principle of proportionality. Nothing in Article 5 or the case law requires admission to be authorized by a court or tribunal, so the current admission procedures are Convention compliant.[5]

However, English law's long-standing non-application of the statutory procedures to mentally incapacitated patients presented a potential problem. Since the MHA 1959, English mental health legislation has provided that the existence of the statutory procedures should not prevent a person being admitted 'informally', meaning that the person is admitted without using statutory powers of detention. Informal admission applies to patients with sufficient mental capacity to consent actively and validly to admission, and also to people who are incapable of consenting to admission but who are not actively resisting it. This approach assumes that there can be no detention unless the person is actively protesting against or resisting confinement. The crucial factor is not consent but absence of dissent, the key indicia of dissent being physical resistance to admission, and persistent attempts to leave.

Detention was to be reserved for the minority of patients who were resisting hospital treatment,[6] as it was thought unseemly and stigmatizing to detain compliant mentally incapacitated people such as elderly patients with dementia or people with profound intellectual disabilities, when often a major reason for their admission to hospital is that there is nowhere else where they can be looked after. This allowed large numbers of compliant incapacitated patients to be admitted without the procedural safeguards available to detained patients, under a statutory permission, that nothing in the Mental Health Act prevents a person from *being admitted* informally.[7]

Only in 1989, in *In re F*,[8] did the House of Lords enunciate the common law doctrine of necessity, conferring a power on doctors to give treatment without consent that is necessary in a mentally incapacitated patient's best interests. In 1999, before the HRA 1998 came into force, the doctrine of necessity was extended by the House of Lords in *Bournewood*[9] to confer a power on a doctor to restrain and detain mentally incapacitated adults if necessary in their best interests. In *Bournewood*, L had been admitted to hospital on the authority of the psychiatrist in charge of his treatment after he

---

5 *HL* v. *United Kingdom* 5 October 2004.
6 For full discussion of this history, see P. Fennell, 'Doctor knows best? Therapeutic Detention Under Common Law, the Mental Health Act and the European Convention' (1998) 6 *Medical Law Rev.* 322–53.
7 Mental Health Act 1983, s. 131.
8 [1990] 2 A.C. 1.
9 *R* v. *Bournewood Community and Mental Health NHS Trust, ex parte L (Secretary of State for Health and others intervening)* [1998] 3 All E.R. 289.

had become disturbed in a day centre. He was kept in hospital, and his long-term carers were told that it would not be in his clinical interests to visit him. The doctor instructed ward staff that if L tried to leave he should be formally detained. The House of Lords ruled by a 3–2 majority that L had not been detained. They also ruled unanimously that, even if he had been, there was a power at common law to restrain and detain a mentally incapacitated person in their best interests.

In *HL* v. *United Kingdom* the Strasbourg Court held that Article 5(1)(e) had been breached in *Bournewood*. The court held that there is a deprivation of liberty where a compliant incapacitated patient is subjected to a strict level of control over residence, treatment, movement, and access to carers, she is deprived of liberty. Whatever the position under English law, removal to hospital, and retention there without access to carers, amounted to a deprivation of liberty under the Convention, and had to be carried out in accordance with a procedure prescribed by law, under Article 5(1)(e). The Court refused to treat compliant incapacitated patients on a par with capable patients who were consenting, affirming that:

> The right to liberty in a democratic society is too important for a person to lose the benefit of Convention protection simply because they have given themselves up to detention, especially when they are not capable of consenting to, or disagreeing with, the proposed action.[10]

The law authorizing detention must be sufficiently precise to allow the citizen to foresee, to a degree that is reasonable in the circumstances, the consequences which a given action might entail. The *Winterwerp* criteria must also be met. There have to be rules specifying a procedure to admit and detain compliant incapacitated persons, indicating who can propose admission, specifying the purpose (assessment or treatment), grounds, and medical evidence needed to justify detention, specifying time limits, and providing for regular review. A nominated representative should be able to make 'certain objections and applications' available under the 1983 Act, especially important for legally incapacitated patients with limited communication abilities.

Under the Convention the common law doctrine of necessity may be used to justify an emergency detention, but not a prolonged deprivation of liberty, because there is no procedure to exercise the common law power. Conferring such a power on a doctor without procedural safeguards risks arbitrary deprivation of liberty based on medical misjudgement.

10 *HL* v. *United Kingdom* 5 October 2004, para. [90].

93

Article 5(4) entitles detainees to take proceedings by which the lawfulness of detention must be decided speedily by a court and release ordered if it is not lawful. In *X* v. *United Kingdom*, the Strasbourg Court held that the court must be able to review the applicability of the *Winterwerp* criteria.[11] If they are not met, the court must have the power to direct the patient's discharge. Review of the 'lawfulness' of detention must be carried out in light of domestic legal requirements, the Convention, and the principle of proportionality. Article 5(4) review is carried out jointly by the High Court and by Mental Health Review Tribunals (MHRTs). The High Court reviews the formal legality of decisions to detain and renew detention via judicial review and habeas corpus. Review of the continued applicability of the *Winterwerp* criteria is done by MHRTs, which have the power to direct discharge. A number of aspects of the MHRTs' functioning were ripe for challenge.

1. *The burden of proof*

Most obvious was the burden of proof on the applicant to satisfy the MHRT of the absence of detainable mental disorder or the absence of risk to the patient's health or safety or to the protection of other people.[12] In a series of cases decided before the HRA 1998 came into force, the the courts emphasized the importance of the reverse burden of proof,[13] departing from Lord Atkin's statement in *Liversidge* v. *Anderson* that 'One of the pillars of liberty is that in English law every imprisonment is prima facie unlawful and that it is for the person directing the imprisonment to justify his act.'[14] This was said to be justified because the MHRT's jurisdiction was to review, not to make the original decision to detain. A tribunal was only required to direct discharge 'if satisfied of a negative, because the tribunal is not intended to duplicate the role of the medical officer, whose diagnosis stands until the tribunal is satisfied that it is wrong.'[15]

The burden of proof was the subject of the first declaration of incompatibility between the MHA 1983 and Convention rights with the decision in *R (H)* v. *Mental Health Review Tribunal North and East London Region and Secretary of State for Health* where Lord Phillips MR held it 'contrary to the Convention compulsorily to detain a patient unless it can be

---

11 (1981) 4 E.H.R.R. 188, at 189. See, also, *Hutchison Reid* v. *United Kingdom* (2003) 37 E.H.R.R. 211.
12 This applied to patients detained for treatment for up to six months renewable under s. 3 of the 1983 Act.
13 *Perkins* v. *Bath DHA*; *R* v. *Wessex MHRT ex p Wiltshire CC* (1989) 4 B.M.L.R. 145. *R* v. *Merseyside MHRT ex p K* [1990] 1 All E.R. 694; (1989) 4 B.M.L.R. 60.
14 *Liversidge* v. *Anderson* [1942] A.C. 206, at 245 (dissenting).
15 *R* v. *Canons Park MHRT* [1994] 2 All E.R. 659.

94

shown that the patient is suffering from a mental disorder that warrants detention.'[16] The burden of proof has now been changed by remedial order[17] and the tribunal is required to discharge a patient if not satisfied that the patient is then suffering from detainable mental disorder of the requisite nature or degree.[18] The Strasbourg Court agreed in *Hutchison Reid* v. *The United Kingdom*,[19] holding that it was 'implicit' in the Convention case law that it was for the authorities to prove that an individual satisfies the conditions for compulsory detention, rather than the converse, [since] detention could only be lawful under Article 5(1)(e) if it could 'reliably be shown that he or she suffers from a mental disorder sufficiently serious to warrant detention.'[20]

These decisions establish a clear improvement in the due process rights of patients, and mark the introduction into the MHRTs of common law procedural safeguards appropriate to cases of deprivation of liberty. They can be said to uphold the non-discrimination, social inclusion agenda

2. *Speedy review*

To comply with Article 5(4) 'speedy' review must be available, and it has been a long-standing concern that MHRTs have not been convened speedily enough. In 1984 the Council on Tribunals noted that already patients were waiting too long for a hearing. In 1988, the Council Annual Report described delays of between 12 and 19 weeks for non-offender patients. In the late 1990s the MHRTs introduced new arrangements to manage case loads, culminating in the conduct of hearings without tribunal clerks but with tribunal assistants employed by an agency. In *R (on the application of C)* v. *the Mental Health Review Tribunal London and South West Region*,[21] listing all cases for a date precisely eight weeks after the application was held to be a breach of Article 5(4), since some cases could be brought on in less than eight weeks, whilst others might legitimately take longer.

In *R (on the application of KB and Others)* v. *Mental Health Review Tribunal*,[22] Stanley Burnton J held that the right of seven applicants to a speedy hearing under Article 5(4) had been breached and that the evidence before him indicated the basic responsibility for the delays experienced by patients was that of central government rather than tribunal chairpersons or

---

16 [2001] 3 W.L.R. 512.
17 Mental Health Act 1983 (Remedial) Order 2001 S.I. 2001 no. 3712.
18 In *Lyons* v. *The Scottish Ministers* 17 January 2002 (First Division of the Court of Session), Scottish Ministers accepted that the Convention required them to bear the burden of proof and argued that section 64 of the Scottish legislation should be read to give this effect.
19 *Hutchison Reid]*, op. cit., n. 11.
20 id., at para. 70
21 (C.A.) [2002] 1 W.L.R.
22 [2002] E.W.H.C. 639.

staff. The disposal of cases speedily has placed the tribunal under tremendous pressure, resulting in clerks being replaced by tribunal assistants recruited though an agency, and in some cases tribunals sitting without a clerk. At the same time, the tribunals' case load has increased steadily from a figure of 3,868 applications, and 2,009 hearings in 1983 to the current level of in excess of 22,000 applications to tribunals for discharge per annum, 11,000 of which result in hearings.[23] Effective enforcement of the speediness requirement is clearly crucial to any system of review and to the psychological well-being of patients awaiting review, but when tribunals sit without professional clerks, there must be risks to the quality of justice.

3. The effects of tribunal decisions

MHRTs have the power of discharge, but an ASW has a duty to apply for the admission of a patient 'where he is satisfied that such an application ought to be made and is of the opinion that it ought to be made by him.'[24] Although a MHRT decision to discharge makes further detention under that authority unlawful, it does not necessarily prevent a fresh application being made for detention or guardianship. Allowing unfettered discretion to 're-section' a patient creates the possibility of professionals countermanding a tribunal decision that had gone against them, in effect an appeal from a judicial body to 'mental health professionals' who have in all probability been parties to the hearing. The courts have had to steer a careful path between fettering the discretion of the 'mental health professionals' to manage a perceived risk to the patient or others, and undermining the authority of the tribunal, which is the competent court for the purposes of reviewing the lawfulness of detention under Article 5(4).

In *ex parte von Brandenburg*[25] the House of Lords established that mental health professionals need not establish a 'change in circumstance' since the tribunal decision before being able to re-section. The ASW must have formed the reasonable and bona fide opinion that he or she has information not known to the tribunal which puts a significantly different complexion on the case as compared with what was before the tribunal. In the overwhelming majority of cases where re-sectioning is in prospect, there will have been a material change of circumstance, but the courts do not wish to place this restraint on discretion to intervene where there is risk to the patient's health or safety or the protection of others.

The other circumstance where re-detention following discharge by the tribunal has been considered, is where the hospital authorities think the

23 Submission of the Mental Health Review Tribunal Chairmen for England and Wales to the Joint Parliamentary Scrutiny Committee on the Mental Health Bill, November 2004, para. 1.
24 Mental Health Act 1983, s. 13.
25 [2003] U.K.H.L. 58.

tribunal has erred in law. In 2002 the Court of Appeal held that to countenance as lawful re-sectioning on the ground that the tribunal was believed to have erred in law would be to permit the professionals and their legal advisers to determine whether a decision by a court to discharge a detained person should have effect, and would contravene Article 5(4). The hospital authorities should instead apply for a stay of the tribunal's decision, pending an application for judicial review.[26] If there are material facts not known to the tribunal, the ASW may re-section, but not if the contention is that the tribunal erred in law. The guiding principles in these cases have been to uphold the authority of the MHRT as the competent court as required by Article 5(4), whilst effectively managing risk by ensuring, as the courts in all these cases have repeatedly asserted, that nothing affected the ability of the professionals to re-section a patient if he or she does or threatens to do something that imperils or might imperil his or her health or safety, or that of members of the public. An important consequence is that the High Court now has power, through the jurisdiction to grant a stay, to allow applications for judicial review by the detaining authority against discharge decisions where those responsible for implementing the decision consider discharge to be too risky. These are important developments. The tribunal has acquired another court-like feature, in that speedy procedures are now available to the detaining authority to seek review of the tribunal decision to discharge.

4. Positive duties under Article 5

The issue in *R* v. *Secretary of State for the Home Department and another ex parte IH*[27] was the extent to which, in addition to creating negative rights not to be arbitrarily detained, Article 5 creates positive rights to treatment in the least restrictive setting. *Stanley Johnson* v *United Kingdom*[28] had established that where a court reviewing the lawfulness of detention finds that a person is no longer suffering from mental disorder, it is not under an obligation to discharge immediately, but may order discharge subject to the provision of after-care support. If this happens, the court must have the power to ensure that discharge is not unreasonably delayed. The scope of the duties of the court and the after-care authorities under *Johnson* was the key issue in *IH*. Resolving it, the House of Lords reaffirmed the funda-mental principle of English law that, regardless of whether psychiatrists are public authorities for the purposes of the HRA 1998, a doctor cannot be

26 *R (on the application of H)* v. *Ashworth Hospital and Others*; *R (on the application of Ashworth Hospital Authority)* v. *Mental Health Review Tribunal for West Midlands and the North West Region and London Borough of Hammersmith and Fulham and Ealing Hammersmith and Hounslow Health Authority* [2002] E.W.C.A. Civ. 923.
27 [2003] U.K.H.L. 59.
28 (1997) 27 E.H.R.R. 296.

97

ordered to do anything against his or her clinical judgement of the patient's best interests.[29] Neither a tribunal nor a health authority could order a doctor to take on the care of a patient if the doctor, in his or her clinical judgement, considered that care could not safely be provided.

In *IH* Lord Bingham maintained a narrow approach to the ruling in *Johnson*,[30] limiting the scope of the duty to ensure that discharge is not unreasonably delayed to cases where the patient is no longer suffering from mental disorder, the '*Johnson* type of case'. In *IH* the second *Winterwerp* criterion was no longer met, because there was still mental disorder but no longer of a kind or degree justifying detention, as long as adequate placement and supervision in the community could be arranged. Hence, the Court of Appeal and the House of Lords in *IH* agreed that, where the basis of discharge is nature or degree of the illness rather than its absence:

> If a health authority was unable, despite the exercise of all reasonable endeavours, to procure for a patient the level of care and treatment in the community that a tribunal considered to be a prerequisite to the discharge of the patient from hospital, the continued detention of the patient in hospital would not violate the right to liberty under Article 5.

Patients will rarely be pronounced 'cured' by psychiatrists or tribunals, so the effect of the ruling is to limit significantly the impact of *Johnson*, and the extent to which Article 5 is capable of imposing positive duties on state authorities to provide after-care to facilitate discharge.

In the United States of America, the Supreme Court dealt with a similar issue in *Olmstead Commissioner, Georgia Department Of Human Resources* v. *LC*.[31] The Court held that, under the Americans with Disabilities Act, states are required to provide persons with mental disabilities with community-based treatment rather than placement in institutions. This duty applies where (i) the state's treatment professionals have determined that community placement is appropriate; (ii) the transfer from institutional care to a less restrictive setting is not opposed by the affected individual; and (iii) the community placement can be reasonably accommodated, taking into account the resources available to the state and the needs of others with mental disabilities.

In the United Kingdom, in the Strasbourg Court, and in the United States, the courts are showing commitment to the idea of a right to treatment in the least restrictive setting, a potential positive obligation in relation to Article 5(1)(e) detentions. However, this is subject to the significant limitation that it must accord with the clinical judgement of the health professionals, and will

---

29 A principle which has since been modified by Munby J in *R (Burke)* v. *General Medical Council* [2004] E.W.H.C. 1879.
30 An approach first adopted by introduced by Lord Phillips of Worth Matravers MR, in paras. [32]–[36] of his judgment in *R(K)* v. *Camden and Islington Health Authority* [2001] E.W.C.A. Civ. 240, [2002] Q.B. 198.
31 527 U.S. 581; 119 S. Ct. 2176.

98

no doubt be subject to the availability of resources, as *Olmstead* makes clear. The *IH* case, like *Olmstead*, shows how the powers of competent courts under Article 5(4) are subject to the important limitation of the clinical judgement of the doctor who will be treating the patient in the community, and his or her view of whether the risk posed by the patient to self or to others can safely be managed in the community. *IH* subjects *Johnson* to strict limits in the interests of risk management.

TREATMENT WITHOUT CONSENT AND THE CONVENTION

In *Herczegfalvy* v. *Austria*, the prohibition on inhuman and degrading treatment in Article 3 was not breached because:

> The established principles of medicine were in principle decisive in such cases; as a general rule, a measure which is a therapeutic necessity cannot be inhuman and degrading.

Nevertheless, the Court emphasized that the 'position of vulnerability and powerlessness' of people detained on grounds of mental disorder called for vigilance on the part of the Court and the national authorities to satisfy themselves that medical necessity had been convincingly shown to exist. Herczegfalvy also claimed under Article 8 that the various treatments given to him, including large doses of neuroleptic medication, infringed his right to respect for private life, which afforded him the right of self-determination. The court rejected his claim, attaching

> decisive weight to the lack of specific information capable of disproving the government's opinion that the hospital authorities were entitled to regard the applicant's psychiatric illness as rendering him entirely incapable of taking decisions for himself.

In other words there was no evidence that he had the necessary capacity to be entitled to refuse treatment. The inference from this is that had Herczegfalvy possessed the necessary capacity, he would have been entitled to refuse treatment as part of his right of self-determination. Then, if doctors wished to impose treatment on him, they would have to find a justification under Article 8(2), 'in accordance with law' and only if necessary in a democratic society for health, or to protect the rights and freedoms of others.

There are various other statements regarding treatment without consent in Council of Europe instruments. To escape criticism by the European Committee for the Prevention of Torture, a member state has to ensure under the CPT Standards that treatment without consent is based on law and only relates to strictly defined exceptional circumstances.[32] Article 6 and 7 of the

---

32 European Committee for the Prevention of Torture, *The CPT Standards*, ch. VI, para. 41.

Bioethics Convention[33] provide that treatment of incapable patients may take place with the authority of their representative or a treatment proxy provided for by law, and treatment without consent of people with serious mental illness should be made subject to supervisory and appeal procedures, and should be based on the likelihood of serious harm to health. Although the United Kingdom has not ratified the Bioethics Convention, following the Strasbourg Court's approach in *Glass* v. *United Kingdom*[34] these provisions should be taken to be a guide to the likely interpretation of Article 8 of the ECHR.

Finally, Article 12 of Council of Europe Recommendation (2004) 10 concerning the protection of the human rights and dignity of persons with mental disorder (again not ratified by the United Kingdom) provides that treatment of a mentally disordered person must be with consent if the patient is capable, and must be authorized by a representative, authority, person or body provided for by law. Treatment in emergencies may be carried out without such authority only when medically necessary to avoid serious harm to the health of the individual concerned, or to protect the safety of others.

The United Kingdom has reserved its right not to comply with the Council recommendation, as explained by the Minister of Health, Rosie Winterton, when she said:

> [B]ecause we are in the process of revising important aspects of legislation in England and Wales on mental health and mental capacity, we were not in a position to identify definitively whether there were specific points in the Recommendation on which we might wish to reserve our right not to comply. We therefore said, at this stage, the United Kingdom wished to reserve its right not to comply with the provisions of the Recommendation generally.[35]

Article 8 of the ECHR requires compulsory treatment to be carried out 'in accordance with law.' This means that the law must be sufficiently clear to be predictable in its effects, so that patients will know the circumstances in which they may be treated without consent, and the grounds on which such treatment must be based (protection of own health or the protection of others). The patient must be able to tell which of the Article 8(2) grounds is relied upon.

The MHA 1983 allows for the compulsory treatment of patients liable to be detained under the Act. A detained patient may be given ECT or medicine for mental disorder without their consent. This applies whether they are incapable of consenting to the treatment or capable but refusing it. If the patient is incapable or is refusing ECT, the treatment may only be given with the approval of a second-opinion doctor appointed by the Mental Health Act

---

33 The Convention for the Protection of the Human Rights and Dignity of the Human being with regard to the application of Biology and Medicine (the Bioethics Convention) opened for signature in 1997; 31 other member states have signed.
34 (2004) 39 E.H.R.R. 15, ar para. [58].
35 R. Winterton, 425 *H.C. Debs.*, col. 796W (20 October 2004).

Commission. The same procedure applies to medicines for mental disorder, but the patient may be required to accept medication for mental disorder for three months before becoming entitled to a second opinion. These are the 'supervisory procedures' where patients are to be treated without consent for mental disorder.

Since 2000, challenges have been brought under Article 3 and Article 8 against the regime of powers to treat compulsorily under Part IV of the 1983 Act. The English courts have accepted that treatment without consent can breach Article 3 if it is not a therapeutic necessity and reaches a minimum level of severity causing physical or recognized psychiatric injury.[36] The test for a second-opinion doctor to approve treatment is whether the treatment should be given, having regard to the likelihood it will alleviate or prevent deterioration in the patient's condition. Following the introduction of the 1983 Act, a circular was issued stating that second-opinion doctors approving treatment without consent should not ask themselves whether the proposed treatment is one they would recommend, but instead ask whether the treatment is one which other responsible psychiatrists would support, in other words, the *Bolam* test.[37] Since the HRA 1998, it has been made clear that second-opinion doctors authorizing treatment without consent must apply the test of therapeutic necessity rather than the *Bolam* test in deciding whether treatment without consent should be given. If a second-opinion doctor authorizes treatment without consent, written reasons must be given why the infringement of the right of respect for privacy is necessary to meet one of the goals in Article 8(2), which include health and the protection of the rights and freedoms of others.[38] There has been a steady move towards establishing the facets of quasi-judicial procedure, a right to be heard, a right to reasons, and tighter criteria to authorize treatment, including a rejection of the *Bolam* test.

The next set of test cases will seek to place further limitations on the power to treat without consent, such as that treatment should only be able to be improved without consent where the patient is incapable and the treatment is necessary to prevent serious harm to health or serious harm to other people which should be the test for authorizing treatment without consent. These developments will have to be achieved by the process of arguing that what is currently 'soft law' under the Bioethics Convention and the Mental Disorder Recommendation 2004 ought to be used, as in *Glass*, as aids to the construction of the Convention.[39]

---

36 *R (on the application of Wilkinson)* v. *Broadmoor Special Hospital Authority* [2002] 1 W.L.R. 419; *R (on the Application of N)* v. *Dr M and others* [2002] E.W.C.A. 1789 [2003] 1 W.L.R. 562; *R (on the application of PS)* v. *Responsible Medical Officer and Another* [2003] E.W.H.C. 2335.

37 *Bolam* v. *Friern Barnet Hospital Management Committee* [1957] 1 W.L.R. 582.

38 *R (Wooder)* v. *Fegetter and Mental Health Act Commission* [2002] E.W.C.A. Civ. 554.

39 An example of such a case is *R(B)* v. *Sarkar Responsible Medical Officer Broadmoor Hospital and the Secretary of State for Health* CO/3489/2004.

101

In *Keenan* v. *United Kingdom*,[40] the Court observed that where a person has been deprived of his liberty, 'recourse to physical force which has not been made strictly necessary by his own conduct diminishes human dignity and is in principle an infringement of the right set forth in Article 3.' Mark Keenan, a mentally ill prisoner, had been placed in solitary confinement when he became disturbed and subsequently killed himself in seclusion. The court held that he had been punished in circumstances breaching Article 3 and there had also been breach of his Article 13 right to a remedy that would have quashed that punishment before it had been executed or come to an end.

No provisions in the MHA 1983 expressly justify seclusion. It is, however, subject to guidance under the MHA Code of Practice, defined as:

> the supervised confinement of a patient in a room, which may be locked to protect others from significant harm. Its sole aim is to contain severely disturbed behaviour which is likely to cause harm to others.

The Code requires that seclusion should only be used as a last resort and for the shortest period possible, reflecting common law necessity and the Convention principle of proportionality. It should never be used as a punishment or threat, as part of a treatment programme, because of shortage of staff, or where there is a risk of suicide or self-harm.[41]

In *Munjaz* v. *Mersey Care National Health Service Trust* and *S* v. *Airedale National Health Service Trust* the applicants challenged their seclusion in breach of the MHA Code of Practice.[42] The case establishes that legal powers to seclude exist under the 1983 Act and outlines the impact of Articles 3 and 8 of the Convention on those powers. The effects had not reached the level of severity necessary to engage Article 3. However, there was a potential breach of Article 8, under *Raininen* v. *Finland* where it was held that respect for privacy under Article 8(1) includes the physical and moral integrity of the individual, and extends to deprivations of liberty, 'affording a protection in relation to conditions of detention that do not reach the level of severity required by Article 3.'

The Court of Appeal upheld both challenges to seclusion, holding that Ashworth were only entitled to depart from the Code with good reason, and that Airedale were not justified in keeping S in seclusion from the time when it ceased to be a necessary and proportionate response to the risk he presented to others. The Court of Appeal held that Convention rights obliged them to afford a status and weight to the Code consistent with the state's obligation to avoid ill-treatment of patients detained by or on the authority of the state. Seclusion would infringe Article 8 unless justified under Article

---

40 *Keenan* v. *United Kingdom* (2001) E.H.R.R. 38.
41 Mental Health Act Code of Practice (1998) para. 19.16.
42 [2003] E.W.C.A. Civ. 1036.

8(2) to protect health or the rights and freedoms of others. Since the justifications under the 1983 Act were very broad, the Code of Practice had an important role to play in securing that they had the necessary degree of predictability and transparency to comply with Article 8(2). Moreover, the need for frequent review of the continued need for seclusion is necessary in order to comply with the requirements of Article 13 as specified in *Keenan*.

If a hospital's policy or actions are in unlawful breach of the Code, legal remedies are available by way of judicial review according to traditional principles and under the Human Rights Act 1998, to declare and if necessary remedy any illegality and to award damages. *Munjaz* is currently under appeal. It establishes a lawful base for seclusion. It also seeks to meet the requirements of Article 13 by affording judicial remedies and requiring review of seclusion by nursing and medical staff and its immediate termination if no longer necessary.

Finally, it will be necessary to consider the way in which the principle in *HL* v. *United Kingdom* applies to Article 8. If the right to liberty is too important in a democratic society to be lost merely because someone gives him or herself up to detention, so too must be the right of self-determination under Article 8(1), leading to the conclusion that treatment and seclusion without consent of compliant mentally incapacitated patients should be carried out in accordance with law and in a proportionate manner, according to ascertainable criteria.

The 1998 Act has undoubtedly strengthened the procedural rights of psychiatric service users under the 1983 Act in important ways. There has been a steady process of juridification of decisions to admit to hospital, to treat without consent, and to seclude. Patients' lawyers have sought to pursue a strategy of upholding what may be called the negative rights, not to be arbitrarily detained, not to be compulsorily treated unless treatment is clinically necessary, not to be secluded unless the safeguards in the MHA Code are observed. There have been significant successes with this approach. At the same the court rulings have ensured that there is an effective legal framework for risk management, reaffirming the power to detain, to treat without consent, and to seclude in a Convention compliant manner. Where the strategy has been to seek to extend patient's positive rights to treatment, support, and facilities which will enable them to be cared for in the least restrictive environment, it has been visited with much more limited success.

HUMAN RIGHTS AND THE DISCOURSE OF LAW REFORM

A protracted process of mental health law reform is drawing to a close. At the time of writing, Parliament is debating the Capacity Bill, a framework for decisions about the care and treatment of people who lack mental capacity resulting from a disturbance or disability of mind. A draft Mental Health Bill is currently undergoing pre-parliamentary scrutiny. This will provide for the compulsory treatment of people who suffer from mental disorder, and who pose a risk to their health or safety or to other persons. The Mental Health Bill pursues an agenda of managing the potential risk posed by mentally disordered people in the community, whether to themselves or to others. Its two principal policy goals are to provide for the indeterminate detention of people with personality disorders, who pose a risk to other people, and to provide greater controls to ensure that mentally disordered patients in the community comply with medication regimes. This will be done by expanding the definition of mental disorder to offer increased possibilities to detain people with personality disorders and drug and alcohol problems by abolishing the so-called 'treatability test' for detention, and by increasing the legal controls which may be imposed on patients in the community, allowing for them to be taken and conveyed to a place where they will be required to accept medication, and requiring them to desist from any specified conduct.

The 2004 Bill defines mental disorder as an impairment or disturbance in the functioning of mind or brain resulting from any disorder or disability of the mind or brain, and in contrast to the Mental Health Act 1983, does not exclude people from being treated as mentally disordered by reason *only* of sexual deviancy, addiction to alcohol or drugs. People with these behaviours are not currently liable to be detained under the Act unless they have some accompanying mental disorder. The Convention concept of unsoundness of mind poses no obstacle to a broad definition of mental disorder. Since Article 5(1)(e) provides for the detention of alcoholics and drug addicts, the removal of the exclusion in respect of these groups will not contravene the Convention.

There are five conditions of compulsion in the Bill.[43] First the patient must be suffering from a true mental disorder from an international diagnostic manual such as the DSM IV or the ICD 10.[44] Secondly, the mental disorder must be of a kind or degree warranting medical treatment. This is a much lower threshold than is required for compulsory admission under the 1983 Act or under Article 5, where the mental disorder must be of a kind or degree warranting confinement. The 2004 Bill is intended to provide a single gateway to compulsory treatment in the community or in hospital, hence the lowering of this threshold. The third criterion, the risk criterion, requires that treatment must be necessary for the protection of the patient from suicide or severe self-harm, or serious neglect of health or safety, or for the protection of others. This raises the threshold of compulsion higher than the 1983 Act test

---

43 Mental Health Bill 2004, cl. 9.
44 American Psychiatric Association, *The Diagnostic and Statistical Manual of Mental Disorders (Fourth Edition) DSM-IV* (1994); World Health Organization, *International Classification of Diseases, Glossary and Guide to the Classification of Mental Disorder in accordance with the Tenth Revision of the International Classification of Diseases (ICD-10)* (1990).

104

of necessary in the interests of the patient's own health or safety or for the protection of others, but only in relation to admissions in the person's own interests, not to those which are in the interests of others.

The fourth criterion is that medical treatment cannot lawfully be provided to the patient without him or her being subject to the provisions of this Act. The other ways of lawfully providing the treatment would be, first, if the patient consents to it, or second, if the patient lacks capacity and is not resisting, and could therefore be treated under common law necessity. This latter avenue has now been closed off, other than in emergencies, by the ruling in *HL* v. *United Kingdom*. The fourth criterion does not apply if the patient is at substantial risk of causing serious harm to others. Every patient who is subject to assessment for the use of compulsory powers will have to be assessed as to whether they pose a substantial risk of serious harm to others. If so it will be possible to detain them even if they consent to admission, and also to dis-apply principles in the Code of Practice, most notably the principle of proportionality, that detention may not be used if there is a less restrictive alternative. This is contrary to the principles established consistently by the Strasbourg Court in Article 5[45] and in Article 8[46] cases that proportionality applies to all deprivations of liberty and interventions with privacy. It is pointless to dis-apply proportionality, because if a patient is high risk, detention will be a proportionate response.

The major effect of this provision is that the government can be seen to be affording fewer protections to patients who are at substantial risk of causing serious harm to others. Its possibly unintended effect will be to reinforce any connection in the public mind between mental ill-health and dangerous behaviour. This sits uneasily with Standard One of the National Service Framework for Adult Mental Health Services which states that health and social services should promote mental health for all, working with individuals and communities to combat discrimination against individuals and groups with mental health problems, and promote their social inclusion.[47]

The fifth criterion is that appropriate medical treatment is available, taking into account the nature or degree of the mental disorder and all other circumstances. This is the replacement of the so-called 'treatability' test in the 1983 Act, and is a key part of the government's public safety agenda. Treatment does not have to alleviate or prevent deterioration in the patient's condition (the 1983 Act test for admission of people with psychopathic disorder or mental impairment). Under the Bill appropriate treatment must be available which is appropriate. This could include psychotherapy or

---

45 *Litwa* v. *Poland*, no. 26629/95 (Sect. 2), E.C.H.R. 2000-III.
46 *Pretty* v. *United Kingdom* 66 B.M.L.R. 147.
47 Department of Health, *A National Service Framework for Mental Health: Modern Standards & Service Model* (1999) accessible at <www.doh.gov.uk/pub/docs/doh/mhmain.pdf>.

counselling which is available, even if the patient is not cooperating with it. The treatability test is seen by many as a bulwark against the use of mental health legislation for preventive detention. The government has drawn support for its abolition from *A* v. *The Scottish Ministers and the Advocate General for Scotland.*[48] There the Privy Council held that it was a matter for domestic law whether a person deprived of liberty on grounds of unsoundness of mind in circumstances which meet the *Winterwerp*[49] criteria should also receive treatment for his or her mental disorder as a condition of detention. So too was the place of detention, so long as it is a hospital, clinic, or other place suitable for the detention of persons of unsound mind. The fact that a person's mental disorder is not susceptible to treatment does not mean that, in Convention terms, his or her continued detention in a hospital is arbitrary or disproportionate.

This view has since been reinforced by the decision in *Reid* that 'No ... requirement [that the mental disorder be amenable to medical treatment] was imposed by Article 5 (1)(e) of the Convention.' The Court held that:

> confinement may be necessary not only where a person needs therapy, medication or other clinical treatment to cure or alleviate his condition, but also where the person needs control and supervision to prevent him, for example, causing harm to himself or other persons.[50]

Both the House of Lords and the Strasbourg Court gave strong support to the public safety agenda, and left no obstacle in the way of weakening the treatability test.

Under the Bill patients may have resident (detained) or non-resident status. Residents are required to accept treatment in hospital. Non-residents may be required to live at a specified place, to grant mental health professionals access to them, and to attend a specified place at a specified time for the purpose of treatment. These powers were available in respect of patients subject to guardianship and subject to supervised discharge under the 1983 Act. The Mental Health (Patients in the Community) Act 1995 added a power to take the patient to the place where he or she is required to attend for treatment. Once at that place, the patient could only be forced to accept the treatment, in the words of the Code of Practice, if it was 'an emergency covered by the common law.' The treating psychiatrist was then entitled to assess the patient for possible readmission to hospital.

The 2004 Bill allows for the imposition of a fourth condition that the patient does not engage in specified conduct,[51] reversing the 'essential powers' approach of the 1983 Act which confined community powers within narrower limits needed for the delivery of care and treatment. Added to the list of potential conditions is the requirement that the patient desist from any

---

48 (2001) S.L.T. 1331 Privy Council.
49 *Winterwerp*, op. cit., n. 2.
50 *Hutchison Reid*, op. cit., n. 11, at para 51.
51 Mental Health Bill 2004, cls. 15(4), 26(5), and 46(7).

conduct specified. This is reminiscent of anti-social behaviour orders, but much more wide ranging, reflecting a return to the breadth of powers conferred by the Mental Deficiency Act 1913 and the Mental Health Act 1959 where the guardian had all the powers of a father over a child under 14. The second extension is that once the patient has attended at the required place for treatment, or has been taken and conveyed there having failed to attend voluntarily, she or he may be treated as a 'compulsory patient' whose consent is not required for treatment described in a care plan which is in force or has been approved by the tribunal.[52] In other words, reasonable force may be used to treat non-resident patients without consent, but only once they have been taken to the hospital or clinic which they are required to attend for treatment. The Bill will undoubtedly widen the scope of compulsory powers, both in terms of the population eligible for compulsion and in terms of the powers available to treat compulsorily. The safeguards against wrongful or overzealous use of these powers therefore become all-important.

1. *Safeguards*

Under the 1983 Act, a person with a mental disorder of a nature or degree warranting detention can be detained if necessary for their health *or* safety *or* for the protection of others. Dangerousness is not a prerequisite of detention. As a counterweight to this strong paternalism, the 1983 Act gives substantive rights to the patient's 'nearest relative' to be consulted and to object to compulsory admission. The nearest relative may request the discharge of a detained patient and the authorities must discharge the patient unless the patient is likely to act in a manner dangerous to self or others. The family can take responsibility for their family member's health needs, but not if the patient is dangerous to self or others, where the state has the power to take over and provide care under detention. Even then the nearest relative retains rights to question the need for detention before the detaining authority and to seek discharge from the Mental Health Review Tribunal.

These rights are taken away in the 2004 draft Bill. The nearest relative gives way to the nominated person, who is not appointed until after compulsory powers have been imposed. The patient can nominate this person, who will not have any rights in the substantive sense, merely the right to express the patient's wishes and feelings to the authorities, and a right to apply to the Mental Health Tribunal for discharge from compulsion or transfer from detention to non-resident status. The mental health professionals will have to consider the patient's wishes and feelings and the views of the nominated person, but will not be bound by them.

In *JT* v. *United Kingdom*,[53] the United Kingdom was held to be in breach of the right to respect for privacy under Article 8 because JT did not have a

---

52 id., cls. 80, 198–200.
53 (2000) 30 E.H.R.R CD 77.

power to apply to court for displacement of her mother who was unsuitable to act as her nearest relative. The Commission stated that the absence of any possibility of applying to the County Court to change the applicant's nearest relative rendered the interference of her rights under Article 8(1) of the European Convention disproportionate to the aims pursued. The judgment of the European Court noted that a friendly settlement was reached between JT and the government, whereby the government undertook to introduce reform proposals to (i) enable a patient to make an application to the court to have his or her nearest relative replaced where the patient objected on reasonable grounds to a particular individual acting in that capacity, and (ii) prevent certain persons from acting as the nearest relative of the patient. Three years later, the government had still not acted, and a declaration of incompatibility was granted in R. (on the application of M) v. Secretary of State for Health.[54] Convention compliance requires that the patient be entitled to apply on reasonable grounds to the court to displace their nearest relative, and disqualifying those who have abused the patient in the past. The government's response is to throw the baby out with the bathwater, and to remove the possibility for carers and family members to act as effective protectors of the rights of their mentally disordered family member prior to detention, especially important if that person lacks mental capacity.

2. The Mental Health Tribunal

The key regulatory body under the Bill will be the Mental Health Tribunal (MHT). Patients will be subject to compulsory assessment and treatment for up to 28 days on the authority of determinations by an Approved Mental Health Professional (AMHP) and two doctors. Any compulsory treatment beyond 28 days will require the authority of the Mental Health Tribunal by treatment order or further assessment order. In making these orders, the tribunal will determine whether a patient should be a resident (detained) or non-resident patient. The tribunal will also approve the care plan indicating what treatment may be given to the patient under the order, and will be required to impose conditions which address the risk by reference to which the patient is subject to compulsion.

This fundamentally changes the tribunal's role. It is to become the detaining authority, not simply the body that reviews lawfulness of detention. It will take over the functions currently performed by second opinion doctors under the 1983 Act, and will authorize electro-convulsive therapy (ECT) for adult patients subject to compulsion who lack capacity to consent or refuse treatment, and for all children under 16. The MHT would exercise functions under both Article 5(1)(e) to authorize detention and under Article 8 to authorize and review treatment. The tribunal will continue

54 [2003] E.W.H.C. 1094.

to exercise functions under Article 5(4) jurisdiction to review the lawfulness of detention, following applications by the patient or the nominated person.

The fact that a judicial body will authorize both the imposition of compulsory powers and compulsory treatment is seen as the acme of human rights protection. However, it is necessary to question this assumption. The current system of compulsory admission is based on checks and balances, where the ASW has a discretion to make an application, and the nearest relative has rights to be consulted, to object to the initial use of compulsion, and to discharge a patient who is not dangerous to self or to others. Under the Bill, if the mental health professionals determine that the conditions are met, the patient automatically becomes subject to compulsory assessment. The patient's carer has a qualified right to be consulted, but no right to object. Once the person is subject to compulsory assessment, they or their nominated person may appeal to the MHT. If, on such an appeal, the Mental Health Tribunal is satisfied that the new broad conditions of compulsion are met, they must make a treatment order or continue the assessment order. If not, they must discharge. Issues of burden of proof are studiously avoided.

It will be difficult for a patient who has been obliged to take medication in the community to convince the tribunal that compulsory treatment is not necessary to prevent serious self-neglect of health. Currently the issue is more straightforward, whether the patient should be discharged from liability to detention in hospital. The conditions under the Bill are so broad that once a person has been subject to compulsion, it will be very difficult for them to achieve discharge. In *A* v. *Scottish Ministers*,[55] the Court of Sessions referred to the 'lobster-pot' effect where it is harder for patients to get out than it is for them to avoid being put in. The Bill's procedures might more accurately be described as a 'dragnet' in that the process of initial compulsion has many fewer safeguards for patients and their families, and once in the system of compulsion, it will be hard to achieve discharge.

It is not necessary to have the MHT authorize compulsion to achieve Convention compliance. It is questionable whether the new framework provides more effective safeguards for patients' rights, given the breadth of the powers of compulsion and the removal of the nearest relative's rights. It is also questionable whether the Bill justifies the government's confidence in its compatibility with Convention rights,[56] considering the dis-application of proportionality to patients at substantial risk of causing serious harm to others With the exception of the procedures in relation to ECT, there are issues concerning the existence of a sufficiently predictable procedure to impose treatment without consent on a capable patient. Perhaps most difficult is the issue of achieving compliance with *HL* v. *United Kingdom*. Estimates of the numbers of compliant incapacitated patients vary between

---

55 *A*, op. cit., n. 48.
56 Department of Health, *Improving Mental Health Law: Towards a new Mental Health Act* (2004) para. 1.4.

20,000 and 40,000. If all these have to be subject to a procedure prescribed by law, this will be difficult to achieve when the procedures for deprivation of liberty in both the Capacity Bill and the Mental Health Bill involve authorization by judicial bodies, the Court of Protection or the MHT.

CONCLUSION

At meetings discussing the 2002 draft Mental Health Bill (substantially the same as the 2004 draft), departmental officials spoke of a 'new human rights agenda', based on the idea that the community should have strong rights to protection against potential depredations visited upon them by mentally disordered people. The rights of the community should be weighed in the balance against those of individual psychiatric patients, and in certain cases should trump those individual rights. The new human rights agenda involves reading up the state's positive duty under Article 2 to uphold the public's right to life under *Osman* v. *United Kingdom*. *Osman* establishes that Article 2 is breached if the authorities:

> knew or ought to have known at the time of the existence of a real and immediate risk to the life of identified individual or individuals from the criminal acts of a third party, and failed to take action within the scope of their powers which, judged reasonably, might have been expected to avoid that risk.[57]

The new human rights agenda reads down the individual rights of psychiatric patients under Article 5 to protection against arbitrary detention, and under Article 8 to protection from arbitrary compulsory treatment. The government has aimed for the minimum level of restraint on compulsory powers consonant with Convention compliance, and has avoided ratifying the Council of Europe Conventions and recommendations that seek to uphold the dignity of mentally disordered people. The 2004 Bill opts for the widest possible definition of mental disorder, further weakening of the treatability test, removal of nearest relatives' rights, and reduction of the rights of patients who are at substantial risk of causing serious harm to others. The main burden of legitimizing this expansion of compulsory powers is on the MHT, and it may prove too great. The 'new human rights agenda' privileges public safety concerns, and leads to reduction of protection for service users and their families. This concept of Convention compliance will result in increased stigmatization and social exclusion of mentally disordered people, and the pre-eminence of public safety risks eclipsing the social inclusion agenda in the National Service Frameworks.

57 [1998] 29 E.H.R.R. 245, at 305.

JOURNAL OF LAW AND SOCIETY
VOLUME 32, NUMBER 1, MARCH 2005
ISSN: 0263-323X, pp. 111–30

Resources, Rights, and Environmental Regulation

ROBERT G. LEE*

Prior to the Human Rights Act 1998, there were significant expectations that it would promote the development of environmental rights and extend remedies for environmental harm. This has not been the case, but then the expectations were probably always false. The paper points to three reasons why: the retention of a strong model of parliamentary sovereignty; the need to mould human rights principles alongside the common law; the traditional reluctance of the courts to determine questions of utility where questions of resource allocation arise. The paper concludes by reflecting on whether one would hope, in any case, to advance the cause of the environment through the mechanism of the Convention and suggests that there may be reasons to doubt the wisdom of this approach.

INTRODUCTION

The Human Rights Act 1998 ('the Act') marks the most significant constitutional development since the passage of the European Communities Act 1972, and, arguably, since the Bill of Rights 1689.[1] The differential between a 30- and a 300-year period arises because much will depend upon the manner in which the courts grasp their new-fledged power of scrutiny over public administration. Expectations have been high among those concerned with environmental law. In June 1999, Sir Nicolas Bratza addressing the implications of the Act for business, including matters of environmental regulation, stated:[2]

* *ESRC BRASS Centre, Cardiff University, 54 Park Place, Cardiff CF10 3AT, Wales*

I am grateful for the assistance of Stuart Bell, Elen Stokes, Stephen Tromans, and the EPR Group at Freshfields, London.

1 L. Clements and J. Young, 'Human Rights: Changing the Culture' (1999) 26 *J. of Law and Society* 1.
2 N. Bratza, 'The implications of the Human Rights Act for Business' [2000] E.H.R.L.R. 1.

Our judges and our lawyers will be able to make their own distinctive contribution to the development of Convention case law, not least in the commercial field. Michael Beloff and Helen Mountfield described our judges as 'straining at the leash'. Soon, mercifully the leash will be released and our courts will be able to roam freely.[3]

Lord McCluskey offered an alternative account during the debate on the Bill describing it as 'a field day for crackpots, a pain in the neck for judges and a goldmine for lawyers'.[4] As Patricia Ryan has rightly pointed out, a review of this type of development is naturally overshadowed by expectations that, on careful reflection, were likely to prove false.[5]

Against the backdrop of environmental claims, this paper examines what one might have expected, because to conclude that the constitutional change has somehow proved disappointing[6] depends on precisely what one expected the Act to achieve. The role of the courts in the constitutional settlement always made it unlikely that environmental claims incorporating human rights' arguments would produce significant review of environmental regulation by a judiciary let off the leash. The paper suggests three reasons for this. First, although the Act encourages the interpretation of legislation in conformity with the Convention, it retains parliamentary supremacy. Secondly, the Convention rights must be made to work alongside established principles of the common law in a context in which the judiciary, viewing environmental law as an area of technical regulation, have adopted a conservative approach to the development of remedies for harm caused by pollution. This has inevitably inhibited approaches to human rights based claims. In the now (in)famous words of Lord Hoffmann: 'the Human Rights Act 1998 was no doubt intended to strengthen the rule of law, but not to inaugurate the rule of lawyers.'[7] Finally, in many environmental claims there are underlying issues of resource allocation. Lord Hoffmann commented in a case involving Article 10 of the Convention that there are legal limits to the courts' power to review administrative or executive decision-making where resource issues are involved:

> Independence makes the courts more suited to deciding some kinds of questions and being elected makes the legislature or executive more suited to deciding others ... The principle that the independence of the courts is

---

3 id., p. 13.
4 R. Purchas and J. Clayton, 'A Field Day for Crackpots? Development Projects and Control' [2001] *J. of Planning and Environment Law* 134, at 134.
5 P. Ryan, 'Court of Hope and False Expectations; Land and Environment Court 21 Years On' (2002) 14 *J. of Environmental Law* 301. As to evolutionary rather than revolutionary change, see D. Feldman, 'The Human Rights Act 1998 and Constitutional Principles' (1999) 19 *Legal Studies* 165.
6 On 'disappointment', see M. Havers and R. English, 'Human Rights: A Review of the Year' (2003) 6 E.H.R.L.R. 587.
7 In *R (Alconbury Developments Ltd)* v. *Secretary of State for the Environment, Transport and the Regions* [2001] 2 All E.R. 929, H.L. *per* Lord Hoffmann, para. 129.

necessary for a proper decision of disputed legal rights or claims of violation of human rights is a legal principle ... On the other hand, the principle that majority approval is necessary for a proper decision on policy or allocation of resources is also a legal principle.[8]

In many instances, arguments about the environment (whether about inputs from or outputs to) will involve resource questions, which the judiciary will approach with great trepidation.

A final section of the paper reflects upon notions of environmental and human rights. The Convention rights are a distinctive if quirky collection of human rights rather than more adventurous, less anthropocentric environmental rights that many advocate. In consequence, approaches to environmental protection using human rights' arguments meet with limited success, provoking a wider debate about whether rights to a healthy and unpolluted environment are best secured through human rights' discourse. The paper argues that it is not churlish to reject the anthropocentric approaches inevitable under the Convention, not least because much of the case law to date smacks of a 'not-in-my-backyard' approach rather than a more lasting or thoughtful concern for the environment. This paper will not rehearse the ways in which Convention rights intersect with environmental interests or review the case law under the Act. There are many such reviews.[9] Relevant authorities are referenced, however, to illustrate points made in the course of the paper.

PARLIAMENTARY SUPREMACY

The government made reference to the British legal influence on the drafting of the Convention in the passage through Parliament of the Bill that became the Act.[10] Yet, during the political process, opposition resistance was based upon the breadth and generality of the Convention, on the basis that the courts would be drawn more deeply into matters of public policy. This is a valid concern. The ethos of the Convention is that there must be limits to the extent of state power to curb rights of the individual. However, while Lord Irvine felt that:

8   *Regina* v. *British Broadcasting Corporation ex parte Prolife Alliance* [2003] 2 All E.R. 977, para. 76.
9   W. Upton, 'The European Convention of Human Rights and Environmental Law' [1998] *J. of Planning and Environmental Law* 315; D. Hart, 'The Impact of the European Convention on Human Rights on Planning and Environmental Law' [2000] *J. of Planning and Environmental Law* 117; K. Cook, 'Environmental Rights as Human Rights' (2002) 2 E.H.R.L.R. 196; M. DeMerieux, 'Deriving Environmental Rights from the European Convention for the Protection of Human Rights and Fundamental Freedoms' (2001) 21 *Ox. J. of Legal Studies* 521.
10   Lord Lester: 'a convention drafted by British lawyers on the basis of traditional common law concepts', Human Rights Bill, 577 *H.L. Debs.*, cols. 1726/30 (5 February 1997) and the White Paper, *Rights Brought Home* (1997; Cm. 3782).

the judiciary will be able to exercise to the full the power to scrutinise legislation rigorously against the fundamental freedoms guaranteed by the Convention but without becoming politicised

he conceded that:

the ultimate decision to amend legislation to bring it into line with the Convention, however, will rest with Parliament. The ultimate responsibility for compliance with the Convention must be Parliament's alone.[11]

Consequently, while the Act envisages that there should be some sort of bulwark against the abuse of executive power, in framing the Act 'the sovereignty of Parliament was absolutely protected'.[12]

Ultimately the Act ensures that Parliament remains sovereign, allowing the primacy of United Kingdom legislation even where Convention rights are offended, and leaving Parliament free to enact or maintain legislation incompatible with the Convention.[13] Such incompatibility would gain higher profile than before and the rights of an individual to pursue a remedy in Strasbourg would remain. Nonetheless, a future Parliament could repeal the Act in its entirety, and no attempt has been made to entrench the legislation.[14] In an early skirmish with the courts over asylum policy,[15] Blair was suggesting on television the need for a fundamental review of obligations under the Act.[16] In contrast, where subordinate legislation appears incompatible with the Convention, then it can be quashed.[17] This has happened in the context of environmental law when the Fur Farming Compensation Scheme (England) Order[18] was found to contravene requirements of Article 1, Protocol 1 that compensation should be related to the value of the property taken. The provisions of the Order as to

11 Lord Irvine, 'Tom Sargant Memorial Lecture: The Development of Human Rights in Britain under an Incorporated Convention on Human Rights' 16 December 1997: <http://www.dca.gov.uk/speeches/1997/speechfr.htm>.
12 J. Straw, 301 *H.C. Debs.*, col. 628 (24 November 1997).
13 J. Limbach, 'The Concept of the Supremacy of the Constitution' (2001) 64 *Modern Law Rev.* 1, and J. Black-Branch, 'Parliamentary Supremacy or Political Expediency? The Constitutional Position of the Human Rights Act under British Law' (2002) 23 *Statute Law Rev.* 59.
14 G. Marshall, 'Parliamentary Sovereignty: The New Horizons' [1997] *Public Law* 1, and M. Zander, 'A Bill of Rights?' (1997, 4th edn.) 111.
15 *R (Q and others)* v. *Secretary of State for the Home Department* [2003] H.R.L.R. 21.
16 'If the measures don't work, then we will have to consider further measures, including fundamentally looking at the obligations we have under the Convention on Human Rights' *Breakfast with Frost* February 2003, from A. Lester, 'The Human Rights Act – Five Years On', Annual Lecture of the Law Reform Committee of the Bar Council (25 November 2003) <http://www.hrla.co.uk/lesterHRA5.pdf>.
17 s. 3(2)(c) of the Act.
18 S.I. no. 2002/221, made under the Fur Farming Prohibition Act 2000. Its quashing led to a negotiated agreement between the breeders and the government.

114

compensation for the value of banned breeding stock was said to operate unfairly as between different farmers, failing to take account of the different values of premium breeds, discriminating without justification, and producing arbitrary effects.[19] Importantly, this was not a case in which the quashing of the secondary legislation deprived the parent Act of effect, or where the defect in the secondary legislation was an inevitable consequence of the parent Act. In contrast, in *Trailer and Marina (Leven) Ltd* v. *English Nature*,[20] a management agreement with the site owners not to use the canal ceased to attract any payment following the passage of the Countryside and Rights of Way Act 2000, but under the authority of primary legislation this classic 'takings' case was said not to offend Article 1 of Protocol 1.

The higher courts can make a declaration of incompatibility. This can necessitate political remedial action[21] where there is a compelling case for a Minister of the Crown to use foreshortened legislative process[22] to amend the offending primary legislation. However, such action (or inaction) on the part of the Minister may be difficult to challenge. There are no mechanisms under the Act to force a Minister to respond to a declaration of incompatibility, but any remedial measure constitutes primary legislation and attracts future protection against judicial review.[23] Under the Act, all courts and tribunals are charged with interpreting the Act and are bound by its provisions alongside other public authorities.[24] Thus the role of the courts in this framework is firmly located in a traditional structure of parliamentary supremacy, and mention of the incorporation of the Convention into United Kingdom law is at best convenient shorthand, but really constitutes sloppy thinking. There has been no incorporation, merely an invitation to the judiciary to review administrative action in accordance with Convention rights.[25]

Prior to the Act, in giving effect to the Convention, courts could intervene only in the face of ambiguity in legislation; the ambiguity came first and the search for compatibility second. Without ambiguity there could be no search for conformity.[26] But the demand of the Act, that 'in so far as it is possible to

---

19 See *Kelsall and Others* v. *Secretary of State for Environment, Food and Rural Affairs* [2003] E.W.H.C. 459.
20 [2004] E.W.H.C. 153.
21 s. 10 of the Act.
22 Schedule 2 of the Act.
23 As originally published, Clause 25 of the Civil Contingencies Bill allowed the making of regulations having the status of primary legislation to protect such measures against human rights' review – see Joint Committee on the Draft Civil Contingencies Bill, *First Report*, HL (2002–3) 184 /HC (2002–3) 1074, para. 156.
24 s. 9 of the Act.
25 The Act speaks of the courts taking 'evidence' of judgments and so on of the ECHR and Commission (s. 2(2)), indicating no direct incorporation of Convention law.
26 *R* v. *Secretary of State for the Home Department ex p Brind* [1991] 1 A.C. 696, though since Lord Goff's lead in *A.G.* v. *Guardian Newspapers (No. 2)* [1990] 1 A.C. 109, judges have been exhorted to interpret English law in accordance with the Convention, when free to do so.

115

do so' all legislation must be read to give effect to the Convention' seems to mandate a *search* for a meaning that accords with the Convention, and a presumption that a consistent interpretation will emerge. The courts will not wish to accept that there is a single plain meaning that leaves no room for the Convention, as this will lead to a declaration of incompatibility.[27] Yet since parliamentary sovereignty is clearly retained, the courts will be reluctant to move towards expansive interpretations of Acts of Parliament, leaving a tension between the interpretive powers of the courts and political reality. The judiciary may have difficulty in handling the broad principles of the Convention in contrast to the precise United Kingdom statutes, such precision being necessary according to Tridimas to ensure that the statute is 'free of ambivalence or equivocation, so the governmental accountability is ensured by Parliamentary, rather than judicial, control'.[28]

This is well illustrated by *Lee* v. *Leeds City Council*.[29] This case concerned a council tenant without a remedy for the conditions of a dwelling,[30] unsuitable for occupation by reason of damp caused by a design defect in its construction. The Court of Appeal rejected invitations to interpret the expression 'to keep in repair the structure', in s. 11 of the Landlord and Tenant Act 1985 to require the landlord to remedy a defect in design, as this would give the tenant greater rights than Parliament had intended. Works to remedy a design defect were not works of 'repair'. This case illustrates the inherent caution of the courts in reinterpretation of statutes where duties are placed on public bodies by Parliament. The Court of Appeal recognized that the question in this individual case needed to be determined with regard to the needs and resources of the community at large, given the possible prevalence of design defects in public housing stock. Chadwick LJ regards such spending as a matter to be determined by democratically ordered priorities.[31] In essence, this is a case on the margin of appreciation to be extended to local authorities in allocating resources to social housing – an issue considered below.

27 A situation that s. 3 of the Act seems keen to avoid, as do the judiciary – see *Regina (Alconbury Developments Ltd and Others)* v. *Secretary of State for the Environment, Transport and the Regions* [2003] 2 A.C. 295.
28 T. Tridimas, 'The Court of Justice and Judicial Activism' [1996] *European Law Rev.* 204.
29 [2002] 1 W.L.R. 1488.
30 Had Lee been a private tenant, then the local authority would have been under a duty to serve an abatement order under s. 80 of the Environmental Protection Act 1990, but an environmental health officer cannot not serve an abatement notices on the housing department run by his employing authority – see *R* v. *Cardiff City Council ex p Cross* [1982] 6 H.L.R. 1.
31 *Lee*, op. cit., n. 29, at para. 49.

As a consequence of its history, many of the 'rights' under the Convention are actually freedoms, guarantees against unwarranted interventions (freedom of expression, assembly, not to be tortured or enslaved, and so on). This sits well alongside English constitutional law,[32] but the rights protected by the Convention may not map onto those recognized by common law. An early example can be found in *Malone* v. *Metropolitan Police Commissioner*. There, Megarry VC stated that in the absence of a tort of breach of privacy, there was no basis for common law protection against telephone tapping.[33] The eventual response came in the Interception of Communications Act, which regulated telephone tapping but introduced no new civil remedies. In the aftermath of the Act we see no appreciable shift in this approach. In *Secretary of State for the Home Office* v. *Wainwright*[34] Lord Hoffmann declined to recognize any tort of breach of privacy. Although, since *Malone*, the tort of breach of confidence had extended remedies, Lord Hoffmann offers limited endorsement to suggestions by Sedley LJ in *Douglas* v. *Hello* that there is no longer a need to 'construct an artificial relationship of confidentiality between intruder and victim'.[35] Lord Hoffmann accepts that the Act may provide remedies to protect the values of privacy where trespass or breach of confidence are not available. But his Lordship rejected invitations to provide an action in tort in the aftermath of *Peck* v. *UK*,[36] a successful claim before the ECHR involving breach of Article 8 rights via CCTV. Lord Hoffmann almost revisited the history of *Malone* suggesting better regulation by Parliament of CCTV, and quoting the words of Megarry VC in *Malone* with approval:

> I readily accept that if the question before me were one of construing a statute enacted with the purpose of giving effect to obligations imposed by the Convention, the court would readily seek to construe the legislation in a way that would effectuate the Convention rather than frustrate it. However ... it seems to me that where Parliament has abstained from legislating on a point that is plainly suitable for legislation, it is difficult for the court to lay down new rules of common law or equity that will carry out the Crown's treaty obligations, or to discover for the first time that such rules have always existed.[37]

---

32 Since it demands specific legal authority for breach of common law rights: *Entick* v. *Carrington* (1765) 2 Will 275, compare K. Ewing, 'The Politics of the British Constitution' [2000] *Public Law* 405.

33 [1979] Ch. 344; and the ruling against the United Kingdom (*Malone* v. *UK* [1984] 7 E.H.R.R. 1) that Malone's right to privacy under Article 8 of the Convention was breached.

34 *Wainwright* [2003] 4 All E.R. 969.

35 [2001] Q.B. 976, para. 126.

36 App. no. 44647/98, January 2003.

37 *Wainwright,* op. cit., n. 34, para. 20, quoting *Malone* (op. cit., n. 33, at p. 379).

As a rights-based system, one might assume that the Act implies a radical departure from Dicey's notion of freedoms under the common law, in which individuals are free to act as they wish subject to the constraints of common law or statute:[38] 'individual rights are the basis not the result of the law of the constitution'.[39] It is unclear, however, why the Act should produce a marked shift in philosophy unless we are to regard the Act as akin to a written constitution – something that Parliament seems not to have intended. Moreover, examining the nature of the rights under the Convention, not all rights work in the same way. Some permit no derogation;[40] for others derogation is limited.[41] The majority of provisions, however, do permit some derogation by reference to a balancing of public as against private interests. Thus, entitlement to a public trial may be restricted in the interests of morals, public order or national security. Similarly rights to peaceful enjoyment of possessions can be restricted in the public interest. This is actually much more akin to Dicey's model. It may be easier to see these articles, especially those most often invoked in the environmental law context (Articles 6, 8, and Article 1 of Protocol 1), as asserting freedoms that may need to be restrained by lawful action. Where such restrictions apply, they must be lawful, and the inference is that restriction of the right will be unlawful unless specifically authorized by law.

If an action is lawful, the purpose of the action might seem legitimate, but the Convention demands further enquiry. There are two criteria that the action must meet. It must be 'necessary in a democratic society' and applied in a non-discriminatory manner. For the first criterion, there is a test of proportionality. Is there a fair balance between the restriction on the right and the legitimate purpose of the restriction? It requires balancing of competing interests in order to show that the response was proportionate – see below. In addition, the Convention allows that, in its application to a wide range of states, there must be some 'margin of appreciation' – some allowance that states will vary in terms of how the public interest may demand a particular restriction. The Strasbourg Court is sensitive to the need to work the margin of appreciation by reference to the practice across Convention states and the significance of the right/restriction in the national context. Austin[42] was deeply sceptical of the possibility of law emanating other than from a sovereign state. Although the events and aftermath of the Second World War created the foundations for the Convention, the need to respect the legitimacy of state interventions runs deep in Convention jurisprudence. The freedoms may be fundamental but they are not absolute.

---

38 A.V. Dicey, *Law of the Constitution* (1885).
39 id., p. 220.
40 For example, Articles 3, 4.
41 For example, Article 2.
42 J. Austin, *Province of Jurisprudence Determined* (1995 edn.).

118

The courts traditionally accept legal constraints on freedoms under the common law. Yet, over time, the courts have become more assertive. The deference shown by the House of Lords to the Home Secretary in cases such as *Liversidge* v. *Anderson*[43] would not be expected today, but not only was that a war-time case involving national security, great play was also placed upon the accountability of the Minister to Parliament. Quite rightly, given the shifting nature of ministerial responsibility, modern Home Secretaries would expect a rougher ride through judicial review, although in the aftermath of the asylum case of *Q*,[44] Blunkett tried to resist judicial review of his actions by asserting his accountability to Parliament: 'Frankly, I am personally fed up with having to deal with a situation where Parliament debates issues and the judges then overturn them.'[45] Moreover the approach of the courts has not changed greatly since the attempt by Blackburn to have the courts declare that the signature of the Treaty of Rome would constitute an unlawful surrender of the sovereignty of Parliament, when the Court of Appeal stated that:

> As to Parliament ... it can enact, amend and repeal any legislation it pleases. The sole power of the courts is to decide and enforce what is the law and not what it should be – now or in the future.[46]

Environmental lawyers are familiar with this approach, for, in cases stretching back over ten years, the House of Lords have not merely declined to extend the common law remedies for environmental pollution, but have consistently reined these in on the basis that 'it is more appropriate for strict liability in respect of operations of high risk to be imposed by Parliament, than by the courts.'[47] These cases have seen a requirement for foreseeability of damage written into the rule in *Rylands* v. *Fletcher*,[48] the assertion that an interest in land be the basis of an action in nuisance, the denial of the possibility of recovery of damages for personal injury in nuisance, the curbing of cases suggesting positive duties to act to abate a nuisance, and the limitation of recovery, by the narrowing of the notion of what constitutes a non-natural user.[49] The general approach to any suggestion that the common law might develop to accommodate environmental concerns is reflected in the words of Lord Bingham:

---

43 [1942] A.C. 246.
44 *Q*, op. cit., n. 15.
45 In Lester, op. cit., n. 16.
46 *Blackburn* v. *Attorney-General* [1971] 2 All E.R. 1380 *per* Lord Salmon, at 1383.
47 Lord Goff in *Cambridge Water Co* v. *Eastern Counties Leather Plc* [1994] 2 W.L.R. 53.
48 (1868) L.R. 3 H.L. 300.
49 *Cambridge Water*, op. cit., n. 47; *Hunter* v. *Canary Wharf Ltd* [1997] 2 W.L.R. 684; *Marcic* v. *Thames Water* [2004] 2 A.C. 42; and *Transco* v. *Stockport MBC* [2004] 2 A.C. 1.

If the law were changed ... the effect might be (one does not know) to falsify the assumption on which Parliament has legislated, by significantly modifying rights which Parliament may have assumed would continue to exist.[50]

As is shown below, this concession to parliamentary authority is marked when decisions about resource allocation are at stake: 'Parliament did not intend the fairness of priorities (for sewerage provision) to be decided by a judge.'[51]

In addition, we see from the case of *Hunter*[52] just how dependent the protection of interests under the common law is upon the notion of property rights. The protection of habitats or species as such is not guaranteed by the common law and any such prospect is remote, not least because this has become an area heavily regulated by Parliament, albeit in the shadow of the European Community. It has been said that the common law perspective is of wrongs to people rather than environmental rights.[53] Even if one wished to attempt to offer such protection judicially, there is little scope in using the Convention: how might the proprietary rights under Article 1 of Protocol 1 or the principles of respect for home and family life be engaged by threats to a species? The best one might hope for is to secure the proper working of any protective regulatory structure using Article 6.

In the light of this, one has to ask how expansive one imagined the approach of the judiciary would be when facing the question whether activity, sanctioned under statutory mechanisms of planning and environmental law, could then said to constitute an interference with (for example) rights of family life. In an early case, *R* v. *Leicester City Council ex p. Blackfordby & Boothcorpe Action Group Ltd*,[54] a residents' group objected to the grant of planning permission for the extraction of coal and clay and for the disposal of waste on a site close to their homes. Richards J was prepared to accept that this would lead to adverse effects on the residents but went on to hold that there was substantial justification for the planning approval, given the benefits to which the permission gave rise. Richards J noted that the planning authority had undertaken an assessment of the effects on health and *environment* that constituted sufficient justification in the Article 8 context. A similar case is that of *R (on the application of Vetterlein)* v. *Hampshire County Council*,[55] though it involved an incinerator rather than a landfill, and was probably given even shorter shrift. Sullivan J ruled that generalized concerns about possible air emissions did not engage the protective rights of Article 8. It had taken ten years to steer the waste

---

50 *Transco*, id., para. 6.
51 Lord Hoffmann in *Marcic*, op. cit., n. 49, para. 70.
52 *Hunter* v. *London Docklands Development Corporation* [1997] A.C. 655.
53 L.M. Soriano, 'Environmental "Wrongs" and Environmental Rights' (2001) 13 *J. of Environmental Law* 297.
54 [2000] *J. of Planning Law* 1266.
55 [2001] E.W.H.C. 560.

incinerator through the planning system by the time of the Vetterlein challenge, using citizens' juries in a model cited as good practice.[56] Had the claim been allowed, it is hard to see that any waste incineration facility could have proceeded in the future, notwithstanding the critical shortage of waste disposal facilities brought on by a general community refusal to minimize or recycle waste. In Miller's words, 'Given the importance of the wider struggle for human rights, it is surely unwise to blunt our most respected weapons on the less deserving targets.'[57]

RIGHTS AND RESOURCES

The environmental justice movement assert that incinerators[58] or landfills impact disproportionately upon people already subject to disadvantage. The environmental justice position is straightforward: 'Everyone has the right to live in a clean and healthy environment. This may be more accurately called environmental equity. In each case, the poor pay more.'[59] This is unsurprising, however regrettable, since such facilities tend to be located in industrial zones that do not border on neat suburbia, and, famously, what is a nuisance in Belgravia may not be such in Bermondsey.[60] Many would look to law to combat this and deliver environmental justice.[61] The Act offers some capacity via the non-discrimination provisions of Article 14, the employment of which is contingent upon the breach of some other Convention right, where Convention rights are denied to a particular group of people, or where certain classes of people face differential environmental standards. This reflects the roots of the environmental justice movement:

> the environmental justice movement developed in the US in response to concerns about the uneven distribution of environmental risks among certain groups of people, especially those of colour.[62]

At this point, however, one hits the problem of which Convention articles, when breached, might support the Article 14 claim. The most likely is Article 8 with the proviso in Article 8(2) concerning 'the economic well-being of the country'. That proviso could be overcome if the threat is to life under Article 2. Right to life under the Convention appears, however, to be restricted to life itself and not those incidents of life that might be cherished

---

56 J. Petts, 'Waste Management Strategy Development' (1995) 38 *J. of Environmental Planning and Management* 519.
57 C. Miller, 'The European Convention on Human Rights: Another Weapon in the Environmentalist's Armoury' (1999) 11 *J. of Environmental Law* 157, 176.
58 FOE, *Incinerators and Deprivation* (2004).
59 P. Stookes, 'What Price Environmental Justice' *New Law J.*, 2 April 2004.
60 *Sturges* v. *Bridgman* (1879) 11 Ch.D. 852.
61 Capacity Global, *Using the Law: Access to Environmental Justice* (2003).
62 J. Agyeman, R. Bullard, and B. Evans, *Just Sustainabilities: Development in an Unequal World* (2003).

or might support and sustain life. In consequence, 'cases under this Article in relation to the environment are sparse.'[63] Although Article 2 may found broader rights to information,[64] in the majority of cases, the impacts are less than life-threatening and fall into the more tricky territory of Article 8 or involve property rights under Protocol 1 Article 1. As explained below, as many such cases involve economic resource issues, courts take the view the political realm is better suited to deciding such allocations.

Nonetheless, human rights can be invoked in matters of environmental concern, not because the Convention addresses environmental rights as such, but because modern environmental law places significant interventionist powers into the hands of regulators. These are public bodies, local authorities, and statutory regulatory agencies, for the purposes of s. 6 of the Act, but s. 6(3) also includes persons whose functions are public in nature. This catches hybrid bodies, which might discharge both private and public functions in the post-Fordist era.[65] The right to take action under s. 6(1) lies with the victim, and here the Convention notions of standing may be narrower than those in administrative law. Pressure groups have not always been accorded standing under the Convention, whereas English admini-strative law has been increasingly liberal,[66] even to the point of suggestions of a prima facie assumption of standing in environmental protection cases.[67] This would not seem to satisfy 'victim' requirements of the Convention, but there has been no hint that English law notions of *locus standi* will be narrowed.

Not surprisingly, a Convention written over fifty years ago took less account of environmental rights than might now be expected. But the states have not addressed this shortfall, except in the EU Charter of Fundamental Rights,[68] which is not yet binding. What remains covers impacts on the human population or its property. In terms of human impact, in the absence of a threat to life itself, one is thrown upon provisions largely dealing with state interference with private and family life or property rights. There are two points to make here. First, the state will not commonly be the polluter, but may be able to exercise regulatory power to restrain commercial interests

---

63 J. Thornton and S. Troman, 'Human Rights and Environmental Wrongs' (1999) 11 *J. of Environmental Law* 35.

64 R.G. Lee, 'Human Rights and Environmental Responsibilities' (2002) 4 *Wales J. of Law and Policy* 335.

65 *Hampshire CC* v. *Beer* [2003] L.L.R. 681; *Poplar Housing Community Association Ltd* v. *Donoghue* [2002] Q.B. 48; N. Bamforth, 'The Application of the Human Rights Act 1998 to Public Authorities and Private Bodies' (1999) 58 *Camb. Law J.* 159.

66 *R* v. *HMIP ex parte Greenpeace (No. 2)* [1994] 4 All E.R. 329; *R* v. *Foreign Secretary ex p. World Development Movement Ltd* [1995] 1 W.L.R. 386.

67 *R* v. *Somerset CC ex p. Dixon* [1997] J.P.L. 1030.

68 Art. 37 states: 'A high level of environmental protection and the improvement of the quality of the environment must be integrated into the policies of the Union and ensured in accordance with the principle of sustainable development.'

122

that cause pollution. The state is left with choices not merely as to mechanisms of control but also as to the balancing of any right against economic welfare under Article 8(2). In the two key successful cases on environmental pollution under Article 8, the violations of the Convention were predicated on a failure of the relevant national authorities to apply and enforce domestic environmental regulation.[69] In *López Ostra* the waste-treatment plant that impacted so greatly on the applicant operated in total contravention of legal requirements of a licence, and legal action by the applicant then led to its closure.[70] In *Guerra*, the applicants had been denied information that the state was under a statutory obligation to provide.[71]

Secondly, the state will consider what is proportionate in relation to the type of interest protected by Article 8. In other words does the pollution complained of really go so far as to invade privacy or the family life dependent on privacy? In some circumstances this could be so, and *Lopez Ostra,* where a waste treatment plant was built with a state subsidy on municipal land twelve metres from the applicant's home, may be such a case. But this is hardly the ideal framework upon which to construct environmental rights. Ultimately this is reflected in the judgment of the Grand Chamber in the Heathrow noise case, *Hatton*:

> Whilst the State is required to give due consideration to the particular interests the respect for which it is obliged to secure by virtue of Article 8, it must in principle be left a choice between different ways and means of meeting this obligation, the Court's supervisory function being of a subsidiary nature and thus limited to reviewing whether or not the particular solution adopted can be regarded as striking a fair balance.[72]

The English courts have fought shy of involving themselves in challenges to administrative decisions involving the allocation of public resources. There are whole areas of welfare provision in which this reluctance to review allocation decisions can be demonstrated. They include: the 'target duties' in providing education to suit the 'age, ability and aptitude' of pupils in a local area;[73] decisions about allocating social housing;[74] or community care.[75] In such instances, it has taken the intervention of Parliament to appease community dissatisfaction with judicial reluctance to intervene by creating

---

69 See Grand Chamber decision in *Hatton* v. *UK, Times,* 10 July 2003, compare D. Hart and M. Wheeler 'Night Flights and Strasbourg's Retreat form Environmental Human Rights' (2003) 16 *J. of Environmental Law* 100, 133.
70 *Lopez Ostra* v. *Spain* (1994) Series A no. 303-C, paras. 16–22.
71 *Guerra and Others* v. *Italy* (116/1996/735/932), paras. 25–27.
72 *Hatton,* op. cit., n. 69.
73 *R* v. *Inner London Education Authority ex p. Ali* (1990) 2 *Administrative Law Rev.* 822, 828 referring to s. 8 Education Act 1944.
74 *Bristol DC* v. *Clark* [1975] 3 All E.R. 976; Part V Housing Act 1957; s. 70 Housing Act 1969.
75 s. 29 National Assistance Act 1948; *R* v. *Islington LBC ex p. Rixon Times* 17 April 1996.

123

specific procedural rights (such as Educational Appeals Tribunals).[76] This inhibition regarding welfare priorities is marked in cases involving medical treatment. *Walker*[77] and *Collier*[78] were cases involving heart surgery for infants, indisputably in need, but repeatedly denied because other cases were given priority; 'the balance of available money and its distribution and use' were not matters which the court could investigate;[79] nor were 'decisions as to staffing'.[80] It was not for the court to substitute its judgment for that of 'those who are responsible for the allocation of resources'.[81] The court was in 'no position to judge', and what was being suggested was no more than 'somehow more resources should be made available'.[82] Later tragic attempts to gain access to life-saving treatment in *Re J* led to Lord Donaldson's stating that: 'Health authorities may find that they have too few resources either human or material or both to treat all the patients when they would like to treat ... it is their duty to make choices.'[83] In *ex parte B*, such applications were described by Lord Bingham as 'wholly understandable but nonetheless misguided (attempt) to involve the court in a field of activity where it is not fitted to make any decision favourable to the patient.'[84]

Environmental claims invoking the Act are inextricably linked with resource issues, reflecting what Miller has described as the 'immanence of the environment'.[85] As the environment is the resource base of human activity, many claims concern access to environmental resources or freedoms from the impacts of using the environmental media as a depository for waste by-products. Judges are drawn into resource-based arguments. In *Marcic*, an obvious and understandable claim by a householder flooded by sewage eight times in a two-year period, the applicant failed in arguments that the water company had breached his rights to family life under Article 8, and to enjoyment of property under Article 1 of the First Protocol.

Lord Nicholls began:

> Sewer flooding is a nation wide environmental problem, arising largely from the building of ever more houses to meet the housing demand. Sewers and drains, sufficient when laid in the 19th century or later, are no longer adequate to cope with the volume of surface water entering the public drainage system ...[86]

76 See Education Act 1980, Housing (Homeless Persons) Act 1977, and Chronically Sick and Disabled Persons Act 1970.
77 *R* v. *Secretary of State for Social Services ex p. Walker* (1992) 3 B.M.L.R. 32.
78 *R* v. *Birmingham Health Authority ex p. Collier* (unreported, see I. Kennedy and A. Grubb. *Medical Law* (1996, 2nd edn.).
79 *Walker*, op. cit., n. 77, p. 34 (*per* Macpherson J).
80 id.
81 id., p. 35 (*per* Lord Donaldson MR)
82 *Collier* quotations taken from C. Newdick, *Who Should We Treat?* (1995) at 125.
83 [1993] Fam. 15.
84 *R* v. *Cambridge HA ex p. B* [1995] 2 All E.R. 129, at 138.
85 C. Miller, 'Environmental law: the weak versus the strong' (1999) 1 *Environmental Law Rev.* 36.
86 *Marcic*, op. cit., n. 49, para. 1.

His Lordship observed that thousands of people suffer in this way and that 6,000 properties in England and Wales are flooded internally each year. At any one time, 15,000 properties are at such risk once every ten years. At an average cost per property of between £50,000 and £70,000, to ameliorate flooding at the 'at risk' properties would cost £1bn. These figures apparently influenced the judgment, if only because the Court showed no desire to become involved in establishing priorities where 'one is dealing with the capital expenditure of a statutory undertaking providing public utilities on a large scale'.[87] The questions of public interest arise, in Lord Hoffmann's view, because capital expenditure on new sewers would have to be financed and could only be met by charges paid by consumers. How much would be spent, and on which claims were decisions that 'courts are not equipped to make in ordinary litigation'.[88] Thus, seemingly simple applications of the Act, such as interpreting the word 'disrepair' to include 'defect' as in *Lee*, turn out to have significant resource implications from which the judiciary turn.

HUMAN RIGHTS OR ENVIRONMENTAL RIGHTS

This cautious approach to the Convention will not displease environmentalists who view environmental protection as a necessary basis for other human rights rather than seeing environmental rights as contingent on human interests. It is possible to promote environmental rights but reject a human rights' discourse. Stone asks the question of whether trees should have standing[89] precisely to place environmental concerns outside the historically anthropocentric legal doctrines. Even if one supported, pragmatically, a human rights' vehicle to deliver better environmental protection, the Convention deals only with questions of immediate violations of the victim's rights. This focus on individual human interests is in tension with wider collective environmental interests that may not encompass human interests. The 'victim' approach does little to address questions of intergenerational equity, commonly seen as a vital component of environmental sustainability.[90] A more ecocentric view would reject completely a link between environmental and human rights. In the words of one commentator:

---

87 id., para. 63.
88 id., para. 64.
89 C. Stone, 'Should Trees Have Standing: Towards Legal Rights for Natural Objects' [1972] *S. California Law Rev.* 450; H. Rolston, *Environmental Ethics, Duties to and Value in the Natural World* (1988).
90 B. Norton, *Searching for Sustainability* (2002) ch. 22.

125

Established human rights standards approach environmental questions obliquely, and lacking precision, provide clumsy tools for urgent environmental tasks. It may be argued that a comprehensive norm, which relates directly to environmental goods, is required.[91]

In some cases, human interests are narrowly drawn and seen as in opposition to the environment, so harm to the environment is tolerated in the wider 'economic interest', with little reflection on the sustainability of human conduct. This opposition occurs the other way around as the cases on travellers demonstrate. In *Turner* v. *UK*[92] and *Buckley* v. *UK*,[93] the Court found little difficulty in invoking the need for environmental protection and upholding planning laws in the denial of (scarcely acknowledged) minority rights. There is not the least conception of the Romany lifestyle as a heritage question that a more holistic approach to our environment might need to accommodate. We see from this, nonetheless, that the realm of the 'environmental' can be recognized as trumping human rights when the mood suits.

This raises the question of placing environmental stewardship in the hands of the judiciary. Griffith[94] doubted the wisdom of entrusting matters to a narrowly drawn, non-elected, and unaccountable body of men. Since that time, political changes (including the growing power of the Executive over Parliament, the dominance of the Prime Minister over Cabinet, the replacement of independent civil servants by political nominees, and the decline of ministerial responsibility) have caused some to put their trust in the judiciary to balance the equation. *Alconbury*,[95] however, represented an example of one arm of the Executive calling in, at the first possible stage, a planning application from which another arm stood to gain significant sums of money. The claimants argued that a decision by the Secretary of State would not constitute a fair hearing by an independent and impartial tribunal as guaranteed by Article 6. Although agreeing that Article 6 was engaged, and accepting that the Secretary of State was not compliant, nonetheless this was rescued by review of a court with full jurisdiction. Full jurisdiction, however, meant 'full jurisdiction to deal with the case as the nature of the decision requires,'[96] and where policy questions were involved, it was inappropriate for a court to review matters as it should not be able to substitute its decision for that of the administrative authority.

91 L. Hagger, 'Current environmental enforcement issues: some international developments and their implications for the UK' (2000) 2 *Environmental Law Rev.* 23; M. Anderson, 'Human Rights Approaches to Environmental Protection' in *Human Rights Approaches to Environmental Protection*, eds. M. Anderson and A. Boyle (1996) 1.
92 (1997) 23 E.H.R.R. CD 181.
93 (1996) 23 E.H.R.R. 101.
94 J. Griffith, *Politics of the Judiciary* (1977).
95 *Alconbury*, where four joined appeals considered the compatibility with Art. 6(1) of the European Convention on Human Rights of decision-making procedures under various planning statutes. The facts here relate to the Alconbury development.
96 id., para. 87, *per* Lord Hoffmann.

In *Begum*,[97] the House of Lords reconsidered this distinction. Laws LJ had found that any lack of independence by a manager rehousing homeless persons was rescued by the availability of appeal on points of law. Lord Hoffmann accepted that he had been 'incautious'[98] in suggesting in *Alconbury* that findings and evaluations of fact would of necessity fall into the policy regime. Nonetheless, His Lordship remains insistent that:

> utilitarian considerations have their place when it comes to setting up, for example, schemes of regulation or social welfare ... in determining the appropriate scope of judicial review of administrative action, regard must be had to democratic accountability, efficient administration and the sovereignty of Parliament.[99]

Loveland had doubted the possibility of a rigid distinction between policy and fact,[100] but even if this has gone, there remains the haziest of notions of when democratic accountability can do its work and when judicial intervention is needed. There is a danger of the housing officer's decision being amenable to review but not that of the Minister. This is not to deny the need for care in ensuring that carefully devised planning procedures, in the politically charged atmosphere of intervening in property rights,[101] are not subject to continual challenge and second guessing by those less able to assess the merits. But something more straightforward was at stake in *Alconbury*: whether it might be an abuse of power for the Minister to call in a decision in which the Executive had a clear and strong financial interest. Ultimately the House of Lords showed no great relish for such a confrontation with the government.

It is a pity that their Lordships were abstemious with this meatier fare because other environmental claims under the Act have provided slim pickings. The tendency is for environmental litigators to invoke the Convention in the face of developments or decisions that their clients regard with distaste. Allowing for the environmental justice claim that environmental hazards are disproportionately spread, and allowing that in *Hunter*[102] this was so, albeit on a temporary basis, for one of the poorest areas of London, few cases seem to have emanated from such communities. The residents of Richmond, Kew, Windsor, and so on, forming the complainants in *Hatton*[103] did not fall into such a category. There is no doubt concerning the noise to which they were subjected, and in an earlier part of

---

97 *Begum (Runa)* v. *Tower Hamlets LBC* [2003] H.R.L.R. 16.
98 id., para. 40.
99 id., para. 43.
100 I. Loveland, 'Comment' *New Law J.*, 18 May 2001, 713.
101 See P. McAuslan, *The Ideologies of Planning Law* (1980).
102 The Art. 8(2) proviso defeated the claimants in *Hunter*, op. cit., n. 52, pursuing their case before the European Commission on Human Rights as the regeneration of the docklands was found necessary for the wider economic well-being: see *Khatun* v. *UK* (1998) 26 E.H.R.R. CD 212.
103 *Hatton*, op. cit., n. 69.

the consultation process the government had raised the temperature by introducing a new regime for night flights which breached the applicants' legitimate expectations, and which was quashed in consequence.[104] Householders in such areas have choices, however, about where they live. The prices paid for the houses presumably reflected the impact of noise from Heathrow Airport, since this is a problem that the most cursory due diligence would discover. In *Chapman*[105] (a case allowing planning enforcement against Romany families occupying caravans on their own land) the Court found no violation of Article 8 in part because it was not persuaded that there were 'insufficient sites which gypsies found acceptable and affordable and on which they could lawfully place their caravans.' *Miller*[106] points out that issues of relocation are no less relevant in cases such as *Hatton*, since 'the possibility of removing oneself from the nuisance cannot be ignored.'[107] The Grand Chamber in *Hatton* rejected arguments that environmental human rights somehow enjoyed a special status:

> Environmental protection should be taken into consideration by Governments in acting within their margin of appreciation and by the Court in its review of that margin, but it would not be appropriate for the Court to adopt a special approach in this respect by reference to a special status of environmental human rights. In this context the Court must revert to the question of the scope of the margin of appreciation available to the State in taking policy decisions ...

To reject this would be to encourage the judiciary to engage in social engineering and welfare distribution on a massive scale and would breach all inhibitions of trespassing on issues of resource allocation.[108] To place responsibility for this in the hands of the judiciary rather than politicians (however poorly accountable) ought to be resisted even if the environmental wrongs complained of are highly troublesome. Often, however, such wrongs are not significant problems of diffuse pollution but are minor and local in nature. In *Furness* v. *Environment Agency*, the courts rejected a claim that the authorization of a waste incinerator in Guildford infringed the right to life under Article 2; the Court took the view that there was no substantial threat to life at all. In *R (on the application of Malster)* v. *Ipswich BC*,[109] the

---

104 *R* v. *Secretary of State for Transport, ex parte Richmond upon Thames Borough Council & Ors* [1995] *Environmental Law Rev.* 390.
105 *Chapman* v. *UK* (2001) 10 B.H.R.C. 48; and see, now, *Coates* v. *South Buckinghamshire D.C.* [2004] E.W.C.A. Civ. 1378 and the dissenting judgment of Sedley LJ.
106 C. Miller, 'Environmental Rights in a Welfare State' (2003) 23 *Ox. J. of Legal Studies* 111.
107 Sir Brian Kerr (dissenting) in *Hatton*, op. cit., n. 69.
108 D. Pannick, 'Principles of Interpretation under the Human Rights Act and the Discretionary Area of Judgment' [1998] *Public Law* 545; R. Cranston, 'The Relevance of the Human Rights Act to Government' (1999) 20 *Statute Law Rev.* 198; compare F. Klug, 'Judicial Deference under the Human Rights Act 1998' (2003) 2 E.H.R.L.R. 125.
109 [2002] P.L.C.R. 251(C.A.).

shadow of Ipswich Town's stadium spoiling the enjoyment of the applicant's garden somehow failed to cross the *López Ostra* threshold for the purposes of Article 8; nor did it infringe Article 1 of Protocol 1. The latter provisions were not offended by the regulatory control of mobile catering vans.[110] In *R v. Camden LBC ex parte Cummins*, the issues at stake under Article 6 were the view from the applicant's flat and the amount of sunshine reaching a playground. The challenge to the Secretary of State's refusal to call in the application here is similar to that in *R v. Secretary of State for the Environment, Transport and the Regions ex p. Adlard*[111] which involved objections by the Fulham residents to the redevelopment of Craven Cottage stadium.

Such claims seem to involve neither very obvious abuses of essential human rights nor major environmental catastrophe. All seem capable of resolution within the ordinary supervisory jurisdiction of the administrative court without resort to human rights' principles. As the Environmental Justice report suggests,[112] public access to the courts is greatly restricted because 'litigation through the courts is prohibitively expensive for most people'.[113] Nonetheless it seems that those able to afford proceedings are unlikely to be (say) those highlighted in a recent Environment Agency report as disproportionately likely to be exposed to toxins through air emissions.[114] Because of the low values of the properties of such people, under the *Hunter* formulation on quantification of loss, litigation based on conditional fees becomes impossible. Only those with the biggest backyards can pursue environmental claims. It is hard to avoid the conclusion that any sensible approach to dealing with the environmental problems that we face – how to dispose of our waste, treat our sewage, prevent global warming, develop contaminated land, and so on – is hindered rather than aided by claims brought to date.

CONCLUSION

Markets allocate goods to their optimal use, and where they fail, perhaps through polluting externalities, it may be necessary to intervene by way of regulation. Such regulation constitutes a political reordering of affairs. Under an unwritten constitution with a strong emphasis on parliamentary supremacy, the courts have historically respected and supported these choices. The greater the level of government regulation, the less likely are the courts to take an expansive approach to the development of the common

---

110 *R (on the application of Davies)* v. *Crawley BC* [2001] 46 E.G.C.S. 178.
111 [2002] 1 W.L.R. 2515.
112 Environmental Justice Project, *Environmental Justice* (2003).
113 R. Carnwath, 'Environment Environmental Litigation – a Way Through the Maze?' (1999) 11 *J. of Environmental Law* 3.
114 Environment Agency, *Environmental Quality and Social Exclusion* (2003).

law, and to second-guess what these political interventions should look like. Where issues concern the allocation of welfare resources, the courts have strongly expressed their preference to sit out the debate. Environmental questions commonly involve all sorts of resource questions ranging from the availability or the protection of natural resources, through the attribution of property rights, to discharges to environmental media. It is unsurprising to see a cautious and tentative approach by the courts to the invocation of human rights arguments involving environmental resources.

This is not necessarily a matter of regret. Those hoping for an ecocentric rather than an anthropocentric approach to environmental protection might not share the pragmatic enthusiasm to introduce environmental claims in the context of human rights. As the paper has attempted to show, more genuine commitments to sustainable development might be hindered rather than advanced through this approach.

JOURNAL OF LAW AND SOCIETY
VOLUME 32, NUMBER 1, MARCH 2005
ISSN: 0263-323X, pp. 131–47

Rights and Rhetoric: The Politics of Asylum and Human Rights Culture in the United Kingdom

SHAMI CHAKRABARTI*

No assessment of the state of human rights today could be complete without some consideration of the situation of asylum seekers and the political trends behind it. Four years after the implementation of the 1998 Act, asylum seekers are perhaps more denigrated in rhetoric and harsh practice than they were even before the first promise that rights would be 'brought home' for all 'people' in the United Kingdom. This piece looks at the undermining of the very concept of asylum, dehumanizing policies such as forced destitution, and attacks on access to legal process for those making asylum claims. It goes on to consider judicial attempts at coping with the arena in which high politics and fundamental rights seem in greatest tension. Finally it considers potential implications for the broader aspiration of building a human rights culture in this country.

> Freedom-loving people around the world must say ... I am a refugee in a crowded boat foundering off the coast of Vietnam. I am a Laotian, a Cambodian, a Cuban, and a Miskito Indian in Nicaragua.
>
> President Reagan, 5 May 1985, at Bergen-Belsen Concentration Camp.

INTRODUCTION

For the greatest part of fifty years, the 1951 Refugee Convention ('the 1951 Convention')[1] remained a relatively sacrosanct legacy of the horrors of the

* Director, Liberty (The National Council for Civil Liberties), 21 Tabard Street, London SE1 4LA, England

This essay is dedicated to the late Roger Bingham, Liberty's much loved former Press Officer who strove for the rights of those seeking asylum in both his professional and personal life. The priority which the organization now gives to this work owes a great deal to his influence. Huge thanks also to Mhairi McGhee for her supporting research.

1 Convention Relating to the Status of Refugees, 28 July 1951, Geneva.

131

Holocaust and the Second World War. In the United Kingdom, the tradition of giving refuge to those fleeing persecution can be traced back considerably further[2] and there seems to have been (at least formal) cross-party consensus as to the moral case for liberal First World democracies providing asylum until about the mid 1990s. The principal 1951 Convention obligation (against *'refoulement'* or return of refugees), was incorporated into domestic law well in advance of the Human Rights Act 1998, just as certain European Convention obligations had been incorporated into the 'soft law' of deportation via a strand of Home Office circulars. Thus it might be argued that much of our polity and judiciary were first introduced to concepts and analysis of fundamental human rights via the 1951 notion of asylum.

The Prime Minister's preface to the White Paper, *Rights Brought Home*,[3] refers to rights recourse for 'people in the United Kingdom' rather than only British nationals or citizens. It goes on to make an express link between human rights policy at home and abroad. How then is it possible that the early infancy of the Human Rights Act should be so associated with the increasing dehumanization of those seeking refuge in the United Kingdom (for the most part from tyrannous regimes which we deplore), with repeated attacks on access to legal process, and the very concept of asylum itself? I suggest that the 'politics of asylum' have operated so as to undermine the developing values and law of human rights in this country. The possible results are damaging not just for those seeking refuge and other 'outsiders' in society, but for human rights and democratic values in society as a whole.

UNDERMINING THE IDEAL

> The UN Convention on Refugees, first introduced in 1951 ... has started to show its age...
>
> Prime Minister Blair, 27 April 2004,
> speaking to the Confederation of British Industry

Dictionary definitions of 'refugee' and 'asylum' present a positive or at least neutral picture of a person in flight from war, persecution or natural disaster and seeking shelter or protection by a receiving state. In our linguistic heritage, the grounds of flight and protection are even broader than the 1951 legal definition of a person who:

> owing to well-founded fear of being persecuted for reasons of race, religion, nationality, membership of a particular social group or political opinion, is outside the country of his nationality and is unable, or owing to such fear, is unwilling to avail himself of the protection of that country ...[4]

---

2 Statutory recognition going back at least as far as the Extradition Act 1870.
3 Home Department, *Rights Brought Home: The Human Rights Bill* (1997; Cm. 3782).
4 1951 Convention, op. cit., n. 1, Art. 1.

132

Indeed, before the advent of the 'asylum seeker' (with or without the express use of the adjective 'bogus'), the term 'refugee' was commonly used in both our political discourse and news media, to cover those in flight as well as those who had been granted legal protection in their destination state.

Article 32 of the 1951 Convention contains an obligation against expulsion (save on grounds of national security or public order – and even then, not without due process). This protects refugees lawfully within the territory. However, Article 31 contains the perfectly logical recognition that some refugees will flee by way of illegal entry to the receiving state and thus immunizes them from penalty as long as they have fled directly from their country of persecution, presented themselves to the receiving authorities without delay, and shown good cause for the illegal method of entry. Finally, Article 33 prohibits return of a refugee to a place where his or her life or freedom would be threatened for a Convention reason (race, religion, and so on), save on reasonable national security or (following a serious criminal conviction), community safety grounds.

The combined effect of this small bundle of protections is hardly the most robust defence from hostility and intolerance in receiving states. However there is a need for states to consider the asylum claims of those who manage to touch their territory (even if only the tarmac or transit lounge of the airport). Summary removal is not possible (as with many other traditional 'illegal entrants' not claiming humanitarian protection) save to so-called 'safe third countries' through which the refugee has travelled. Even in this latter situation, traditional public law principles of rationality and fairness would require some degree of judicial satisfaction that the third country was indeed 'safe' rather than likely to return the refugee to danger. The assumption of safety as a third country has not always been free from doubt, even in relation to the leading member states of the European Union.[5]

Arriving refugees have not always been regarded as a problem in the United Kingdom. It is true that Jewish refugees fleeing the Holocaust (in whose memory the 1951 Convention is almost dedicated), did not always enjoy the warmest reception in this country. However for much of the Cold War, refugees enjoyed the cachet associated with defecting spies, ballet dancers, and sportsmen, a relatively small number of white European heroic figures who existed to remind us of the evils of Communism and the superior and free society that we enjoyed in the West. For much of this period, asylum casework was dealt with by a small single unit in the Home Office

---

5 See I. Macdonald and F. Webber, *Immigration Law and Practice* (2001, 5th edn.) at para. 12.128:

> During the period between 1993 and 1996, special adjudicators on occasion rejected certificates of the Secretary of State relating to every member state of the EU, and consistently rejected certificates relating to removals to France and Belgium. The Secretary of State desisted from removing asylum seekers to Italy, Greece and Portugal following adverse decisions and in the light of the evidence produced at appeals as to the practice in these states.

133

(rather than the gargantuan directorates of a subsequent generation). The greater number of – sometimes demonized – migrants of this period were new Commonwealth (and, for the most part, lawful) 'economic migrants'. That term then, like others, had yet to acquire its pejorative connation at the hands of our political elite.

Asylum folklore suggests that the tide began to turn against wholehearted support for the concept of asylum protection with the arrival of the first airliner containing fifty-four Sri Lankan refugees in 1986. There certainly seems to have been some time correlation between this event and the passage of what became the Immigration (Carriers' Liability) Act 1987. We have seen how the principal and express obligations of the 1951 Convention relate to the treatment of refugees who successfully flee from their own country to the state in which they claim protection. Summary removal of asylum claimants would be in flagrant violation of the 1951 Convention, but what of making it harder for refugees (those whose 1951 claims are likely to succeed as well as those likely to be less well-founded) to reach your territory and make their claims for protection? The late 1980s and 1990s saw the increasing use of visa restrictions as a relatively subtle (by contrast with later policies) impediment to the flow of refugees. Carriers' liability provided the teeth behind such visa regimes. Airlines bringing 'inadequately documented passengers' to the United Kingdom were liable to pay a hefty fine for each such passenger as well as possible detention and eventual removal costs. Thus the United Kingdom's border control began almost imperceptibly to shift beyond our shores, with the small force of Immigration Directorate 'Airline Liaison Officers' who exercised no legal power of their own at foreign ports, but 'advised' diligent carriers on the discharge of their new burden of immigration control.

There were of course other crucial developments during this period. The greater and greater accessibility of affordable airline transport made crawling across a local land border (perhaps to a life not dissimilar from that escaped from) no more obvious than the aeroplane that created a new accessible border to the multi-cultural United Kingdom. Further, non-asylum related migration from a whole host of former British colonies was becoming almost impossible, the door on the Commonwealth having gradually closed as the door to Europe had opened. Finally of course, then as now, there was a very great deal of strife up to and including serious persecution of various people in the bulk of the countries from which large numbers of refugees came to the United Kingdom.

By the early 1990s, visas and carrier' fines were not thought to go far enough. A visa was only required by a relevant national who declared a desire to enter the United Kingdom in advance of travel. London's Heathrow Airport in particular, was a hub of international routes with very many passengers changing planes in transit to final destinations beyond the United Kingdom and with no need ever to pass 'land-side' (as opposed to 'air-side') beyond the Immigration Officer's desk. Understandably however, the legal

134

fiction of the 'transit lounge' found no analogy in a 1951 international instrument concerned with granting protection to refugees. It was therefore possible for a refugee or asylum seeker to buy a ticket with an eventual destination country which required no visa, but which necessitated a change of aeroplane in London. Once on British soil, the refugee could then make his claim for asylum in the United Kingdom. So the Immigration (Carriers' Liability) Act of 1987 was amended to create an express power to require 'transit visas' – an even more draconian visa regime requiring certain nationals to obtain a visa in order even to change aircraft in the United Kingdom. This step constitutes a very important but hardly discussed development in the history of asylum policy in this country. Unlike traditional visas, transit visa regimes have no real application in relation to any class of unwelcome migrants other than those likely to claim asylum in Britain, and being so keen or desperate so to do, that they (assisted or not by a facilitator or 'trafficker') would go to the expense of an onward passage. By 1998, the list of unwelcome refugees or nationals requiring transit visas for a trip to a Heathrow lounge included those from Afghanistan, Iraq, and the Federal Republic of Yugoslavia.[6]

The most blatant turn of the screw came with the 'piloting' of 'pre-clearance' in 2001.[7] For the first time (and by agreement with a foreign power), Britain's border control formally moved to a foreign shore by way of Immigration Officers posted at Prague Airport for the principal or sole purpose of preventing Czech Roma asylum seekers from travelling to the United Kingdom and making 1951 Convention claims. Under the new legal regime, Immigration Officers were able to grant or refuse leave to enter the United Kingdom just as they might at Heathrow Airport. In contrast with the United Kingdom port, however, requests to enter the United Kingdom for the purposes of asylum were met with summary and routine rejection on the basis that asylum was not a valid basis for travel to the United Kingdom under the Immigration Rules. Such claims when made within the United Kingdom, are referred to the Secretary of State (in practice, Home Office Asylum caseworkers), rather than being dealt with by the border police. The logic applied was ruthless and simple. The claimants in question had yet to escape from the territory of alleged persecution and thus were not yet *'outside'* their country of nationality and worthy of 1951 Convention protection. An equally simple and ruthless logic dictates that if every 'safe' country in the world employed such policies in relation to foreign territories generating refugees/asylum seekers, the Jews of a future Holocaust – as

---

6 See the Immigration (Transit Visa) (Amendment No. 2) Order 1998 (S.I. no. 1998/ 1014). The 2003 Order (S.I. no. 2003/1185) made under the Immigration and Asylum Act 1999 includes, amongst others countries, Afghanistan, the Democratic Republic of Congo, Iran, Iraq, and Zimbabwe.
7 Via the Immigration and Asylum Act 1999 and the Immigration (Leave to Enter and Remain) Order 2000 (S.I. no. 2000/1661).

provided for by the drafters of the 1951 Convention – might never escape to the safety anticipated by the post-war community of civilized nations.

As if this new development in British asylum policy were not chilling enough, it was accompanied by the New Labour government's attempt to reconcile tough asylum measures, not merely with the infant Human Rights Act, but with the Race Relations (Amendment) Act 2000. The latter statute (a political legacy of Stephen Lawrence's murder and the enormous scandal of discriminatory and negligent policing which followed) attacked an anomaly of decades by bringing public matters such as policing and immigration control within the framework of race equality protection. Understandably, perhaps, as all immigration control necessarily requires some discrimination based upon nationality, some exemption was allowed as required by immigration legislation and by express 'Ministerial authorization' made under the Race Relations Act. Such authorizations expressly provide for discrimination against certain ethnic or national groups (the latter being more easily explained by the inherent nature of national borders and immigration control). The authorization in place at the time of the Prague experiment[8] targeted Kurds, Somalis, Albanians, and Afghans (amongst others) alongside the Roma for discriminatory treatment in the context of immigration examination. The Home Office has maintained that the authorization was not in fact relied upon because discrimination did not actually take place. Nonetheless, such a list makes particularly distasteful reading when one remembers the home- and foreign-policy human rights promise of the preface to *Rights Brought Home*. One imagines that, distasteful or not, such lists must become an increasing part of any political future which champions the human rights of some rather than others in contrast with more universal post-war ideals. It may go without saying that the vast majority of Roma passengers were refused entry to the United Kingdom under this experiment, regardless of their stated reason for travel.

At the time of writing, the House of Lords Judicial Committee is considering a Liberty challenge to the legality of the Prague policy experiment as to its compatibility both with the 1951 Convention and domestic race discrimination principles.[9]

---

8 The Race Relations (Immigration and Asylum) (No. 2) Authorization 2001.
9 *European Roma Rights Centre* v. *Secretary of State for the Home Department*.

DEHUMANIZATION

Refugees are flooding into the United Kingdom like ants.

Daily Express, 7 November 2001.

In the mid 1970s, anti-immigration sentiment at the highest levels of political debate, echoed in the popular press, created a climate where the people thought to be the subject of 'the problem' were so robbed of their human identity and dignity, that almost any policy device in pursuit of stemming the flow became imaginable. How else could Immigration Officials at Heathrow Airport ever have been authorized and instructed to conduct virginity testing of Hindu brides arriving in the United Kingdom to join their partners?

In January of 2003, as much of Britain endured sub-zero and blizzard conditions, section 55 of the Nationality, Immigration and Asylum Act 2002 was brought into force. The provision contained an obligation upon the Secretary of State to deny state support to asylum claimants who had not (in his view) made their claims *'as soon as reasonably practicable'* after arrival in the United Kingdom. Crucially, asylum seekers are also barred from lawful employment. Forced destitution had been used as a lever against asylum by the previous Conservative government.[10] At that time, and even without the Human Rights Act, the policy had provoked one of the greatest of the then Home Secretary's staged battles with the senior judiciary. Now a Labour government was forcing desperate people (including, in some instances, vulnerable teenage girls) onto the streets before even an initial assessment of the merits of their asylum claim. The argument put before Parliament had related to stories of 'abusers' of the immigration and asylum system who come to Britain in one lawful capacity, stay and overstay for many months or years before claiming asylum only in the face of deportation. Yet early evidence revealed that people who had claimed asylum within hours or days of arrival in the United Kingdom were being denied all effective and lawful means of support under the new regime. Further, ministerial media justifications for the policy by the time of implementation focused more on the idea of 'sending signals' and 'changing behaviour' of potential asylum seekers beyond our shores than the objective of separating worthier claimants from those thought to be 'abusing the system'.[11]

It is fascinating for present purposes however, that this infamous provision of primary legislation contained a narrow exception so that it would not prevent:

> the exercise of a power by the Secretary of State to the extent necessary for the purpose of avoiding a breach of a person's Convention rights (within the meaning of the Human Rights Act 1998).[12]

---

10 ss. 9–11 of and Schedule 1 to the Asylum and Immigration Act 1996.
11 In particular, a number of print and broadcast press statements by the then Minister, Beverley Hughes MP.
12 Section 55(5).

137

This single legislative policy or drafting choice could warrant an essay in itself. What were the factors behind this decision? Was it made at official or ministerial level? Does it constitute one of the best examples of a human rights' schizophrenia at the heart of New Labour thinking or was it a clever but rather mundane legal device to limit the extent of any subsequent dust-up with the judiciary? It may be some years before the answers to these questions are in the public domain. However some observations are possible even now. It is a political curiosity (to say the least), to provide for a policy of deliberate, targeted, and forced destitution against a section of humanity, to do so by the most ruthless means possible (that is, by way of primary legislative *duty* – which therefore may not be overturned by the courts on either traditional or even Human Rights Act grounds), and yet to create such a deliberate and accessible ejector seat for any High Court judge brave enough to flick the switch. This stands in contrast with Mr Howard's pre-Human Rights Act strategy of the mid-1990s. In that case, destitution was initially achieved by secondary legislation which was then struck down by the courts. The governmental response was to transcribe the same policy into primary legislation (robust from judicial attack), though the attempt was perhaps botched, as other and overlooked primary legislative duties in older statutes were unearthed by lawyers seeking to save their clients from starvation and hypothermia.

Perhaps Mr Blunkett relished the idea of revisiting the populist appeal of both the destitution policy and any subsequent battle with the judges. However, the Human Rights Act's moral and political remedy of the 'declaration of incompatibility'[13] in relation to incompatible primary legislation may have been thought (by the Home Secretary or his advisers) to have upped the ante beyond the Howard scenario. Perhaps the government had become over-confident in the developing doctrine of so-called 'judicial deference', and particularly so in such a politicized environment as that relating to asylum. In that event, the constant presence of an unused safety-valve could perhaps serve as a defence from liberal and humanitarian criticisms of the policy. Alternatively, perhaps the provision defines a policy which lacks the courage of its convictions, being prepared to starve a human being to the point of illness but not death.[14] In any event, the employment of an explicit human rights saving of this kind marks a real contrast with the confidence in the human rights aspirations of each limb (rather than just the judicial branch) of the Constitution displayed in the delicate scheme that is the Human Rights

---

13 s. 4 of the Human Rights Act 1998.
14 Support for this rather distasteful proposition can be found in some of the government's legal arguments in the face of various challenges brought to s. 55 under Article 3 (the right against inhuman and degrading treatment) of the ECHR, as contained in the Human Rights Act.

Act itself.[15] Some of us had once hoped that the beautifully crafted and thoroughly British constitutional settlement of the Human Rights Act might be used to invigorate a parliament that could strive to be the first (if not the last) Court of Human Rights in this country. Section 55 of the Nationality, Immigration and Asylum Act could not be further from this vision. Not only did Parliament agree to deliberate, targeted, and forced destitution as a means of further undermining the efficacy of the 1951 Convention, it did so on the basis that it might always rely on the judges to save the day if the policy which it had sanctioned ever got really unpleasant.

That is eventually what happened and yet, policies of forced destitution as a means of influencing desperate human beings have not been consigned to the history books, as we have since seen the advent of the chillingly titled Asylum and Immigration (Treatment of Claimants, etc.) Act 2004 ('the 2004 Act'). One cannot be sure whether failed asylum seekers constitute claimants or some part of the etcetera. What is clear, however, is that these people and their children may be the subject of forced destitution[16] at the behest of the Secretary of State, should they refuse to make a voluntary departure from this country. A few days before the Queen's Speech in 2003,[17] the *Observer* carried a report bearing all of the apparent hallmarks of a special adviser's briefing:

> Asylum seekers will have their children taken into care in a draconian attempt to force them to go home, under a government crackdown ... Parents whose claims have been rejected will be offered a stark choice: take a 'voluntary' flight to their native country, paid for by the state, or lose all benefits in the UK and have their children taken.[18]

The report triggered a predictable outcry from the refugee assistance and human rights' community. The relevant section in the Queen's Speech of the following week was silent as to the gory details. Nonetheless, the parliamentary debate which followed suggested that the *Observer* piece had provided sufficient ammunition for a perhaps surprising rebuke from none other than Mr Howard (by now leader of the Opposition):

> ... this time they've gone further than any civilised government should go. Earlier this week we read in our newspapers that the Government proposes to use the children of asylum seekers as pawns to cover up their failure to get a grip on their asylum chaos.[19]

---

15 Preservation of Parliamentary Sovereignty via ss. 3, 4, and 6, ministerial statements in relation to Bills under s. 19, and so on.
16 ss. 9 and 10.
17 26 November 2003.
18 G. Hinsliff, 'Asylum children may be forced into care' *Observer*, 23 November 2003.
19 M. Howard, 415 *H.C. Debs.*, col. 18 (26 November 2003).

Sadly Mr Howard's subsequent promise that Conservatives would vote against such an illiberal measure were not to be borne out in the parliamentary session to come. It may have been that the opposition (and perhaps even parts of government), had originally anticipated a specific new legislative power (or even duty) for social services to take the children of failed asylum seekers. Perhaps Conservatives would indeed have voted against such a measure. However such an explicit provision proved unnecessary, existing child protection legislation being sufficient to enable the taking of children facing destitution and starvation. The eventual legislation contains merely the necessary provision of allowing for failed asylum seekers (including, for the first time, those with children) to be denied support as a cowardly and cruel alternative to forced removal from the country.

Some may argue that such a policy of 'encouraging voluntary departure' is somehow more humane than the forced removal of families with children. Those of that view should perhaps imagine trying to explain it to a small child taken from parents who (rightly or wrongly) see the trauma of separation as more in the child's interests than a return to whatever life awaits in their country of origin. An alternative basis for the policy may lie in the way in which families facing deportation have often aroused the sympathies of even the most apparently xenophobic local communities. There is perhaps nothing which greater connects any of us to the rest of humanity than our children. This is as true of migrants as it is of anyone else. Once children attend school and play with other children, the despised person facing removal acquires a human face. A few extra children driven away from their homes in the custody of social workers may be politically more palatable than whole families dragged away by immigration officers and the police. Further, destitution policies will surely lead to begging, crime, and prostitution on the part of their targets, activities which are likely to increase sympathy for the authorities rather than the asylum seekers. Ultimately, whilst politically expedient, forced destitution is a greater attack on what is left of the dignity of a failed asylum seeker than arrest and removal after full and fair legal process.

It is impossible however to leave the 2004 Act without mention of a few more of its dehumanizing measures. The Act creates new criminal offences catching asylum seekers with no passports or forged documents save where the authorities are satisfied in the explanation given. People at various stages in the immigration and asylum machine will be the first human beings outside the criminal justice system to be electronically tagged by the authorities. There are no detailed criteria as to who may be subjected to tagging in the primary legislation. There are also restrictions on the ability of foreign nationals marrying in the United Kingdom – an aspect of immigration control now being shared with those whose normal professional task is to celebrate and solemnize the union of marriage.

140

> Changing the law on asylum is the only fair way of helping the genuinely persecuted – and its best defence against racism gaining ground ... we should cut back on the ludicrously complicated appeals process, de-rail the gravy train of legal aid, fast-track those from democratic countries, and remove those who fail in their claims without further judicial interference.
>
> Prime Minister Blair, 30 September 2003,
> Labour Party Conference, Bournemouth.

The attack on due process for asylum seekers (up to and including political criticism of any serious judicial defence of asylum seeker's rights) has formed an obvious part of asylum policy since the late 1990s. It is perhaps this aspect of governmental policy and practice that may have some of the gravest implications for human rights and the rule of law beyond the field of asylum.

It has often been observed that it has taken a Labour government so enriched by the skills and experience of commercial lawyers to launch the greatest ever attack upon the public service enterprise of legal aid practice and the representation of asylum seekers in particular. In truth, the levels of morale and poor remuneration associated with asylum legal aid practice make it much more akin to nursing or teaching than the practicing lives of the last two Lord Chancellors. Yet the myth serves the politics well. If legal aid lawyers may be reduced to greedy, unscrupulous, and self-interested caricatures in the popular consciousness, pleas for their clients may be more muted in effect. Further, cutting back on legal norms and process, let alone the 'gravy train' of legal aid, becomes a positive virtue rather than a sin when the most vocal critics of the policy are almost as hated as their clients. In May 2004, legal help for the preparation of an asylum claim was reduced to five hours in each case. How many members of wider society would feel satisfied with that amount of advice in preparation for an acrimonious divorce, let alone a decision which might result in return to death or persecution on the other side of the world? It is far from surprising that recent months and years have seen some of the most respected asylum lawyers leaving practice or moving into more sustainable areas. Asylum constitutes one of the most complex and serious (in terms of consequences for a client) areas of public and human rights law. One can only wonder from where the future generations of legal specialists capable of conducting this work with skill and integrity will come?

However, one can see that asylum legal aid might not be a particular priority for a government bent on reducing the system to one of purely administrative and summary decision-making. Clause 10 of the Asylum and Immigration (Treatment of Claimants etc.) Bill, as originally introduced into Parliament,[20] contained a provision ousting the review jurisdiction of the

---

20 At times, the placement of the clause rendered it clause 11 and 14.

Higher Courts in all asylum and immigration cases from the new single-tier Immigration Tribunal. The true magnitude of the meaning behind the Prime Minister's rhetoric as to 'judicial interference' stood in plain view. Such attempted 'ouster' provisions had previously proved unsuccessful over the years. However, the government may have been emboldened by the success of recent examples in the national security context.[21] Thus the most explicit, comprehensive and therefore robust ouster provision imaginable, sought to prevent:

> ... a court, in particular, from entertaining proceedings to determine whether a purported determination, decision or action of the Tribunal was a nullity by reason of
> (i)   lack of jurisdiction,
> (ii) irrationality,
> (iii) error of law,
> (iv) breach of natural justice, or
> (v)   any other matter ...[22]

It is perhaps particularly worrying for the human rights culture in this country that in the subsequent public debates on the issue, the bulk of non-legal opinion (of many political persuasions) seemed content to categorize such a broadside on the jurisdiction of the Higher Courts as little more than the 'streamlining' of a convoluted appeals process.

In the end, it was legal and judicial opinion that came together to force a government rethink. None other than the Lord Chief Justice described the clause as 'fundamentally in conflict with the rule of law and should not be contemplated by any government if it had respect for the rule of law'.[23] This development, in particular, suggested to various commentators that the passage of such a measure could well create a constitution crisis. Some remarked on the very idea of parliamentary sovereignty itself being a creature of the common law and therefore of judicial abstinence. If Parliament (led by an overzealous executive) showed such distain for the judicial branch and its vital role in any democracy, perhaps the paradigm of legislative supremacy might have to be revisited to the point of a wilful flouting of the 'ouster' provision by the Higher Courts.

Interventions from the former Lord Chancellor (Lord Irvine of Lairgs, who had of course presided over the passage of the Human Rights Bill) and a number of other lawyers of all generations and party political persuasions will also no doubt have made an impression on the final governmental judgement to replace the ouster with a severely curtailed right of statutory appeal to the Higher Courts. However, this worrying chapter in the asylum

---

21 See s. 67 of the Regulation of Investigatory Powers Act 2000 and Part 4 of the Anti-Terrorism, Crime and Security Act 2001.
22 To have been inserted as s. 108A of the Nationality, Immigration and Asylum Act 2002.
23 Speech to the Law Faculty of Cambridge University, 3 March 2004.

story says little very positive about human rights' or even rule-of-law values in wider society, or indeed at the heart of government.

Overreliance on judicial defence of the rights of asylum seekers (whether in court or extra-legal comment) is particularly dangerous given the ferocity of some of the political attacks on judges themselves (both as individuals and as the institution of the independent judiciary). Mr Blunkett's sour grapes about early successful challenges to his application of section 55 of the 2002 Act, provides one of the worst examples of this phenomenon:

> Frankly, I'm personally fed up with having to deal with a situation where Parliament debates issues and the judges overturn them ... I don't want any mixed messages going out so I am making it absolutely clear today that we don't accept what Justice Collins has said.[24]

It is impossible to discuss attacks upon due process for asylum seekers without some mention of the conflation that has been made between asylum and threats to national security since the declaration of the 'War on Terror'. Successive Home Secretaries had mentioned asylum and criminal policy in the same stanzas of speeches to their party faithful. Further, the tradition of denying entry to or deporting foreign nationals suspected of posing a threat to national security is a long and not altogether illegitimate one. However, the post-September 11 policy of interning foreign nationals suspected of 'links' to international terrorism[25] marks a complete blurring of lines between traditional criminal justice and asylum policy, quite possibly to the long-term detriment of both. Under the 2001 regime, a dozen or so asylum seekers and refugees have been detained without police interview, charge or trial for nearly three years (at the time of writing). In contrast with indefinite detention without trial in the American law-free zone that is Guantánamo Bay in Cuba, here a fig leaf of legal apparatus is provided by a tribunal originally intended to improve the lot of those who previously enjoyed no appeal in National Security denial of entry or deportation cases.[26] The Special Immigration Appeals Commission is charged only with second-guessing the Home Secretary's 'suspicion' which, if reasonable, may form the basis for indefinite incarceration in circumstances where any British national would be entitled to charge, trial, and the presumption of innocence, reasonable suspicion being a basis for a pre-charge detention of no more than 14 days.[27] Further, the suspicion must be disputed by a detainee and lawyers who will never see the secret intelligence (quite possibly contributed to by torture[28]). Only a Special Advocate, appointed by the Attorney General and

---

24 From the 'World at One', BBC Radio 4, 3 February 2003.
25 Under Part 4 of the Anti-Terrorism, Crime and Security Act 2004.
26 See the Special Immigrations Appeals Commission Act 1997.
27 Under the Terrorism Act 2000.
28 A possibility conceded by the government and upheld in legality terms by the Court of Appeal.

enjoying no lawyer-client relationship with the detainee, may probe the case in the interests of justice.

The only real governmental justification for this abrogation of normal human rights principles[29] is built on the internees' immigration status as foreign nationals and, in particular, asylum seekers. Great virtue is made of the fact that the internees may not be returned to their countries of origin because of the likelihood that they would face ill-treatment of Article 3 (ECHR) gravity there. It is of course to be remembered that unlike Article 5, Article 3 is a non-derogable right and this sheds another light on governmental claims that detention is actually a form of kindness to the men concerned. Equally, however, the government argues that the policy does not really constitute detention at all. After all, as with all immigration-related detention, the inmates are free to leave the country at any time of their own volition. Crucially for present purposes, however, both government Law Officers attempt to resist the argument of blatant and inexcusable discrimination in relation to grave suspicions of criminality of British citizens on the one hand, and these foreign nationals on the other, with their fundamentally differential status as 'asylum seekers'. This argument is not merely saved for media comment but employed in legal proceedings as well. When the Judicial Committee of the House of Lords heard argument as to the alleged discriminatory nature of this policy, the Attorney General suggested that the 'man on the street' would not find the differential treatment of asylum seekers discriminatory. So policy and politics stoke a public hostility for asylum seekers which is then cited in legal defence of further such policies.

JUDICIAL RESPONSES

If evaluation of the state of asylum seekers' rights were made from the strength of the hostile political rhetoric, one would be forgiven for thinking that judicial activism were in danger of riding rough-shod over the legislature and undermining the very fabric of this country's border controls. Senior Ministers rail against 'judicial interference' and the official opposition openly contemplates an end to both the Refugee Convention and the Human Rights Act. Ironically, any real analysis of the post-Human Rights Act asylum case law suggests a mostly meek defence of the relevant rights. One might always have expected a relatively nervous judicial approach to the application of Article 8 of the Convention in an immigration context and, in the event, such an expectation has not been disappointed. Too much loose talk of post-1998 constructs (designed so as not to frighten the politicians), such as the 'discretionary area of judgement' and 'judicial

---

29 Necessitating a derogation from Article 5 of the European Convention on Human Rights.

144

deference' in the immigration and asylum spheres in particular, has at times been in danger of reducing the relatively vigorous and disciplined scrutiny of administration embodied in the principal of proportionality, to little more than the traditional *Wednesbury* test. It took a judicial committee hearing in a prisoner's privacy case to point out the wider dangers for the developing rights discipline:

> In other words, the intensity of the review, in similar cases, is guaranteed by the twin requirements that the limitation of the right was necessary in a democratic society, in the sense of meeting a pressing social need, and the question whether the interference was really proportionate to the legitimate aim being pursued. ... The differences in approach between the traditional grounds of review and the proportionality approach may therefore sometimes yield different results. It is therefore important that cases involving convention rights must be analysed in the correct way.[30]

Further, whilst Human Rights Act judgments of all varieties have frequently referred to 'context being everything', one wonders whether 'context' serves to help or hinder the protection of asylum seekers in a space where high politics and fundamental rights come into such sharp conflict.

This is even more worrying outside the ambit of 'balanced rights' such as Article 8 and into the realms of the Convention's more jealous protection of due process. The House of Lords decision in *R* v. *Secretary of State for the Home Department, ex parte Saadi and others*[31] remains one of the bitterest disappointments of the early infancy of the Human Rights Act. In that case (which had sparked its own bitter political controversy when before the Administrative Court), the House of Lords upheld the administrative detention, for up to ten days, of Iraqi asylum seekers (Kurds in the instant case), as a job lot, for the purposes of early and speedy processing of claims, and without the need for an individuated decision about any absconding or other risk posed by a particular asylum seeker. In coming to this decision, their Lordships significantly contorted the immigration specific detention ground under Article 5 of the Convention. Asylum seekers whose claims had yet to be considered might be detained 'to prevent ... an unauthorised entry into the country',[32] the logic being that some of those detained might turn out to be fraudulent or otherwise ineligible for asylum. If such logic were applied more widely, large numbers of citizens might be detained for the swift completion and assessment of our tax returns. The rationale would no doubt be to justify such administrative detention on the basis that some of us would inevitably lie and commit tax offences in the completion of our returns, so the detention could be said to be for preventing the commission of offences or of flight thereafter.[33]

---

30 *R* v. *SSHD, ex parte Daley* [2001] U.K.H.L., Lord Steyn's speech commenting upon *R (Mahmood)* v. *Secretary of State for the Home* Department [2001] 1 W.L.R. 840.
31 [2002] U.K.H.L. 41.
32 ECHR Art. 5.1(f).
33 ECHR Art. 5.1(c).

Ironically perhaps, the boldest judicial championing of asylum seekers' rights to date has come, not in the context of due process protection but in effectively defeating the use of the socio-economic lever of forced destitution contained in section 55 of the 2002 Act as applied by Mr Blunkett.[34] The majority of the Court of Appeal found that claimants need not show the actual onset of severe illness or suffering in the effective absence of charitable or other support. There was a presumption of severe suffering sufficient to engage Article 3 of the Convention, and render the government's section 55 policy unlawful. This constitutes the dramatic, tragic but ultimately uplifting Human Rights Act story of how supposedly lofty and remote unelected judges taught a Labour government about the evils of deliberately attempting to starve human beings into submission.

CONCLUSION

The greatest disappointment of the infancy of the Human Rights Act lies in the way in which its values have failed sufficiently to take root in wider society. This is not surprising, given the neglect of its political parents and the various countervailing pressures which tempt us and them away from the values contained in the Act itself and the wider post-war Human Rights legacy of which the Refugee Convention is a vital part. Political rhetoric relating to asylum seekers and refugees has been particularly damaging, not only to their interests, but to respect for Human Rights values more generally. There is increasing talk of the rights and interests of British citizens rather than of universal Human Rights. Further, the rhetoric of 'rights and responsibilities' suggests rights that are earned by citizen and bestowed by political community, rather than those which are inalienable and inherent in humanity. A newly-arrived, impoverished, and demonized asylum seeker is unlikely to score very highly in a calculation of 'earned' rights. Whilst there is immediate danger of the development of a two-tier system of human rights (due-process rights, in particular) for Britons on the one hand and asylum seekers on the other, a more likely longer-term outcome would be the politically expedient dilution or complete rejection of human rights values as a whole. Still, there are some limited sources of optimism. The senior judiciary have shown some potential for the defence of asylum seekers when policy crosses lines of common decency and the rule of law. To some extent, human rights law exists to protect society when politics lets its down. However, law cannot operate in a vacuum or promulgate human rights values unassisted. The British public shows some very real concern for flagrant human rights abuses beyond our shores. The bulk of

---

34 See, in particular, *R (on the application of Limbuela and others)* v. *SSHD* [2004] E.W.C.A.

asylum applicants to the United Kingdom in 2003 came from Somalia, Iraq, China, Zimbabwe, and Iran.[35] Surely it is just a matter of time before the penny drops as to the connection between foreign and home human rights policies. When it does, a less schizophrenic and more enlightened discourse will surely unfold.

35 T. Heath, R. Jeffries, and J. Purcell, *Home Office Statistical Bulletin: Asylum Statistics 2003* (2004, 2nd edn.).

147

JOURNAL OF LAW AND SOCIETY
VOLUME 32, NUMBER 1, MARCH 2005
ISSN: 0263-323X, pp. 148–68

Human Rights in the Scottish Courts

TOM MULLEN,* JIM MURDOCH,* ALAN MILLER,**
AND SARAH CRAIG***

This article looks at the use made of the human rights legislation in the Scottish courts since the devolution of legislative and executive power to Scotland, based on research undertaken in all the ordinary courts, but excluding tribunals. It concludes that the incorporation of the Convention via the human rights legislation has had significant effects within the Scottish court system and on policy development without amounting to a major upheaval.

INTRODUCTION

This article presents an overview of the use made of the human rights legislation in the Scottish courts since the devolution of legislative and executive power to Scotland, May–July 1999, and offers some further comments on the impact of that legislation in Scotland. Throughout, the phrase 'human rights legislation' refers to the Human Rights Act and to related provisions of the Scotland Act which are discussed below. It draws on research funded and published by the Scottish Executive.[1] The research covered the period from May 1999 to August 2003 and covered cases in all the ordinary courts (the District Court, sheriff court and High Court for criminal matters and the sheriff court and Court of Session for civil matters) but not cases heard by tribunals. Its scope was also restricted to the European Convention on Human Rights ('the Convention') and did not consider other

* *School of Law, University of Glasgow, Stair Building, 5–8 The Square, Glasgow G12 8QQ, Scotland*
** *Law School, University of Strathclyde, Stenhouse Building, 173 Cathedral Street, Glasgow G4 0RQ, Scotland, and Director of McGrigors Rights*
*** *Dept. of Accounting, Finance and Law, University of Stirling, Stirling FK9 4LA, Scotland*

1 P. Greenhill, T. Mullen, J. Murdoch, S. Craig, and A. Miller, *The Use of Human Rights Legislation in the Scottish Courts* (2004).

international human rights instruments to which the United Kingdom is a party.

It is important to begin by explaining the differences in the legal framework for the protection of human rights in Scotland as compared to the rest of the United Kingdom. Until shortly before the enactment of the Human Rights Act 1998, the Scottish courts were even less responsive to arguments based on the Convention than the courts in the rest of the United Kingdom. In *Kaur* v. *Lord Advocate*,[2] Lord Ross appeared to suggest that the Convention could not be referred to even as an aid to interpretation of a statute. However, just in time for the Human Rights Act, in *T, Petitioner*,[3] the Inner House of the Court of Session adopted a position essentially the same as that in English and Welsh law, namely, that the courts should presume that the United Kingdom Parliament intended to legislate in conformity with the Convention so that, where legislation was ambiguous, an interpretation compatible with the Convention should be preferred.

The Human Rights Act 1998 applies in Scotland in the same way as it does in the rest of the United Kingdom so, in general, any plausible argument that Convention rights have been infringed can be made in terms of the Human Rights Act. The differences arise from the fact that there are also provisions protective of human rights in the Scotland Act 1998. These provisions came into effect on 20 May 1999 and 1 July 1999 so that litigants in the Scottish courts were able to rely on an enhanced status for Convention rights significantly earlier than those litigating in England and Wales. However, what is of more significance in the long run is that the protection given to the Convention rights by the Scotland Act goes *further* than that provided by the Human Rights Act. Section 29 of the Scotland Act makes clear that the Scottish Parliament has no power to legislate incompatibly with the Convention rights or with Community law[4] and the courts have power, therefore, to invalidate provisions of Acts of the Scottish Parliament.

Section 57(2) of the Scotland Act states that a member of the Scottish Executive has no power to make any subordinate legislation, or to do any other act so far as incompatible with any of the Convention rights or with Community Law. This is broadly equivalent to section 6 of the Human Rights Act which states that it is unlawful for a public authority to act in a way which is incompatible with a Convention right, although it has a narrower scope in that it applies only to the Scottish Executive and not to public bodies generally. However, it goes further than section 6 of the Human Rights Act in that there is no general proviso, as there is to section 6, excusing acts which are required to be done by primary legislation. There is instead a specific proviso which states that the Lord Advocate benefits from the proviso to

---

2 *Kaur* v. *Lord Advocate* 1980 S.C. 319.

3 1997 S.L.T. 724.

4 There are other restrictions on legislative competence which need not concern us here.

149

section 6 in relation to his functions as head of the systems of criminal prosecution and investigation of deaths. The proviso has limited practical impact because it applies only to the Lord Advocate, and also because there will be few situations where a prosecution decision infringing human rights is *required* by primary legislation rather then merely permitted by it. Outside the sphere of criminal justice and investigation of deaths, there is an absolute prohibition on members of the Scottish Executive making subordinate legislation or taking any action which the infringes Convention rights. It is important to note that section 57 covers all powers of the Scottish Executive, that is, not only powers which have been conferred since devolution by Acts of the Scottish Parliament, but also powers under United Kingdom legislation and prerogative powers which have been transferred to the Scottish Executive as part of the general scheme of devolution under the Scotland Act.[5]

The other way in which devolution has affected the protection of Convention rights in Scotland is a consequence of the position of the Lord Advocate, the senior law officer in Scotland. As indicated earlier, the Lord Advocate heads the system of public prosecution in Scotland. Before devolution, the Lord Advocate was a minister of the United Kingdom government. The Scotland Act made the Lord Advocate a member of the Scottish Executive and, therefore, brought his or her actions within the scope of section 57(2). In a series of cases including *Starrs* v. *Ruxton*,[6] *Brown* v. *Stott*,[7] and *R* v. *HMA*,[8] the Scottish courts took a broad view of what constitutes an 'act' of the Lord Advocate. For example, in *Starrs* v. *Ruxton* the accused argued successfully that, where his trial was conducted by a temporary sheriff, this was a contravention of his Article 6 right to be tried by an independent and impartial tribunal because of the judge's lack of security of tenure. The accused could not rely on the Human Rights Act and argue that the court was a public authority acting unlawfully in terms of section 6 as that Act was not yet in force. However, the accused could rely on section 57(2) of the Scotland Act which was in force. The Lord Advocate was acting unlawfully in prosecuting a case before a tribunal which did not meet the requirements of Article 6. The effect of these cases has been that any claim of violation of a Convention right in the context of criminal prosecution is likely to be treated as governed by the Scotland Act as well as by the Human Rights Act. This was particularly important in the period between the entry into force of section 57 and the entry into force of the Human Rights Act, but also has long-term significance in the way it opens up the acts of public prosecutors to challenge.

Claims that legislative or executive action is invalid in terms of section 29(2) or 57(2) have procedural as well as substantive consequences. Such

---

5 See Scotland Act 1998, ss. 52–6.
6 2002 J.C. 208.
7 2001 S.C. (P.C.) 43.
8 2003 S.C. (P.C.) 21

claims are 'devolution issues'. They must be intimated to the Lord Advocate and the Advocate General for Scotland, either of whom may enter the proceedings, and the issue may be referred to a higher court for decision.[9]

There are, therefore, important differences in the arrangements for protection of Convention rights in the different parts of the United Kingdom both in relation to substance and procedure. Many human rights claims may be made only under the Human Rights Act. Equally, many claims of human rights violations may be made both under the Human Rights Act and under the Scotland Act with the latter offering a greater degree of protection (at least in law) for Convention rights.

OBJECTIVES OF THE RESEARCH

The objectives of the research were to:

- collect data about both civil and criminal cases raising human rights issues under the Convention;
- estimate the volume of such cases in Scotland;
- analyse how the human rights legislation was being used including analysis of trends and developments in the case law;
- analyse other factors relevant to the wider context; and
- make recommendations on the feasibility of a nationwide system for tracking and recording cases.

The research was, therefore, designed to provide both quantitative and qualitative analysis of the use made of the human rights legislation since devolution. The methods were essentially the collection of data on both reported and unreported cases, and the analysis of that data. Both unreported and reported cases were subjected to quantitative analysis. The reported cases were also subjected to doctrinal analysis. We also carried out some interviews of court staff in relation to the last objective (feasibility of tracking and recording cases) but this aspect of the research will not be discussed further.

QUANTITATIVE ANALYSIS

There were significant methodological difficulties in carrying out the research which require us to distinguish between civil and criminal cases. We are confident that, subject to the possibility of a small degree of error, we have been able to identify all criminal cases raising human rights issues over the period of the research. As indicated above, the raising of a human rights

---

9 Scotland Act 1998, s. 98 and Schedule 6.

argument by the accused in a criminal prosecution is treated as a 'devolution issue' requiring intimation to the Lord Advocate. The Crown Office had been keeping a record of all such intimations (referred to as 'devolution minutes') since May 1999 and we were given access to this data.

There was no such 'short cut' to identifying civil cases in which human rights issues arose and our information on civil cases was, as a result, much less comprehensive. We had two sources of data for our analysis of civil cases. First, we identified all reported cases, raising human rights points, meaning all such cases reported in hard copy, or in electronic databases including the Scottish Courts Service website. Second, we sampled a limited range of court records from both the Court of Session and two sheriff courts. Whilst these exercises provided useful data, they did not provide as reliable a basis for drawing conclusions on a range of issues as did the criminal cases data. However, the reported cases do provide an overview of the whole four-and-a-quarter-year period under study, and the sample cases a 'snapshot' of the position in early 2002. The value of the sample was that it provided a check on the database of reported cases and gave some indication of whether reported case were representative of cases generally. So, taken together, the overview and the snapshot give some indication of the level and nature of the use of human rights arguments on the civil side and allowed some tentative conclusions to be drawn, albeit without the same degree of certainty as was possible for criminal cases.

1. The volume of cases

Over the whole period of the study there was a total of 1,581 criminal cases in which a human rights argument was raised, an average of around 360 cases per annum. Although we were unable to date cases from early in the period, information provided earlier to the Scottish Parliament[10] had shown that there was an initial surge of cases, with 587 in the first year after devolution and 969 in the first eighteen months. After that the number of cases raising human rights issues declined sharply but, as Table 1 indicates, has stabilized at around 175–200 cases per annum.[11] Whilst this may seem a substantial number of cases in absolute terms, it is important to put the figures in context. This caseload represents a little over a quarter of 1 per cent of the total criminal courts caseload over the period of the study.[12]

The frequency with which human rights arguments were raised corresponded directly with the relative position of the court in the hierarchy,

---

10 See Scottish Parliament RP 01/03, *ECHR Incorporation Into Domestic Law: The Human Rights Act 1998 and the Scotland Act 1998* (2001).
11 As the figure for 2003 is a part-year figure, the total for the whole year would almost certainly have exceeded 200.
12 See Scottish Executive Statistical Bulletins CrJ/2004/1, CrJ/2002/9, CrJ/2001/7, and CrJ/2000/9.

152

Table 1: Total criminal cases raising human rights issues

20 May 1999–end December 2000	2001	2002	2003 (January–end August)	Total
1011	176	204	190	1581

Source: Crown Office Devolution minutes

with human rights arguments being made most frequently in trials in the High Court of Justiciary, which deals with the most serious crime, at 4.7 per cent of all cases, followed by jury trials in the sheriff court (3.0 per cent), summary trials in the sheriff court (0.26 per cent), and summary trials in the District Court (0.038 per cent).[13]

As indicated above, there was no short cut to identifying civil cases in which human rights arguments were raised, and, therefore, no way of producing an exact count of the total number of such cases since devolution. In fact, we were not able to produce even a reliable estimate of civil cases raising human rights issues for any given period. This was due to the inherent difficulties of the enterprise coupled with resource constraints. Most socio-legal research in the courts has a particular focus such that the data gathering can be confined to a limited range of procedures. However, human rights points could, in principle, arise in any civil court and under any procedure. There being no short cut to identifying human rights cases, the only way to produce a reliable estimate would have been to trawl through all the records in all forms of procedure for an appropriate period in a sufficiently large number of courts. Resource constraints would, therefore, have been an issue at any conceivable level of funding. In the event, the resource constraints on the project allowed for sampling of cases only in two sheriff courts and in the Court of Session, rather less than would have been necessary to produce a reliable estimate. Apart from the resource demands, the wide variety of forms of civil procedure results in considerable variations in the way records are kept, particularly for concluded cases, which means that a retrospective data gathering exercise would in any event fail to identify some cases in which human rights arguments were raised.

The total number of reported[14] civil cases raising human rights issues over the whole period of the research was 105. We would have expected reported cases to be only a small fraction of the total in which human rights arguments were raised. The sampling exercise tended to support this assumption. It identified 38 civil cases, 23 in the Court of Session and 15 in the two sheriff courts in the first quarter of 2002. Assuming that the first

13 Figures produced by comparing the average annual number of cases over the period of the study with the criminal statistics for 1999/2002.
14 As defined above.

quarter of 2002 was not atypical, there may have been approximately 92 cases in the Court of Session and 60 cases in the two sheriff courts in the whole year. Bearing in mind that the two sheriff court areas together cover only 13.2 per cent of the population of Scotland, it seems reasonable to conclude that there were at least several times as many unreported as there were reported civil cases in which human rights issues were raised over the period of the study. Although it is difficult to draw inferences from such a limited sample, the sample figures appear at least to rule out the possibility that there are substantially fewer civil than criminal cases raising human rights issues.

We analysed reported cases to determine how human rights points were distributed across courts and procedures. Judicial review procedure was responsible for the largest number of cases at 51 (37.1 per cent of the total). Given the relative size of the case loads, it is clear that human rights points were arising far more frequently in judicial review proceedings than in other types of case. This is not surprising in the light of the function of judicial review as a general purpose remedy for unlawful action by public bodies. The pattern of courts and procedures in the sample is consistent with this, suggesting that the prominence of judicial review is not a peculiarity of reported cases. What is also worth noting is the significant number of reported cases (31 out of 105) in which none of the parties to the case was a public body, suggesting that the Convention has had a significant role in private law litigation.

2. Subject matter: Convention rights

We analysed the civil and criminal cases to determine the extent to which they related to different Convention rights. Table 2 summarizes the results for criminal cases. It shows the number of issues raised rather than the number of cases. The former, at 1,712, is greater than the number of cases at 1,581 because some cases raised more than one distinct human rights issue.

The predominance of fair trial issues under Article 6 is striking. Fully 86 per cent of the Convention arguments raised were based on Article 6. The largest category within Article 6 was allegations of undue delay in bringing a case to trial (39 per cent of all issues raised). On the criminal justice side it is, therefore, clear that the Convention has been primarily used to raise questions of process and procedure (including complaints about the independence of judges) rather than questions of substantive criminal law.

As Table 3 shows, the pattern in the reported civil cases is rather different. Article 6 was again the most frequently raised article (36.9 per cent of issues raised) but it did not predominate to nearly the same degree as in criminal cases.

The other articles which figure prominently in the reported cases are Article 8 (respect for private and family life), accounting for 18.8 per cent of the issues raised, Article 3 (freedom from torture and inhuman or degrading

Table 2: ECHR Articles raised in criminal cases

Article	No. of issues	Percentage
Article 6 delay	673	39
Article 6 substantive fair hearing	375	22
Article 6 equality of arms	175	10
Article 6 access to independent and impartial tribunal	108	6
Article 8 respect for private and family life	84	5
All other Articles and Protocols (twelve)[15]	80	5
Article 5 right to liberty and security	64	4
Article 6 relief from self-incrimination	61	4
Article 6 presumption of innocence	50	3
Article 6 right to remain silent	42	2
TOTAL	1712	100

Source: Crown Office Devolution Minutes

Table 3: ECHR Articles in reported civil cases

Article	No. of issues[16]	Percentage
Article 8	31	18.8
Article 6 substantive fair hearing	28	17.0
Article 6 access to independent and impartial tribunal	17	10.3
Article 3	16	9.7
Protocol 1, Article 1	14	8.5
Article 6 delay	8	4.8
Article 6 equality of arms	8	4.8
Other[17]	43	26.1
TOTAL	165	100

Source: Human Rights in Scottish Courts Database

15 The 12 articles and protocols included in this category were Articles 2, 3, 10, 11, 13, 14, Article 1 of Protocol 1 and Article 4(1) of Protocol 7.
16 The number of issues (165) exceeds the number of cases (105) as some cases raised more than one human rights issue.
17 The 12 Articles and Protocols included in this category were Articles 1, 2, 4, 5, 7, 9, 10, 11, 14, 17, and 53, and Articles 1 and 2 of Protocol 1. There were also four cases in which an unspecified human rights issue was raised.

treatment) accounting for 9.7 per cent, and Article 1 of the First Protocol (peaceful enjoyment of possessions) accounting for 8.5 per cent of the issues raised. The figures for the sample were broadly comparable suggesting that the reported cases give a reasonable indication of the relative frequency with which different Articles are relied upon.

3. Subject matter: areas of law and policy

We also analysed the reported cases and the sample civil cases to determine in which areas of domestic law and policy human rights arguments were being used. It was clear, of course, that criminal justice was the area of policy to which the largest number of cases related. As Table 4 indicates, the largest group of *reported* civil cases related to asylum and immigration control (21.7 per cent of issues raised), followed by civil court procedure (18.9 per cent), and child law and property rights (both 9.8 per cent). The

Table 4: Reported Civil Cases by Subject

Subject	No. of issues	Percentage
Civil procedure	27	18.9
Asylum	20	14.0
Child	14	9.8
Property rights	14	9.8
Immigration	11	7.7
Delict	7	4.9
Adoption	6	4.2
Broadcasting/media	5	3.5
Contract	5	3.5
Planning	5	3.5
Education	4	2.8
Licensing	3	2.1
Mental health	3	2.1
Prisons	3	2.1
Public order	3	2.1
Road traffic	3	2.1
Other	10	7.0
TOTAL[18]	143	100

Totals do not add up due to rounding
Source: Human Rights in Scottish Courts Database

18 Where a case could be related to more than one subject area, both appear in the table. This is why the number of issues (143) is greater than the number of reported civil cases (105).

figures from the sample were broadly comparable suggesting again that the reported cases are a reasonable guide to the distribution of human rights cases across different areas of law and policy. Consideration of both sets of data (human rights issues by Article and issues by law/policy area) suggests that the full range of Convention rights were being raised in litigation, and that such rights were being raised in a wide variety of legal and policy contexts.

We can give a little more detail than does Table 4 about the sorts of issues that were coming up. Within the criminal justice area, the vast majority of the cases concerned issues of process and structure rather than challenges to aspects of substantive criminal law. In addition to the flood of cases on delay in bringing cases to trial, there was litigation concerning release on bail, pre-trial publicity, sentencing, and the independence of judges.

There was a considerably smaller number of cases dealing with the processes of civil courts and tribunals. These involved, amongst other issues, cases on the independence of judges, the role of juries, the imposition of a requirement to find security for expenses (caution) as a condition of proceeding with litigation, the lack of availability of legal aid for children's hearings, and the application of procedural fairness in professional disciplinary tribunals.

There was little use of the Convention in relation to substantive rules of private law, although Convention issues were raised, for example, in the context of claims by unmarried fathers for the award of parental rights and claims by parents for contact with children.

Criminal justice apart, the area of public administration giving rise to the largest number of cases was immigration control and asylum. Most of these cases turned on their facts, and the Convention arguments raised did not call into question existing laws and policies. However, that may not remain true for the future, as a consequence of restrictions on access to the courts in recent legislation, and proposals to remove financial support and accommodation from asylum seekers and their families as possible objects of legal challenge.[19]

There were also a number of cases in the area of development planning, generally invoking Article 6 in the context of appeal procedures, including a challenge to the role of Ministers in making decisions. However, there were large areas of public administration, including education, health care, and social security, which experienced little impact from human rights litigation either in terms of numbers or the nature of the issues raised, although there were some challenges in each of these areas.

19 See the criticisms made by the Parliamentary Joint Committee on Human Rights, Fourteenth Report, *Asylum & Immigration (Treatment of Claimants, etc.) Bill: New Clauses*, HL (2003–4) 130/HC (2003–4) 828.

157

4. *Geographical distribution*

In view of the limitations of the sampling exercise, it is appropriate to discuss geographical distribution only for criminal cases. The Crown Office records indicated the local Procurator Fiscal office responsible for the preparation of the prosecution. These offices correspond to the jurisdiction of the sheriff courts, although the cases originating in the local offices would include prosecutions in any of the criminal courts. The records indicate an uneven distribution of human rights cases across Scotland with 'hot spots' such as Glasgow which had one human rights case for every 49 prosecutions and Edinburgh (one case for every 54 prosecutions), and comparatively 'cold spots' such as Dundee (only one case for every 278 prosecutions) and Greenock (one for every 374).[20] The research was not designed to establish the causes of this uneven distribution.

5. *Outcomes*

We analysed outcomes by determining whether the courts granted a remedy for an alleged human rights violation. This analysis was confined to the reported cases, as the Crown Office database of criminal cases did not systematically record outcomes. Such a remedy was awarded in 39 (16.8 per cent) of the 232 reported cases (both criminal and civil). We cannot, of course, assume that remedies were being awarded at the same rate in unreported cases. The success rate in the sample cases was very much lower with remedies awarded in three out of 95 cases (3.16 per cent). However, two comments are appropriate here. First, a number of cases were still continuing at the conclusion of the study and some of these were ultimately successful. Second, it would not be very surprising if the success rate were lower in unreported cases. Cases are only likely to be reported if the human rights arguments, even if ultimately unsuccessful, have some merit. Cases in which the argument is spurious or highly speculative are less likely to be reported. However, it is clear that we cannot estimate the success rate in cases generally, as opposed to the success rate in reported cases, from our data.

Whether the success rate in reported cases was appropriate is a separate question. The qualitative analysis (discussed in more detail below) suggested that decisions of the Scottish courts were in general in line with Strasbourg jurisprudence. So, even if the success rate appears low, the reported cases provide no grounds for concluding that the Scottish courts are being too strict in their interpretation of the Convention. It is also worth pointing out that we treated a remedy as awarded on human rights grounds only where there was

---

20 Based on unpublished figures for numbers of prosecutions in each local authority area supplied by the Scottish Executive. The areas chosen are those in which the local authority area corresponds exactly or very closely with the jurisdiction of the relevant PF Office.

158

a specific indication to that effect in the report. There may have been cases in which the human rights arguments influenced the granting of the remedy but this is not reflected in the judgment(s).

QUALITATIVE ANALYSIS

We have already indicated that the issues raised in the reported cases span the full range of Convention rights. In the full report of the research,[21] we presented a doctrinal analysis, which summarized the legal issues that have arisen for decision by reference to the Articles of the Convention. It would not be appropriate to produce even a reduced version of that discussion here. We also analysed the reported cases according to the area of domestic law or policy concerned in order to give more information about the nature of the cases in which human rights issues were being raised, and also to assess the significance rather than simply the volume of challenges for each area. We included comment also on challenges to existing laws and practices which might have been expected but had not in fact been made. Again, it would not be appropriate to reproduce that detailed account here.

However, we do think it useful to discuss here some general issues relating to the impact of the human rights legislation in Scotland using both the data gathered for the research and other material already in the public domain.

THE IMPACT OF THE HUMAN RIGHTS LEGISLATION

The process of the incorporation of the conversion into domestic law aroused conflicting expectations. Many were broadly supportive of enhancing the legal status of Convention rights. Others were more sceptical of the merits of the enterprise. There was a separate disagreement over whether the human rights legislation would make much difference, with some expecting a major impact not just on the courts but on legal thinking generally and perhaps also the development of a human rights culture,[22] but others had rather different expectations.[23] It seems appropriate, therefore, to try to assess some of the effects of the human rights legislation in Scotland, in so far as we can do so.

There are potentially many dimensions to the impact of the legislation. It might be assessed by reference to its effects on:

21 Greenhill et al., op. cit., n. 1.
22 Lord Irvine of Lairg, Tom Sargant Memorial Lecture 1997, <http://www.open.gov.uk/lcd/speeches/tomsarg.htm>. H.W.R. Wade, 'Human rights and the judiciary' [1998] E.H.R.L.R. 520.
23 See, for example, T. Campbell, K.D. Ewing, and A. Tomkins, *Sceptical Essays on Human Rights* (2001).

- the business of the courts (for example, volume of cases, changes in administrative practices);
- the legal profession (for example, volume and nature of case load, awareness of human rights issues);
- the public (for example, awareness and understanding of human rights issues, propensity to seek legal advice or to litigate);
- policy development and the legislative process (for example, human rights proofing in policy development; changes to legislative procedure, ministerial awareness of human rights issues);
- the implementation of policy by public bodies (for example, changes to sub-legislative policy-making, changes to operational procedures, awareness amongst officials of human rights
- the judicial function (for example, how judges use human rights arguments, weight given to Strasbourg case law);

This list emphasizes the wide range of persons, institutions, and processes potentially affected by the human rights legislation. It also indicates that the potential effects are of many types. Space does not permit comment on all of the above so we will confine our comments to the business of the courts, the judicial function, and policy development, policy implementation, and the policy process.

1. *Effects on the courts*

Although we were unable to estimate precisely the volume of civil cases raising human rights issues, it seems clear that human rights legislation has had little effect on the volume of business in the courts. Cases raising human rights points have been only a tiny fraction of the total caseload of the Scottish civil and criminal courts. There were other resource implications for the justice system in terms of judicial training, but overall, the incorporation of the Convention into Scots law does not appear to have had major continuing resource implications for the justice system.

Human rights cases have not been evenly distributed across procedures, and human rights issues have been raised far more frequently (relative to total caseload) under judicial review procedure than under other procedures. However, it is doubtful if there has been a substantial redistribution of resources towards judicial review procedure as the absolute numbers are small, and, in most cases, the application in which the human rights argument was included would have been made on other grounds anyway.

However, although numbers are small in relation to cases generally, it is clear that human rights arguments have become an established category of argument in the Scottish legal system and feature prominently in the law reports. It is noteworthy that the full range of Convention rights has been deployed in argument, and equally noteworthy that Article 6 was the Article most frequently resorted to. Its predominance in criminal cases and the very

160

high number of claims of unfairness based on delay in bringing a case to trial are particularly striking, although we cannot say on the basis of our data whether this indicates any systemic problem within the criminal justice system.

2. *The judicial function*

The attitude and approach of the judges was a matter of great interest around the time of the enactment of the human rights legislation. It was assumed that judicial attitudes would be crucial to the impact of the human rights legislation. However, establishing criteria for the assessment and evaluation of judicial performance is not a straightforward task. The underlying problem is the nature of the Convention as a set of rather general and open-ended guarantees of rights which will inevitably leave room for debate about whether the Convention has been violated in many particular contexts. It is true that the substantial case law built up by the Strasbourg authorities has given considerably more specific content to the Convention rights than the bare text itself supplies, and therefore, argument about what the Convention requires may be less contested than it would be in the absence of such a large body of case law. However, although that case law is clearly a constraining factor in determining the range of arguments about human rights that it is legally plausible to make, there still remains a greater level of uncertainty and room for argument than is the case in most areas of domestic litigation, meaning that the judicial role is more pivotal.

The uncertainty in determining what Strasbourg doctrine is arises not only from difficulties in interpreting the meaning of particular cases or groups of cases, but also from aspects of the general approach of the Strasbourg authorities to interpretation of the Convention's guarantees which acknowledge, and even celebrate, uncertainty in determining its meaning. The first of these is the notion that the Convention is a living instrument to be given a 'dynamic' or 'evolutive' interpretation,[24] so that the court must take account of changing social attitudes and conditions in applying the Convention. Second, there is the concept of margin of appreciation,[25] which gives the state discretion in taking legislative, administrative, or judicial action in relation to a Convention right, for example, in deciding whether interference with a right is necessary in terms of Articles 8–11. Strictly speaking, this doctrine has no application to national courts specifying as it does the relationship between international institutions and national authorities. However, although national courts are not required to defer to legislative and administrative bodies within a state on account of this doctrine,

---

24 See, for example, *Tyrer* v. *UK* [1979–80] 2 E.H.R.R. 1 and D. J. Harris, M. O'Boyle, and C. Warbrick, *Law of the European Convention on Human Rights* (1995) 7–9.
25 Harris et al., id., pp. 13–15.

161

both the Scottish and English and Welsh courts have developed the idea of judicial deference to legislative choices on general democratic grounds.[26]

The terms of the Human Rights Act arguably add to the uncertainty. Section 2 makes clear that, although Strasbourg case law must be taken into account by our judges, it is not binding on them, which leaves open the possibility of our judges departing from the approach taken by the Strasbourg authorities. However, without trying to wish away the uncertainty of Strasbourg doctrine, it is important not to overemphasize these difficulties. There is a degree of predictability about what the Strasbourg authorities will do when faced with claims, and lawyers frequently find it possible to give clear advice about the compatibility of existing practices with the Convention. We therefore think that it is appropriate to use Strasbourg doctrine as a yardstick for measuring the performance of judges in Scottish cases – with the caveats noted above – and to ask whether they are in general terms deciding cases consistently with the doctrine developed by the Strasbourg authorities.

Our conclusions on that issue are based on a detailed review of the whole of the post-devolution case law up to August 2003. Space does not permit a full analysis of the case law here but the published report contains such an analysis.[27] There was a small number of cases in which the courts appeared to apply either a more or a less protective approach to the protection of rights than would the Strasbourg court. Three examples are given here. The most celebrated case in which it has been alleged that a less protective approach was taken was probably *Brown* v. *Stott*[28] in which the issue was whether information as to the identity of the driver of a car at the time of an offence, which the owner was compelled to give under section 172 of the Road Traffic Act, could then be used in evidence at a subsequent trial of the owner for that offence. The High Court of Justiciary had found this to be a violation of the right to silence and the right not to incriminate oneself both implicit in the fair trial guarantee of Article 6. The Privy Council reversed this decision on the grounds that these rights, not being mentioned expressly in the legislation, were open to modification and restriction where this served a legitimate purpose (public safety) and that the means were proportionate. It has been forcefully argued that this reasoning is incompatible with Strasbourg case law,[29] but not all commentators agree,[30] so even this is not a clear-cut example of failing to protect Convention rights.

It is also arguable that the Scottish courts have been too ready to reject claims based on the alleged bias of jurors in different contexts including

---

26 See, for example, *R* v. *DPP, ex parte Kebilene* [2000] 2 A.C. 326; *A* v. *Scottish Ministers* 2001 S.C. 1; *Brown* v. *Stott* 2001 S.C. (P.C.) 43.
27 Greenhill et al., op. cit., n. 1, chs. 3 and 4.
28 op. cit., n. 7.
29 S. Naismith, 'Human Rights, Self-incrimination: the case law of the European Court of Human Rights' (2001) 2 *Human Rights and UK Practice* 3.
30 R. Pillay, 'Self-incrimination and Article 6' [2001] E.H.R.L.R. 78.

adverse pre-trial publicity. Thirdly, it may be argued that in *S* v. *Miller (No 2)*[31] in deciding that a secure accommodation order made under the Children (Scotland) Act 1995 was a lawful detention under Article 5 because it could be regarded as 'for the purposes of educational supervision', the court did not have sufficient regard to the Strasbourg case law which would not authorize detention under this heading if the essential nature of the regime was punitive rather than educational.[32]

Thus far, there have been only two areas in which the Scottish courts have arguably applied stricter standards, that is, more protective of human rights, than the Strasbourg authorities. The first is in relation to immigration and asylum cases. The Scottish courts, like the English and Welsh courts, have acted as if these cases involve the determination of a civil right and, therefore, it is appropriate to apply the Conventions requirement of a fair hearing, whereas the Strasbourg case law is fairly clear that these issues fall outside the scope of Article 6 protection because immigration decisions are not regarded as determining civil rights.[33]

The second example is less clear cut. The failure to upgrade conditions in Scottish prisons sufficiently quickly to eliminate the practice of 'slopping-out' stimulated a number of cases alleging a violation of Article 3, and one such claim was successful in *Napier* v. *Scottish Ministers*.[34] It is doubtful whether the Strasbourg Court would consider conditions in Scottish prisons to meet the minimum level of severity required for an Article 3 violation. However, whether *Napier* should be seen as 'going further' than the Strasbourg Court would is difficult to say. Lord Bonomy's opinion stresses the particular circumstances of the applicant so the case may be seen as one that turns on its own facts and does not have wider application. It is, in any event, under appeal to the Inner House.

There have also been cases in which the Scottish courts have in effect been invited to apply a stricter standard for assessing violations than the Strasbourg case law but have refused to do so. This has happened, for example, in cases involving the disclosure of evidence by prosecutors, admissibility of evidence obtained in violation of Article 8, challenges to the role of juries in assessing awards of damages in personal injury claims, and challenges to the role of Ministers in planning appeals.[35]

---

31 2001 S.L.T. 34.
32 *DG* v. *Ireland* R.J.D. 2002-II.
33 See, for example, *Asifa Saleem* v. *Secretary of State for Home Department* [2000] 4 All E.R. 814.
34 2004 S.L.T. 555.
35 *County Properties Ltd* v. *Scottish Ministers* 2002 S.C. 79. The argument that current arrangements were incompatible with Article 6 succeeded at first instance in the Court of Session but that decision was reversed on appeal following the decision of the House of Lords in *R (On the application of Alconbury Developments Ltd* v. *Secretary of State for the Environment* [2001] 2 W.L.R. 1389.

163

However, viewing the post-devolution case law as a whole, there is little evidence in the domestic human rights jurisprudence of the Scottish courts diverging from the doctrine of the Strasbourg Court either by construing the Convention rights more narrowly or more broadly than would the Strasbourg court.

3. Policy development, the legislative process, and policy implementation

A further important measure of the impact of the human rights legislation is the extent to which it has required changes to public policy. Such changes might be forced as responses to litigation or be pre-emptive measures to ensure compliance with the Convention before any legal challenges are mounted.

As to the first possibility, of course, 'Strasbourg-proofing' is not new. It was a well established process within the United Kingdom before devolution. However, it is worth noting that several aspects of the devolution scheme impose legal requirements for pre-enactment human rights-proofing of the legislation. These impose separate obligations on the Parliament and the Scottish Executive. Section 31(1) requires that the Minister in charge of an Executive Bill shall state on its introduction that in his/her view it is within legislative competence. The Presiding Officer must also state his or her opinion on the competence of the Bill,[36] and standing orders require that any Executive Bill must be accompanied by a policy memorandum which, amongst other things, must include an assessment of the effects of the Bill on human rights. There is also the possibility of referring a Bill to the Judicial Committee of the Privy Council, after it has been passed but before it is sent for Royal Assent, to determine whether it is within competence.[37] The research was not designed to assess how such procedures were working in practice.

However, we can point to several examples of the incorporation of the Convention leading to significant changes in public policy which were not necessitated by litigation. The Scottish Executive promoted the Bail, Judicial Appointments, etc. (Scotland) Act 2000. One aspect of the Act was a response to litigation but the following were not. The Act altered the law on bail in several respects (removal of excluded crimes, automatic consideration of bail at first appearance in court) and excluded local authority councillors from trying criminal cases in the district court as justices of the peace. The other important pre-emptive legislation was the Convention Rights Compliance (Scotland) Act 2001 which, amongst other things, changed the rules for release of adult mandatory life prisoners and the constitution of the Parole Board, provided for a limited extension of the legal advice and assistance scheme to cover representation at certain tribunal hearings, and

36 Scotland Act 1998, s. 31(2).
37 id., s. 33.

164

amended the law on sexual offences so that it is no longer an offence for more than two adult males to engage in consensual homosexual acts in private.

Changes have also been made as a direct consequence of litigation under the Act. The most clear cut example of policy reversal has been the abolition of the position of temporary sheriffs (who had been increasingly used in recent years to try cases), by the Bail, Judicial Appointments, etc. (Scotland) Act 2000. This followed the decision in *Starrs* v. *Ruxton*[38] that their lack of security of tenure was incompatible with Article 6. Article 6 had also been used, in *Buchanan* v. *McLean*,[39] to attack the fixed fee regime for legal aid introduced by regulations made under section 33(3A) of the Legal Aid (Scotland) Act 1986 which capped the fee that could be claimed for a summary trial at £500. The court rejected the head-on challenge holding that the fixed fee regime was not, in itself, contrary to Article 6. However, it did accept that there were some cases in which the fixed fee would compromise the fairness of the trial, and since then the Scottish Legal Aid Board has had discretion to award a higher fee in appropriate cases.

Another important policy change required a fresh interpretation of the law rather than a change to it. As indicated above, the Convention Rights Compliance (Scotland) Act 2001 changed the law on the release of life prisoners to bring it into line with the Convention. The Act created a new regime for determining the punishment period in life sentences. It made transitional provisions for adult mandatory life prisoners sentenced under the old procedures. Following earlier decisions of the High Court of Justiciary,[40] the transitional provisions were being applied in such as way that existing life prisoners might have to spend longer in prison. In *Flynn and others* v. *Her Majesty's Advocate*, a majority of the Privy Council took the view that such an interpretation would violate life prisoners' Article 7 rights.[41] However, the majority also thought, applying the rule that an Act of the Scottish Parliament is to be construed as narrowly as is required for it to be within competence,[42] that an alternative interpretation could and should be given which would not have the effect of extending the period in prison beyond that which would have been served under the prior legislation.

However, reviewing the whole post-devolution case law, the majority of the more significant challenges (in policy terms) to existing policies and legislation have been unsuccessful. The challenges to the planning appeal system, to the provisions for the preventative detention of persons suffering

---

38 op. cit., n. 6.
39 2000 S.C. (J.C.) 603.
40 *Stewart* v. *HM Advocate* 2002 S.L.T. 1307; *McCreaddie* v. *HM Advocate* 2002 S.L.T. 1311.
41 2004 J.L.T. 863; Lord Rodger of Earlsferry preferred to rest his conclusion on ordinary principles of statutory interpretation.
42 Act 1998, s. 101(2), which is broadly equivalent to s. 3 of the Human Rights Act.

from psychopathic personality disorders,[43] to the ban on hunting wild animals with dogs,[44] and the use in road traffic prosecutions of evidence as to the identity of the driver of a car which had been obtained under compulsion all failed.[45]

Of course not all claims of violation of human rights call into question legislation or policy. Many will relate to the implementation of policy rather than to major substantive issues or the terms of legislation. Probably, the most significant implementation challenge was the series of cases on slopping-out in prisons. As noted above, in *Napier*, Lord Bonomy found there to have been a violation of Article 3, but the finding appeared to rest on the particular facts of Napier's case and fell short of stating that the practice of slopping-out was, in itself, in breach of Article 3. In any event the decision has been appealed by the Scottish Ministers and the outcome is awaited. However, there were not many cases arising from the implementation of policy which clearly had implications going beyond their own circumstances. However, the research was not designed to assess the effects of the human rights legislation on the implementation of policy in any depth, and we did not go beyond information in the public domain in considering either the consequences of particular cases, or the more diffuse effects of the legislation such as the possible development of a pro-human rights culture amongst administrators.

The final issue worth discussing in relation to the effect of human rights litigation on the content of public policy and the policy process is a constitutional one, and it involves assessing the effect of human rights litigation, not according to the importance of the changes required in policy or terms, but according to the hierarchy of legal norms. Many successful cases have little or no wider impact. For example, a finding of undue delay in bringing a case to trial amounting to a violation of Article 6 might well be based on facts peculiar to that case. Conversely, a successful challenge may require a change of policy, including cases where a change in the accepted interpretation of legislation was required. If a change in the law is required the nature of that change might be a development of the common law, amendment or repeal of subordinate legislation, or even amendment or repeal of primary legislation. The last possibility is the most significant in constitutional terms, bearing in mind the perennial debate over the legitimacy of courts using human rights guarantees to invalidate the enactments of elected legislatures.

This is a more pressing issue in Scotland than it is in England and Wales given that the Scotland Act requires provisions of Acts of the Scottish

---

43 Mental Health (Public Safety and Appeals) (Scotland) Act 1999. See *Anderson* v. *Scottish Ministers* 2002 S.C. (P.C.) 63.
44 Protection of Wild Mammals (Scotland) Act 2002. See *Adams* v. *Advocate General* 2003 S.C. 171 and *Whaley* v. *Lord Advocate* 2004 S.L.T. 425.
45 Road Traffic Act 1988, s. 172. See *Brown* v. *Stott* 2002 S.C. (P.C.) 43.

Parliament which conflict with human rights to be treated as invalid, whereas it is not possible to invalidate Acts of the United Kingdom Parliament,[46] although the superior courts may make a declaration of incompatibility. Three Acts of the Scottish Parliament have been subject to challenges to their competence: the Mental Health (Public Safety and Appeals) (Scotland) Act 1999, the Protection of Wild Mammals (Scotland) Act 2002, and the Convention Rights (Compliance) (Scotland) Act 2001. None of these challenges has been successful, although in the third case the challenge was only repelled because the Privy Council adopted a different interpretation of the legislation from that of the High Court. So, it appears that the ultimate weapon of the courts – the invalidation of primary legislation – has not yet been wielded.[47]

Nor have the courts made any declarations of incompatibility in relation to United Kingdom statutes in Scottish cases. However, the unsuccessful claim of a violation of Article 6 in *Brown* v. *Stott* (discussed above) points the way to the seemingly paradoxical possibility that an Act of the United Kingdom Parliament can effectively be nullified, despite the terms of the Human Rights Act and the underlying constitutional principle of parliamentary sovereignty. Section 172 of the Road Traffic Act 1988 makes it an offence to refuse to say who was driving a motor vehicle at a time when an offence had been committed. This power is essential in practice to the prosecution of many motoring offences because, without the admission of the owner of the vehicle, it would often be impossible for the police and prosecutor to prove who was driving the vehicle when the offence was committed. As noted above, the Privy Council reversed the finding of the High Court that this violated Article 6. However, had the challenge succeeded, section 172 would have become a dead letter in Scotland. This is because, as indicated above, any step in the prosecution process is an act of the Lord Advocate and covered by section 57(2) of the Scotland Act: a finding in favour of Brown would have made it impossible for any future prosecution to be mounted on the basis of section 172.

Although it has not yet arisen, this is an important issue for the future. Provisions of United Kingdom Acts of Parliament which depend for their effective enforcement on action by members of the Scottish Executive may be rendered nugatory by a finding that enforcement by the Executive is incompatible with a Convention right.

---

46 Special considerations would apply where the human rights argument was based on the human rights principles protected by Community law, given the principle of supremacy of Community law.

47 Acts of the Scottish Parliament are defined as subordinate legislation for its purposes by s. 21(1) of the Human Rights Act. However, we may treat this as a matter of form. Functionally they may be regarded as primary legislation. See *Adams*, op. cit., n. 44.

CONCLUSION

Our research was a study of the ordinary courts. It did not cover tribunals as it would not have been feasible to include both in the same study. However, it is clear that human rights arguments are raised regularly in some tribunals. The lack of systematic information about tribunals is a gap that could usefully be filled by further research, and we should be aware that looking at the courts alone might produce a skewed impression of the extent and nature of the use of human rights arguments in legal disputes generally, and in the context of particular areas of public administration. With that qualification our general conclusion is that the incorporation of the Convention via the human rights legislation has had significant effects within the Scottish court system and on policy development without amounting to a major upheaval. The numbers of cases were not such as to disturb the balance of the court system, and there has been only a small number of successful human rights challenges which required significant policy changes. The required changes to the policy process (as opposed to the outcomes of that process) should probably not be regarded as fundamental for two reasons: first, Strasbourg proofing is a long-established process; second, the additional procedures required by the Scotland Act are part of a broader scheme of testing the *vires* of legislation required by the scheme of devolution. On the evidence of the opinions delivered in reported cases, the judges (at least the senior judges) appear to have adapted without great difficulty to the demands placed on them by the human rights legislation, and their approach appears to be generally consistent with the Strasbourg jurisprudence.

JOURNAL OF LAW AND SOCIETY
VOLUME 32, NUMBER 1, MARCH 2005
ISSN: 0263-323X, pp. 169–86

An Equality and Human Rights Commission Worthy of the Name

ANTHONY LESTER* AND LYDIA CLAPINSKA**

The Human Rights Act 1998 came fully into force on 2 October 2000, enabling the European Convention on Human Rights (ECHR) to be relied on directly in our domestic courts.[1] The Act lacked provision for a Human Rights Commission to advise and assist alleged victims in bringing proceedings for breaches of Convention rights, to research, intervene in court proceedings, and promote a culture of human rights, although such a Commission had been created for Northern Ireland. A White Paper has now been issued outlining plans for a Commission for Equality and Human Rights. This paper considers the future role and potential impact of the Commission and highlights opportunities that have been missed since October 2000 in its absence. We focus on its human rights aspects and summarize key conditions for the new Commission's success.

THE HUMAN RIGHTS ACT 1998

In December 1996, Jack Straw MP, the then-Shadow Home Secretary, and Paul Boateng MP, produced a consultation paper, *Bringing Rights Home*,[2] which set out the Labour Party's proposals to incorporate the Convention rights into United Kingdom law. In March 1997, the Labour and Liberal Democrat Joint Consultative Committee on Constitutional Reform, co-

---

* *Blackstone Chambers, Blackstone House, Temple, London EC4Y 9BW, England, Liberal Democrat peer and member of the Joint Committee on Human Rights*
** *Barrister and Parliamentary Legal Officer at the Odysseus Trust, 193 Fleet Street, London EC4A 2AH, England*

1 The Scotland Act 1998 and the Northern Ireland Act 1998 had already brought the European Convention on Human Rights into United Kingdom law in 1998.
2 J. Straw and P. Boateng, *Bringing Rights Home: Labour's Plans to Incorporate the European Convention on Human Rights into UK Law* (1996), text published in [1997] E.H.R.L.R. 71–80.

chaired by Robin Cook MP and Robert Maclennan MP, published its report. It envisaged that there would be a human rights commissioner or commission, or similar public body, to advise and assist those seeking protection of their Convention rights, and to bring proceedings in its own name. On 1 May 1997, the Labour Party was returned to power. In October 1997, the new government published a White Paper,[3] together with the Bill itself. Neither White Paper nor Bill made provision for a human rights commission. The government explained that it was not yet persuaded of the need for such a body.

During the passage of the Human Rights Bill, there were many calls for a commission to be established. Baroness Amos argued that:

> we need a body which will raise public awareness, promote good practice, scrutinise legislation, monitor policy developments and their impact, provide independent advice to Parliament, and advise those who feel that their human rights have been infringed.[4]

Lord Woolf of Barnes, at that time Master of the Rolls, stated that:

> The most important benefit of a Commission is that it will assist in creating a culture in which human rights are routinely observed without the need for continuous intervention by the courts. Human rights will only be a reality when this is the situation.[5]

During the Committee stage of the Bill, Baroness Williams of Crosby warned of 'an extraordinarily uncoordinated structure of concern for human rights, with wide gaps between the organisations that currently exist';[6] such gaps would not be filled without a human rights commissioner or commission; she continued, 'I fear we may lose a great opportunity created by the Bill ... because of our unwillingness to take the final step.'

However, when the Human Rights Act was brought into force on 2 October 2000, there was no provision for a human rights commission and no government commitment to establish such a commission. The time when a human rights commission was most needed was in the period following enactment of the Human Rights Act, when a culture of respect for human rights could have been promoted, to give real meaning to the Act and to ensure that its purposes were widely understood.

THE JOINT COMMITTEE ON HUMAN RIGHTS

The government, whilst resisting proposals for establishing a human rights commission, suggested instead that the proposed parliamentary committee

---

3 Home Department, *Rights Brought Home: The Human Rights Bill* (1997; Cm. 3782).
4 583, *H.L. Debs.*, col. 846 (24 November 1997).
5 Foreword to S. Spencer and I. Bynoe, *A Human Rights Commission, the Options for Britain and Northern Ireland* (1998).
6 583, *H.L. Debs.*, col. 843 (24 November 1997).

on human rights should consider the question and come forward with recommendations. After much delay, the Joint Committee on Human Rights met for the first time on 31 January 2001. Its remit is to consider matters relating to human rights in the United Kingdom (but excluding consideration of individual cases) and proposals for remedial orders made under section 10 of the Human Rights Act. One of the earliest decisions taken by the Joint Committee was to launch an inquiry into the case for establishing a human rights commission for the United Kingdom; a call for written evidence was issued in April 2001.

The Joint Committee published an interim report in July 2002.[7] The call for evidence had netted protean responses from a variety of sources. The majority of responses expressed strong support for the establishment of a human rights commission.[8]

In December 2001, before the Joint Committee's interim report had been made, the government published a consultation paper, *Towards Equality and Diversity.*[9] The government expressed the view that there were good arguments to move towards a single equality commission. This consultation did not mention the possibility of a human rights commission. The Joint Committee's interim report concluded that:[10]

> ... it would be a serious omission for the Government's forthcoming consultative proposals on a single equality body to fail to give full weight to the element of the project's terms of reference relating to the promotion and protection of human rights. If any proposals for measures to protect and promote equalities fail to address the relationship between those powers and functions and arrangements for promoting and protecting human rights, they are likely to be incoherent, incomplete and ineffective.

The interim report was followed by a substantive report published in March 2003,[11] in which the Joint Committee concluded that the case for establishing a commission was compelling.

---

7 Joint Committee on Human Rights (JCHR), Twenty-second Report, *The Case for a Human Rights Commission: Interim Report*, HL (2001-02) 160/HC (2001-02) 1142.
8 id., ev. 16: written evidence by JUSTICE expressed forceful concern about the lack of a human rights commission, 'Without a Human Rights Commission, it is likely that the UK's conception of human rights will be an impoverished one. The Human Rights Act will be viewed narrowly, as a legalistic document to be developed primarily through litigation.'
9 Cabinet Office, Department of Trade and Industry, Home Office, and Department for Work and Pensions, *Towards Equality and Diversity: Implementing the Employment and Race Directives* (2001).
10 JCHR, op. cit., n. 7, p. 7.
11 JCHR, Sixth Report, *The Case for a Human Rights Commission*, HL (2002–03) 67/ HC (2002–03) 489.

A HUMAN RIGHTS CULTURE

The Joint Committee regards a culture of human rights as having institutional and ethical dimensions. This means that human rights should shape the goals, structures, and practices of public bodies, and that the legislature, the executive, and the judiciary should share responsibility for the protection and promotion of human rights. It also means that individuals need to understand their rights and responsibilities and to be able to seek advice, assistance, redress, and protection if they believe that their rights have been violated.

MISSED OPPORTUNITIES

The focus of the Joint Committee's substantive report was upon the need for a human rights commission. The pivotal questions were whether there was evidence that the Human Rights Act had spurred the process of cultural change, and whether a human rights commission could contribute substantially towards achieving this goal. The Committee adopted a two-pronged approach. First, it examined the extent to which the Human Rights Act is observed and informs the practices of all public authorities. Second, it considered the practical benefits of seeking to create a culture of respect for human rights, and the role a commission might play in that task. The results of research commissioned by the Joint Committee painted a dismal picture. The Committee concluded that:

> There is no vision, no administrative framework and scant guidance reaching public authorities to tell them how a culture of respect for human rights might look or how it can be delivered.[12]

The Committee found virtually no examples of public authorities having adopted a culture of respect for human rights in their work, other than in terms of formal legal compliance. In public sector bodies concerned with the state in its coercive, rather than enabling, roles there was greater awareness of human rights issues. The supervisory organizations in the policing, prisons, and mental health sectors all saw human rights as important grounding principles for the legislative framework or standards of good practice within which they inspected or adjudicated. However, this was an approach taken by a minority of public authorities overall. Public authorities such as hospitals and local councils did not put human rights at the heart of their policies.

These findings are in marked contrast to the way in which race equality has been woven into the fabric of public authorities and their work. Research commissioned by the Joint Committee indicated that the mainstreaming of

12 id., p. 29.

172

race equality has been spurred by the new public sector 'duty to promote' racial equality contained in the Race Relations (Amendment) Act 2000 and the steps taken by the Commission for Racial Equality to give the duty real and practical effect through the implementation of race equality schemes in public authorities.[13] In July 2003, the Commission for Racial Equality published the results of its research into the practical impact of the new positive duty to promote race equality.[14] Almost 70 per cent of respondents to this survey felt that their work on the positive duty had produced positive benefits, including increased awareness of race equality in policy making and service delivery; this figure rose to 89 per cent in central government and 83 per cent in higher education.

As the Joint Committee concluded, 'agents of state cannot be expected to embrace a human rights culture that they do not know about'.[15] By failing to create a human rights commission at the inception of the Human Rights Act, the government had missed the early opportunity to build a culture of respect for human rights. If human rights had been given a champion from the outset, by establishing a commission, then there would have been a powerful body to counter negative and misleading media reporting and commentary,[16] and other political cynicism.[17]

The second prong of the Joint Committee's approach considered the practical benefits of seeking to create a culture of respect for human rights, and the role a commission might play in that task. The Joint Committee found that a commission could satisfy the unmet need for citizens to be assisted in understanding what their rights are, how those rights must be balanced with those of others, and how to assert their rights without necessarily having recourse to litigation. The commission would provide an effective and efficient way of developing public awareness, beyond the very limited remit of the tiny Human Rights Unit within the then-named Lord Chancellor's Department.

---

13 id., and see, also, JCHR, op. cit., n. 7, ev. 250-234.
14 Commission for Racial Equality (CRE), *Towards Racial Equality: An evaluation of the public duty to promote race equality and good relations in England and Wales* (2003), referred to and summarized in JCHR, Eleventh Report, *Commission for Equality and Human Rights: Structure, Functions and Powers*, HL (2003–04) 78/HC (2003–04) 536, 15.
15 JCHR, op. cit., n. 11, p. 32.
16 See Lord Lester and D. Pannick, *Human Rights Law and Practice* (2004, 2nd edn.) ch. 1, para. 1.43.
17 For a recent example, see Sir Oliver Popplewell, 'You can have too many human rights' *Sunday Times*, 29 August 2004, 7. On 23 August 2004, in a political party press release, the Conservative Party Shadow Home Secretary, David Davis MP promised to establish a Commission to conduct a review into the Human Rights Act, which he believes has given rise to 'too many spurious rights' and has 'fuelled a compensation culture out of all sense of proportion'.

In October 2002, the government published a second consultation paper, *Equality and Diversity: Making it happen*.[18] The paper noted the 'complementary nature of equality and human rights', which was 'reflected in the Government's vision of a society based on fair and equal treatment for all and respect for the dignity and value of each person.'[19] The Joint Committee's Sixth Report also served as their response to this consultation. Some Committee members[20] were concerned that it would be difficult to create a successful equality commission without overloading it with an even broader mandate to tackle abuses of human rights generally, especially if the commission were to be lopsided with strong powers to tackle inequality and few, if any, powers to tackle wider human rights abuses. They tended to prefer two linked commissions. However, after protracted debate on the respective merits of separate, linked commissions or a joint body for equality and human rights, the Joint Committee concluded that:

> A powerful argument for bringing all the strands of the human rights agenda into a single body is that this would strengthen the ability to promote a culture that respects the dignity, worth and human rights of everyone. Provided that this were done in a way that did not blunt the cutting edge of the specialised compliance work in tackling unjustifiable discrimination by means of monitoring and law enforcement, we consider that, on balance a single body would be the more desirable of the two options.[21]

The proviso was that the option of separate bodies was a viable alternative, provided that they were closely linked in their work. The Joint Committee considered that such a model had been successfully adopted in Northern Ireland and the Republic of Ireland.

The government accepted the compelling case for a single commission, identified and firmly endorsed by the Joint Committee. On 30 October 2003, the Secretary of State for Trade and Industry and Minister for Women, Patricia Hewitt announced government plans to create a Commission for Equality and Human Rights.[22] On the 16 January 2004, Baroness Prashar of Runnymede introduced a debate on the Joint Committee's report in the House of Lords. The government's announcement received a cautious welcome. This was attributable in part to the lack of detail in the government's statement about the commission's structure and powers. There was also a sense of frustration at the prospect of further delay with a task force set up to advise the government, before any parliamentary time would be devoted to the necessary legislation. This meant that there would be no

---

18 Women and Equality Unit, *Equality and Diversity: Making it happen* (2002).
19 id., para. 9.3.
20 Including Anthony Lester.
21 JCHR, op. cit., n. 11, p. 68.
22 P. Hewitt, 412 *H.C. Debs.*, col. 17WS (30 October 2003).

prospect of a commission being set up before 2006. This delay unsettled the leadership and staff of the existing equality commissions.

MINIMUM CONDITIONS FOR SUCCESS

During the 16 January debate, we welcomed the decision to set up a commission, with the crucial proviso that certain conditions are met. We believe that these important conditions are of continuing relevance in advance of final decisions about the way in which the commission is structured and will function.

1. *The first condition*

The first condition required for the very foundations of a new commission is that the tangled and incoherent mess of existing equality laws is replaced as a high priority by a comprehensive, coherent, and user-friendly Equality Act, covering all the main types of unjustifiable discrimination on grounds of gender, sexuality, ethnicity, disability, religious belief or lack of it, and age, not only in employment but also in education, housing, goods, and services. The Hepple report[23] which preceded our Equality Bill, advised that:

> In Britain the first step must be to harmonise the substantive law into a single equality statute. This will then provide a sound basis for a single commission.[24]

Britain's equality code is a tangled thicket of inconsistent and incomplete legislation in urgent need of coherent reform. Its complexity makes it especially difficult for small businesses to comply with their legal obligations and hinders victims in their access to justice. Equality legislation has developed in a piecemeal fashion and is itself unequal in the varying levels of protection it provides to different groups of people. Even the basic concepts of discrimination differ without rhyme or reason in the hotchpotch of different statutes and regulations. The equality agencies that were created to tackle entrenched discriminatory practices by means of strategic law enforcement have never treated that as their main priority, and are not resourced to do so.

However, rather than introduce an Equality Bill to clarify and simplify the law, the government has used cramped, delegated legislation to give effect to the European equality directives. By deciding not to bring in primary legislation, it has fettered Parliament's ability to legislate to tackle unjustifiable discrimination, in the words of New Labour's 1997 election

---

23 B. Hepple et al., *Equality: A New Framework – Report of the Independent Review of the Enforcement of UK Anti-Discrimination Legislation* (2000).
24 id., para. 2.91.

manifesto, 'wherever it exists'. The government has put the cart before the horse for reasons of short-term political expediency.

On 14 January 2003, we introduced an Equality Bill as a Private Member's Bill in the House of Lords. The Bill sought to address the serious defects of current equality legislation, setting out a single framework for eliminating discrimination and promoting equality between different people, regardless of their racial or ethnic origin, religion or belief, sex, marital or family status, sexual orientation, gender reassignment, age or disability. The introduction of the Bill was preceded by a thorough consultation exercise and enjoyed widespread support. The Bill passed successfully through the House of Lords[25] and moved to the House of Commons. The Bill was supported by Angela Eagle MP (former Minister for Race Relations) along with Vera Baird QC MP and Norman Lamb MP (Liberal Democrat Treasury Spokesperson). The Bill received a tremendous welcome in the Commons with over 246 MPs signing an Early Day Motion in support. Without the necessary government support, the Bill fell at the end of that session. Subsequent calls for a Single Equality Act have been made by the equality commissions and by a large number of organizations and charities concerned with equality and human rights, so far in vain. It will be impossible to achieve parity across the equality strands within a new commission if it is underpinned with legislation which does not provide an equal level of protection against different forms of discrimination. It will also hamper the effectiveness of the commission's work if it has to work with the existing mess of legislation.

2. *The second condition*

That the commission's leadership is chosen to ensure that it is, and is seen to be, independent of government. Many in the field have expressed concern that the new commission will not be genuinely independent but will be subject to government interference. What is required is a whole new approach to the structure and composition of the commission to ensure uncompromising independence and accountability to Parliament. In its Eleventh Report, the Joint Committee on Human Rights considered different models which would be capable of achieving these aims. It was convinced that the new commission should not be modelled on the standard non-departmental public body but should have the character of a constitutional watchdog like the Parliamentary Commissioner for Administration, the National Audit Office, and the Electoral Commission.[26]

The Joint Committee went on to recommend that the chair of the commission should be defined in statute as an 'officer of Parliament'. There should be between eight and fifteen commissioners. Dismissal of a

25 Lord Lester, 645 *H.L. Debs.*, col. 525 (28 February 2003).
26 JCHR, Eleventh Report, op. cit., n. 14, p. 45.

commissioner within the fixed term of appointment should be effected only by a Joint Address of both Houses, or otherwise only on the recommendation of a statutory committee, which should be appointed to approve and oversee the commission's budget and strategic plan. There should be no power of direction or veto over the commission, in relation to the promotion and protection of human rights, either by Minister or by Parliament. The statutory committee should recommend commissioners for appointment whom the Secretary of State for Constitutional Affairs would recommend for appointment by Her Majesty. The commission should be required to make an annual report to Parliament, which should be laid before each House and there should be a committee of both Houses charged with considering the reports of the commission.[27] These elements would ensure that the new commission is independent and accountable. The vision for the new commission must be of a fully professional body, which is not permitted to become unwieldy, with commissioners and senior staff appointed for their expertise, knowledge, and experience to enable them to further the aims of the commission.

3. *The third condition*

This concerns resources. In terms of the commission's funding and staffing, the resources must be sufficient to ensure that it is able to tackle unjustifiable discrimination wherever it exists, as well as tackling breaches of human rights beyond the equality field. Resourcing is crucial for the credibility of the commission as well as ensuring that the focus of the work of the commission is on achieving its aims rather than struggling to stretch its budget between competing equality strands and human rights. Without adequate resources the commission will not achieve the necessary professional standards required for its demanding tasks.

4. *The fourth condition*

The chair and other members of the commission and their staff must be both able and willing to carry out their vital strategic law enforcement functions as a main priority and not as an optional extra, and to do so to the best professional standards that one finds in other enforcement agencies. The existing equality commissions have not treated strategic law enforcement as a priority and are not currently staffed to do so. The mandate in the White Papers, *Equality for Women*[28] and *Racial Discrimination*,[29] has not been

---

27 id., pp. 45–7.
28 Home Office, *Equality for women. A policy for equal opportunity* (1974; Cmnd. 5724) see para 110: 'The Commission's main functions will be strategic: to identify and eliminate discriminatory practices.'
29 Home Office, *Racial Discrimination* (1975; Cmnd. 6234).

implemented. New legislation needs to tackle this too. The new commission must not be an amalgamation of the existing equality commissions and their staff but a genuinely new and powerful body. The dead weight of custom and practice for over 30 years and the protection of jobs for the staff of the old commissions must not be allowed to rule the future commission; otherwise, it will be doomed from the start to a lack of effective law enforcement.

5. *The fifth condition*

The commission must have sufficient powers to investigate practices and procedures that are incompatible not only with equality standards but also with human rights standards, including the power to obtain information and to bring legal proceedings for breaches of the Convention rights. There is little point in creating a toothless human rights commission as a statutory pressure group.

6. *The sixth condition*

The commission's task in promoting a culture of respect for human rights must not weaken effective action to tackle discrimination. There must be no levelling down of existing protection against discrimination, but a levelling up. This will be vital, but difficult to achieve. This levelling up is linked not only to the need for a Single Equality Act but also to the recognition that the promotion and protection of equality itself in the context of human rights should be the core aim of the commission, and the priority of the commissioners. Obviously tensions exist between particular equality strands, for example, sexual orientation and religion or belief, but it will be easier to overcome these tensions if there is a common shared vision of equality for all.

7. *The seventh condition*

The commission must give and be seen to give equal protection to all the victims of the different forms of discrimination. This must be done in a way that will not tear the fabric of the commission and make it into a body of separate, competing compartments.

8. *The eighth condition*

The commission's mandate must cover not only human rights in the context of equality but all the human rights, economic and social as well as civil and political, protected by the international human rights treaties by which the United Kingdom is bound. That is particularly important in the light of a European Charter of Fundamental Rights. If the commission is to deal only with human rights in the context of equality, it will not be a human rights commission worthy of the name.

178

Following the government's announcement, the Joint Committee published a report in April 2004 considering in detail the functions, powers and structure of the proposed commission as they relate to human rights.[30] The Joint Committee hoped that the government would take its report into account when drawing up their White Paper. However, the White Paper, *Fairness For All*,[31] was published only days after the Joint Committee report, and did not take it into account at all. This led to an exchange of reports, with the Joint Committee producing another report,[32] commenting on the White Paper, and the government, in July 2004. responding to the Joint Committee's April report.[33] There are several areas of agreement between the Joint Committee's recommendations and government proposals. However, there are critical gaps in the government's proposals which need to be plugged if the commission is to be effective.

The White Paper is lopsided in its treatment of equality and other human rights, with a marked focus on the former. The key functions of the commission in its equality agenda, beyond providing support for all six equality areas (age, disability, gender, race, religion or belief, and sexual orientation), are identified as encouraging awareness and good practice on equality and diversity, promoting equality of opportunity, working towards eliminating unlawful discrimination and harassment, and promoting good relations. The strategic law enforcement powers are played down.

On the human rights side, the emphasis is on promotion. There is currently no institutional support for human rights and it is plainly important for the commission to promote a culture of respect for human rights. Indeed, promotion is the primary competence required of national human rights commissions by the UN Paris Principles.[34] The White Paper sets out laudable aims, with the expectation that the commission will spread good practice and promote support for human rights throughout the public sector, in addition to providing public education and promoting good community relations through a human rights framework. But the first competence required by the Paris Principles is not just promotion; they recommend that, 'a national institution shall be vested with competence to promote *and protect* human rights.' In its Eleventh Report, the Joint Committee expressed concern that the White Paper does not deal adequately with the precise nature of the general duty to be

---

30 JCHR, Eleventh Report, op. cit., n. 14.
31 DTI, *Fairness For All: A New Commission for Equality and Human Rights* (2004; Cm. 6185).
32 JCHR, Sixteenth Report, *Commission for Equality and Human Rights: The Government's White Paper*, HL 156/ HC 998 (2003–04).
33 *Government Response to the Joint Committee on Human Rights Eleventh Report of Session 2003–04, Commission for Equality and Human Rights: Structure, Functions and Powers* (2004).
34 UN Doc. A/RES/48/134 (20 December 1993).

179

placed upon the new commission in relation to the promotion and protection of human rights. The Joint Committee stated:

> We remind the Government that we said in our [Eleventh] Report that the new body should be given the general duty 'to promote understanding and awareness, *and to help secure the protection*, of human rights in Great Britain'. It would not be sufficient if the mandate of the new commission were to be without reference to helping to secure the *protection* of these rights, or if this aspect of its mandate were to be couched as a function rather than a duty.[35]

Furthermore, the White Paper does not deal with the introduction of a public sector duty relating to human rights, which was recommended by the Joint Committee as a way of ensuring the advancement of a culture of respect for human rights, and providing a statutory framework within which the commission would be responsible for giving guidance to public authorities on the implementation of the duties. In its response to the Joint Committee's Eleventh Report, the government stated that it 'is not persuaded that positive statutory duties in relation to human rights, going beyond those contained in the Human Rights Act, are needed.'[36] They did not give their reasons for this negative conclusion.

The overwhelming majority of responses generally support the establishment of a commission.[37] The exceptions are black and minority ethnic organizations and most notably, the Commission for Racial Equality (CRE). In August 2004, the CRE published its response to the White Paper, rejecting the proposals contained within *Fairness For All*. In the foreword to the response, CRE chair Trevor Phillips described the tests the CRE had applied to the proposed body, specifically 'is it right in principle?', 'will it work in practice?', and is 'it better than what we have now?' He concluded that the 'proposed Commission for Equality and Human Rights, as set out in the White Paper, Fairness for All, fails the test.'[38] The CRE is of the opinion that implementation of the White Paper would:

> weaken the cause of equality overall, and racial equality specifically, and offer so little to the so-called 'new strands' that the relevant groups would receive second class protection ... For the CRE specifically, the proposals would reduce our (or a successor body's) impact and authority; and the process of merger would destroy our capacity to reduce conflict within communities to combat the rise of racist sentiment and organisations, and to meet the challenging objectives set for us by the government itself.[39]

The CRE has not recognized the potential value of a single commission as a one-stop shop for people who may have been discriminated against on more than one ground. A black woman claiming discrimination currently has

---

35 JCHR, Sixteenth Report, op. cit., n. 32, p. 8.
36 *Government Response,* op. cit., n. 33, p. 3.
37 *Summary of Consultation Responses* in DTI, op. cit., n. 31.
38 See <www.cre.gov.uk>.
39 *Summary of Consultation Responses* in DTI, op. cit., n. 31.

to approach two separate commissions, the CRE and the EOC. Further complications arise if religious belief is also a factor. The resistance by the CRE to a single commission is damaging and divisive, and will not benefit the victims of discrimination.

Many of the responses to the White Papers from charities, NGOs, and other interested organizations share the Joint Committee's concerns about the lack of a public sector duty, including Help the Aged and Liberty, who believe that a positive duty is necessary to ensure optimum public authority compliance and urge the government to reconsider its position.[40] As the Joint Committee observed:

> the central task of 'promotion' of human rights does not just mean effective public relations, advertising and education, but also effective, credible inquiries backed up by necessary investigative powers.[41]

INVESTIGATIONS

A potentially powerful tool for the new commission will be the ability to conduct public inquiries into matters of public policy and practice relating to human rights. As the Joint Committee emphasized:

> the power to conduct public inquiries should be a novel, free-standing power in relation to matters of public policy which engage human rights, not dependent on equality issues being engaged and the use of the existing anti-discrimination powers that will be vested in the new commission.[42]

The government agrees with this, although the commission will not perform named investigations[43] into human rights cases.[44] The White Paper proposes that the commission will:

> have a power to carry out general inquiries into issues of public interest relevant to the groups protected by discrimination legislation and to human rights.[45]

The Joint Committee has emphasized the importance of adequate investigatory powers for the new commission. This conviction was strengthened following the Joint Committee's recent visit to the South African Human Rights Commission.[46] That Commission has powers to call

---

40 See Liberty's response to the DTI, op. cit., n. 3, in August 2004, and also the response of Help the Aged.
41 JCHR, Eleventh Report, op. cit., n. 14, p. 22.
42 id., p, 23.
43 That is, investigations into a named individual, company, or organization where there is a reasonable suspicion that an unlawful act of discrimination or harassment has taken place. See DTI, op. cit., n. 31, paras. 4.24–4.30.
44 *Government Response*, op. cit., n. 33, p. 5.
45 DTI, op. cit., n. 31, para. 4.3.
46 JCHR, Sixteenth Report, op. cit., n. 32, p. 12.

for persons and papers, and to enter and search premises. Its members view these powers as extremely important. It has used its powers on occasion to require information from government departments, and to subpoena provincial government leaders, a Cabinet Minister, and the head of the defence force. The Commission has also found it necessary to use its powers of entry, on one occasion, to gain access to private sector premises. Like the CRE or the EOC, the South African Commission uses these coercive powers only in the last resort. But it is essential to possess them if the new commission is to be taken seriously in tackling human rights problems beyond the equality field.

JUDICIAL REVIEW

The White Paper is silent on the question of whether the commission should have any judicial review power in relation to human rights. The Joint Committee has clearly stated that:

> We remain convinced that it will be essential to give the power to seek judicial review under the Human Rights Act to the Commission for Equality and Human Rights. Without it, it will be neutered.[47]

The Joint Committee has identified the benefits of permitting the commission to seek judicial review – before individuals are victimized.[48] In their *Eleventh Report,* the Joint Committee reasoned that:

> In the long run it could help reduce demand on court resources, which would be required to deal with less well-informed and more partial challenges. The bringing of one focused public interest claim by a body such as the commission might actually prevent the courts from being unduly burdened ... an inquiry power without the long-stop of any enforcement mechanism (or route to test the findings in the courts) would be damaging to the credibility of the commission. Finally, and perhaps most importantly ... there is a wider public interest in ensuring that public authorities comply with the law. It would be an indefensible situation in which a commission set up for the express purpose of promoting and protecting human rights was able to identify what it believed were threats to those rights, and no steps were available to enable it to apply to the courts to remove those threats.[49]

The Joint Committee concluded:

> We recommend that the commission should have a power, notwithstanding the provisions of section 7(3) and (4) of the Human Rights Act, to seek judicial review of the policies or actions or omissions of a public authority where it has reason to believe that such policies or actions or omissions have resulted, or are likely to result, in a violation of the Convention rights.[50]

47 id., p. 15.
48 JCHR, Eleventh Report, op. cit., n. 14, p. 36.
49 id., para. 91.
50 id., p. 36, para. 92.

The Joint Committee went on to explain that it would be desirable to achieve this aim by amending section 7 of the Human Rights Act itself (to allow the new commission to bring cases in which there is no individual victim).

Many organizations, including JUSTICE, the Institute for Public Policy Research (IPPR), and the Equality and Diversity Forum, have voiced support for the commission to have judicial review powers in human rights cases. Liberty agrees with the Joint Committee and specifically disagrees with the government in its assessment that allowing such powers would give the commission a 'distinctly litigious character'. The Law Society also supports the case for judicial review and moreover, would like to see the commission able to seek, in judicial review proceedings, interpretative declarations under section 3 of the Human Rights Act or declarations of incompatibility under section 4.

However, the government has concluded that:

> the balance of the argument is against such a power, even in the slightly limited form proposed by the Committee ... Empowering the Commission, additionally, to judicially review public authorities on human rights grounds would undoubtedly give the body a distinctly litigious character, which the Government wishes to avoid. It would also be likely to place the new body under considerable pressure from all other bodies who wish to see judicial review on human rights grounds but are themselves subject to the general ban.[51]

We are wholly unpersuaded by these arguments. They fail to understand the safeguards that exist against the abuse of judicial review, or the history of the effective use of judicial review by the CRE and the EOC. Without the power to seek judicial review, the commission will be unable to tackle human rights abuses effectively in the public interest.

THE REPUBLIC OF IRELAND[52]

The powers and functions of the Irish Human Rights Commission are set out in the Human Rights Commission Acts 2000 and 2001. Chapter 6 of the Good Friday Agreement, 1998, sets out the roles of the Human Rights Commission, the Northern Ireland Human Rights Commission, and the Joint Committee of Representatives of the two Human Rights Commissions. The Human Rights Commission Act 2000 confers a wide-ranging jurisdiction on the Commission to promote and protect human rights as defined both in international agreements to which Ireland is a party and in the Constitution. The functions of the Commission include conducting enquiries. The Commission has the means to obtain information, with recourse to the courts, if necessary. The Commission can also offer its expertise in human

51 *Government Response*, op. cit., n. 33, p. 8.
52 See <www.ihrc.ie>.

rights law to the courts in suitable cases as *amicus curiae*, in cases involving human rights issues and take legal proceedings to vindicate human rights in the State or provide legal assistance to persons in this regard.

NORTHERN IRELAND

The Northern Ireland Act 1998 created the Northern Ireland Human Rights Commission as a central part of the Belfast/Good Friday Agreement. There is a separate Equality Commission for Northern Ireland. The Chief Commissioner for the Northern Ireland Human Rights Commission, Professor Brice Dickson, has commented that although the Human Rights Commission plays an important role in trying to ensure that the laws and practices of Northern Ireland comply with internationally recognized human rights standards, the Commission is still primarily an advisory body and it cannot guarantee that its advice will be implemented by other public bodies.[53] However, the Commission does have power to take cases to court.

One lesson that the government should learn from Northern Ireland is the importance of the detail and clarity of the legislation that establishes the powers of the new commission for Great Britain. The Northern Ireland Act 1998 has been criticized for making insufficiently detailed provision for the Commission's powers, as well as for failing to arm the Commission with any investigatory powers to require the production of evidence to it inquiries. This has resulted in a number of refusals by public bodies of requests for information and the involvement of the courts in helping to determine the scope of the Commission's powers.[54]

To give a recent example[55] of how the Northern Ireland Human Rights Commission's investigatory powers have been hampered, in March 2002, the Commission published research reviewing the conditions under which children and young people are detained in the criminal justice system in Northern Ireland. The report contained some 170 recommendations aimed at improving the care of children in custody. Since last year, the Commission has attempted to obtain permission to visit Rathgael Juvenile Justice Centre to carry out research on how those recommendations have been implemented. The Northern Ireland Office (NIO) refused the Commission access, claiming it had no right of access under its powers. In July 2004, the Commission was granted leave to take judicial review proceedings against the Secretary of State, challenging the decision of the NIO to refuse the Commission access to Rathgael. Lord Justice Weatherup granted leave for the Commission to review the Secretary of State based on two key points:

---

53 Lester and Pannick, op. cit., n. 16, p. 581.
54 See Joint Committee on Human Rights, Fourteenth Report, *Work of the Northern Ireland Human Rights Commission*, HL (2002–03) 132/HC (2002–03) 142.
55 See <www.nihrc.org>.

first, that the Commission has a legitimate expectation of cooperation from the government given its previous commitment to cooperation, clearly stated to Parliament, and, secondly, that the NIO has wrongly assumed that the Commission's powers in this case may only be exercised where no other statutory provisions exist for the type of work proposed by the Commission.

The Chief Executive of the Northern Ireland Human Rights Commission, Paddy Sloan said:

> It is very disappointing that we should have to resort to the courts to secure the co-operation of the NIO on this matter. The Secretary of State has been considering a Review of the Commission's powers since March 2001, without any definitive response. It is quite unacceptable that despite Parliamentary assertion of full co-operation, a simple follow-up exercise such as is proposed should be blocked by the NIO. The Commission has a supportive, not inspectorate role and is very conscious of its responsibility to protect and promote the human rights of the children and young people who are currently held in custody.[56]

After five years in operation, there is much to learn from the Northern Ireland experience and yet, 'the Commission's very existence appears to have eluded the authors of the White Paper'.[57] However, the Commission has wise advice for the government on litigation and judicial review:[58]

> The NIHRC ... has power to bring proceedings to court in its own name. This too is an extremely important provision. It means that the Commission can take cases over and above those in which it would already have a sufficient interest for the purposes of the law of standing in judicial review. Some would argue that endowing a statutory equality and human rights body with the power to go to court in its own name is the best possible indication of such a body's independence and effectiveness. If it cannot access the courts in an attempt to correct human rights abuses allegedly perpetrated by public authorities, the government included, then it would be a poor watchdog indeed. For the avoidance of doubt it might also be advisable to specify in the legislation that the CEHR has the power to apply for judicial review of decisions by public authorities which may breach the European Convention on Human Rights.

We agree with this advice.

POTENTIAL ROLE AND IMPACT

The new commission has the potential to make a significant impact on the development of a culture of human rights in Britain, provided that the government meet the concerns summarized in this paper. The government's decision to proceed with the setting up of the commission provides an

---

56 id.
57 See *'Fairness for All' – Response of the Northern Ireland Human Rights Commission to the Consultation on a New Commission for Equality and Human Rights* (2004).
58 id., para. 25.

important opportunity to design and create an independent and really effective body. The Canadian Human Rights Commission has interpreted its mandate to advance equal opportunity broadly. The human rights laws, the Equal Employment Act, and the Charter of Rights and Freedoms have all played a part in creating a culture of human rights in Canada. Surveys have shown that the Charter enjoys a high level of support across the country. Canadians are proud of their Charter and for the majority it has become an important symbol of Canadian identity.[59] There is no reason why, similarly, we cannot build a culture of respect for human rights in this country. There is a pressing need for a new and effective Commission for Equality and Human Rights, but the government has yet to demonstrate that it is willing to create a body worthy of the name.

SUMMARY OF RECOMMENDATIONS

A Commission for Equality and Human Rights worthy of the name needs:

- **A single Equality Act**, to replace the incoherent tangle of existing legislation;
- **Uncompromising independence** from government interference, and accountability to Parliament;
- **Sufficient resources** to tackle unjustifiable discrimination and breaches of human rights beyond the equality field;
- **Strategic law enforcement** to be treated by the new commission as a priority;
- **Adequate powers**, including the power to obtain information and apply for judicial review;
- **No levelling down of existing protection against discrimination**, but a levelling up;
- **Equal protection to all victims of discrimination** and the avoidance of separate competing compartments within the commission;
- **Broad human rights mandate** to cover the economic, social, civil, and political rights protected by international human rights treaties by which the United Kingdom is bound.

59 JCHR, Sixth Report, op. cit., n. 11, p. 26.

JOURNAL OF LAW AND SOCIETY
VOLUME 32, NUMBER 1, MARCH 2005
ISSN: 0263-323X, pp. 187–201

Constitutional Reform, the Lord Chancellor, and Human Rights: The Battle of Form and Substance

ROGER SMITH*

This article examines the impact of the Human Rights Act on the government's constitutional proposals for reform of the role of the Lord Chancellor and the appointment of the judiciary. It also looks at the uncertain acceptance of a 'human rights' culture by the department charged with lead responsibility for its implementation. It concludes that the government went further than was required in reforming the role of the Lord Chancellor. As a consequence, considerable – and possibly undue – weight now hangs on the enlarged role of the Lord Chief Justice. Meanwhile, the Department of Constitutional Affairs and its ministers have rejected the 'rule of law' brief of the Lord Chancellor without clarity as to where such responsibilities might now be adequately located within government.

The Human Rights Act 1998 delivered three landmines with sufficient potential to shudder the foundations of the constitution. None of the three have yet fully detonated – though the initial reforming blasts are beginning to be felt. The three were:

(i) The disguised, but real, shift of power to the judiciary implemented by section three and the accompanying tremor to the doctrine of parliamentary sovereignty – with judges injuncted: 'So far as it is possible to do so, primary legislation and subordinate legislation must be read and given effect in a way which is compatible with Convention rights';[1]

(ii) The delayed effects of incorporation of the fair trial rights in article six for constitutional conventions governing the role of the Lord Chancellor and the appellate committee of the House of Lords;

(iii) The overall creation of a 'human rights culture', extolled both by the Act's author, Lord Irvine, and his successor, Lord Falconer, as its most

* Director, JUSTICE, 59 Carter Lane, London EC4V 5AQ, England

1 s. 3(1) Human Rights Act 1998.

important objective, with the former confidently predicting, in his speech to the House of Lords on the Second Reading of the Bill: 'A culture of awareness of human rights will develop'.[2]

As to the first, the judiciary are working their way through the implications. The House of Lords has recently urged more boldness, with a comprehensive analysis of decided cases leading Lord Steyn to conclude that the law had 'taken a wrong turn' and that 'a broad approach' was required.[3] As to the second, the fate of the Constitutional Reform Bill has dominated the work of the Department of Constitutional Affairs since it was so surprisingly announced in June 2003. The third is perhaps the most powerful in the longer term. Here, government ministers have taken to berating lawyers as diverting the Human Rights Act into the courts but some attention is required in their own articulations – if not formulations – of policy.

THE LORD CHANCELLOR: ENDGAME (ALMOST)

The role of the Lord Chancellor was under strain well before the advent of the Human Rights Act. Its fusion of executive, legislative, and judicial powers flew in the face of political ideas of the separation of powers in countries more influenced by the French Revolution than the United Kingdom. However, their merger in the role of Lord Chancellor increasingly manifested a wider range of difficulties than could be dismissed as academic, abstract, and theoretical. Lord Mackay of Clashfern, Lord Irvine's predecessor, recognized the tensions but gave a characteristically elegant defence of the time-honoured mix of roles in his Hamlyn lectures. He stressed, as had other holders of the office, such as Lord Hailsham, the value of his own very personal role in the making of judicial appointments:[4]

> The importance of appointments, and the nature of the tenure to which judges are appointed, has meant that those who have this responsibility [of judicial appointment] have discharged it with a close, strong and personal interest and a feeling of immense responsibility. To diffuse that responsibility would, I believe, lose an essential element to the system which has produced a judiciary of very high standing.

Force was given to Lord Mackay's argument because there could have been no doubt as to the integrity of his own approach to the appointment process. His successor, Lord Irvine, ran into accusations of cronyism, at least in relation to appointment of Treasury Counsel, but was similarly unimpressed by arguments for reform:

2 Lord Irvine of Lairg, *Human Rights, Constitutional Law and the Development of the English Legal System* (2003) 8-9.
3 *Ghaidan* v. *Godin Mondoza* [2004] U.K.H.L. 30, at paras. 39 and 41.
4 Mackay of Clashfern, *The Administration of Justice: The Hamlyn Lectures of 1993* (1994).

188

Judicial independence in principle and practice is fundamental to the functioning of a parliamentary democracy and to freedom under the law. And ... our constitutional settlement, including the Law Lords, and the office of Lord Chancellor, provides for both independence and accountability ... These features of our constitution have as relevant and useful a part to play in the future as they do in the past.[5]

Lords Mackay and Irvine deployed the traditional defences of the role, as it has developed over the centuries and subject to the conventions which had developed around it by the late-twentieth century. The office is, of course, extremely old. A credible claim can be made for Angmendus as the first office-holder in the year 605, though something more like the modern combination of roles is better dated from the eleventh century. Amongst a galaxy of stars, the 296 Lord Chancellors (including the reluctant Lord Falconer) included at least three saints, Thomas à Becket, Swithin, and Sir Thomas More, together with the somewhat more venal Cardinal Wolsey (an ironic self-comparison with whom was to dog Lord Irvine's reign). The only gap in succession was for five years after the Glorious Revolution in 1688 when the post lapsed.[6]

In truth, of course, the office evolved considerably over that time. Mid-twentieth-century apologists tended to deploy the justification, articulated by its inter-war permanent secretary Lord Schuster, that the role provided 'some kind of link or buffer' between executive and judiciary, or that of his successor, Sir Albert Napier, that it was a form of constitutional 'hinge'.[7] That hinge, link or buffer existed not only at a bureaucratic level: it was manifest in the judiciary themselves at the highest level. Experience as a politician was seen as desirable for appointment to high judicial office. Lord Halsbury was famously observed 'almost invariably to put service to the Conservative Party above judicial qualities'.[8] As late as 1974, half of the ten Law Lords had political experience.[9] Fashions and constitutional conventions change. By contrast, in 2004, none of the twelve Law Lords had been a Member of Parliament.

The Human Rights Act, with its incorporation of Article 6 rights to trial by 'an independent and impartial tribunal', was always going to be a threat to some part of the Lord Chancellor's multiple roles – though more directly to the Lord Chancellor sitting as a judge than his role in appointment of the judiciary. A report to the Parliamentary Assembly of the Council of Europe by a Dutch jurist, Erik Jurgens, in 2002 provided a well argued indictment of the office – based expressly both on the effect of Article 6 and separation of

5 Irvine, op. cit., n. 2, p. 208.
6 BBC News, 13 June 2003, 'End of Historic Post'.
7 For example, G. Drewry, 'Thatcherism catches up with the judiciary' <www.fu.uni-lj.si/egpa2004/html/sg5/SG5_Drewry.pdf>.
8 B. Abel Smith and R. Stevens, *In Search of Justice* (1976), quoted in D. Woodhouse, *The Office of Lord Chancellor* (2001) 139.
9 Woodhouse, id., p. 140.

powers. He reported to the Legal Affairs and Human Rights committee that the position in the United Kingdom:

> May ... cause confusion, or be abused, in the new member countries of the Council of Europe, where the Council of Europe is repeatedly stressing the judiciary should be a completely independent branch of government.[10]

It was somewhat embarrassing to the United Kingdom government to be held as supporting a basic constitutional flaw that would not be accepted by the Council in the case of countries like Romania and Bulgaria, newly freed from the yoke of communism and tentatively emerging into the European democratic space.

The concern of the Council of Europe was not necessarily terminal of the Lord Chancellor's office: it was concerned with only two aspects:

(i) at present, the Lord Chancellor continues actively to engage in his judicial role – albeit infrequently and apparently only in cases not involving government interests – creating a potential conflict of interest with his executive position and thus calling into question the independence and impartiality of the head of the judiciary and of the highest court;

(ii) he also continues to play an important, if limited, role in the legislative process as Speaker of the House of Lords, creating a potential conflict with his judicial position (accentuated by the fact that all other 'Law Lords' are also members of the House of Lords capable of intervening in legislative activity).[11]

The Parliamentary Assembly received Mr Jurgens report only after the United Kingdom government announced its reform programme in June 2003. No doubt with some relief, the Assembly was able to say that it 'very much' welcomed the government's proposals.[12]

Some teeth were given to the reflections of Mr Jurgens by a decision of the European Court of Justice in 2000 but, again, the issue at stake was just one of the Lord Chancellor's roles: that of sitting judge. The court decided that the multiple roles of the Bailiff of the Royal Court of Guernsey fell foul of the provisions of Article 6. The case was taken by a Mr McGonnell. The factual and substantive basis of his claim were, perhaps, dubious. He converted a packing shed into a house or land zoned for agricultural use, having been refused planning permission for residential use on a number of occasions. Subsequently, the Deputy Bailiff of Guernsey had presided over a debate in the legislature ('the States of Deliberation') over whether the land should be rezoned. The States rejected the idea. There seems to be no

---

10 'Office of the Lord Chancellor in the constitutional system of the United Kingdom', Doc. 9798, 28 April 2003.
11 Parliamentary Assembly, Council of Europe, 'Office of the Lord Chancellor in the constitutional system of the United Kingdom', Resolution 1342 (2003).
12 id., para. 6.

190

suggestion that the Bailiff actually spoke in the debate or even expressed a personal view. Some time afterwards, then promoted to Bailiff, the same man presided over the court that rejected a further challenge by Mr McGonnell to the effects of the failure to rezone – a judgment that again does not appear to have been substantively incorrect. Nevertheless, the majority of the European Court (20–5) found that:

> The mere fact that the Deputy Bailiff presided over the States of Deliberation when [planning zoning was upheld] is capable of casting doubt on his impartiality when he subsequently determined, as the sole judge of law in the case, the applicant's planning appeal. The applicant therefore had legitimate grounds for fearing that the Bailiff may have been influenced by his prior participation ... That doubt, however slight its justification, is sufficient to vitiate the impartiality of the Royal Court. It follows that there has been a breach of Article 6(1).[13]

This applied an extremely tight test, over which a number of judges on the court expressed some reservation. Sir John Laws, sitting as an ad hoc judge, made it clear that he based his decision on the facts that the same actual person had performed the role of judge and legislator. He specifically stated:

> If it were thought arguable that a violation might be shown on a wider basis, having regard to the Bailiff's multiple roles, I would express my firm dissent from such a view.[14]

It is important to note that the core strictures of the McGonnell judgement and the Jurgens opinion could have been met if the Lord Chancellor had ceased to sit as a judge in the House of Lords. It might also have been necessary for the Law Lords to have taken a vow of silence in parliamentary debate. In such a case, the storm might have passed and the old arrangements evolved into something new. However, even the most modern Lord Chancellors demanded the right to sit and would not renounce their historic rights. Lord Mackay might have had some justification since he had been a Lord of Appeal in Ordinary in his own right before appointment as Lord Chancellor. He sat for 60 days during his decade as Lord Chancellor. Lord Irvine, more rarely described as judicial in character, carried on the tradition and sat for 18 during his five years.[15] Both asserted that they did not sit in cases that would cause conflict of interest, though Lord Mackay found himself in *Pepper* v. *Hart*[16] which concerned whether records of parliamentary debates could be referred to as an aid to statutory construction – a matter on which a government minister might be thought to have a particular view.

Voices for reform from concerned interest groups were slowly joined by senior members of the judiciary and the Bar. A head of steam for some measure of reform was building up. JUSTICE was early in the field, arguing

13 *McGonnell* v. *UK* (2000) 30 E.H.R.R. 289, at para. 2(k).
14 id., at para. 64.
15 <http://www.wordiq.com>.
16 *Pepper* v. *Hart* [1992] 3 W.L.R. 1032.

since the early 1970s for reform of judicial appointments and the Lord Chancellor's role. The Legal Action Group joined the chorus for a Ministry of Justice in the 1990s. More recently, senior Law Lords began to agitate for reform. Lord Steyn called for a Supreme Court separate from the House of Lords in his Neill lecture of 2002. Lord Bingham made a series of speeches in which he agreed, suggesting also that the Lord Chancellor might curtail his sitting as a judge. He was, however, supportive of the continuation of the Lord Chancellor's responsibility for judicial appointment and also 'as the guarantor, at the highest level of government, of the values of the legal system and the rule of law.'[17] Other influential voices added themselves to this refrain. For example, Lord Alexander of Weedon QC backed a Supreme Court and a somewhat similar role for the Lord Chancellor:

> What I believe would strengthen government and open accountability would be the transfer of the more overtly political functions of the Lord Chancellor to other departments, leaving him to have the still-large role of court administration with responsibility for non-political law reform and for appointing judges. In the latter task, he could, and I believe should, be assisted by an appointments commission which advises him and presents him with choices of names for individual posts.[18]

Another force for change was, however, at work that would have made Lord Alexander's solution difficult to provide constitutional stability. Increasingly, the pressures of modern government – and, in particular, those of resources as well as free market ideology – brought the office holder into conflict with the legal world of which he was such a doyen. Lord Alexander himself, when Chairman of the Bar Council, had mounted a successful legal challenge on the level of remuneration offered by Lord Hailsham to barristers on legal aid. In consequence, the direct statutory link between payments for legally aided work and privately funded cases was abolished. As legal aid expenditure climbed through the 1990s – hitting an annual £1 billion early in the decade and rising to almost £2 billion in the next – no Lord Chancellor could meet the expectations, legitimate or otherwise, of both branches of the legal profession. Legal aid rates inevitably fell relative to privately funded work. Furthermore, Lord Mackay's proposals for reform of the profession brought down a firestorm on his head that exposed a breach between the legal profession and any ministerial advancement of policies that were seen as hostile to its interests. Lord Lane called a Judges' Council meeting to discuss Lord Mackay's proposals, effectively closing the courts for its duration and prompting press comparison with a strike. Lord Ackner, then a sitting Law Lord, complained that proposals to breach the monopoly of the Bar's advocacy rights:

---

17 'The Evolving Constitution', JUSTICE Annual Lecture, 4 October 2001.
18 Denning Society Lecture, 30 October 2001.

raised serious constitutional questions about the interference of the executive, both directly, with the legal profession and, thus, indirectly with the judiciary.[19]

If senior members of the judiciary were seriously to equate the constitutional imperative of judicial independence with maintenance of a strong (and largely publicly funded) Bar then a measure of conflict was bound, sooner or later, to be inescapable.

Meanwhile, there was another source of attack. Empirical information was emerging that questioned the professionalism of the process of the time-honoured system of judicial appointment. Lords Mackay and Irvine had seemed to have cleaned this up as much as was possible with reforms such as an extension of public advertisement of posts. However, close examination was to expose practices that were difficult to justify. The procedures for appointment had more defects in them that had been apparent. These emerged as the result of continued pressure, particularly from the Law Society which had an institutional interest in broadening appointments beyond the Bar. The Society participated in a wider group that produced a report, *Equal Opportunities in Judicial Appointments and Silk*,[20] which called for a 'wider range of positive action measures'.[21] Pressure reached a level to which Lord Irvine felt he had to respond and he did so in the classic way. He requested a report and appointed Sir Leonard Peach to review the system of appointment. Sir Leonard duly expressed his satisfaction: 'My assessment is that the procedures and execution are as good as any which I have seen in the Public Sector.'[22] He suggested, however, that: 'Confidence will be increased ... by the appointment of a Commissioner for Judicial Appointments and a number of Deputy Commissioners.'[23]

Thus, it looked as if matters might be amicably resolved by the appointment of a committee. Lord Irvine, no doubt hoping that the criticism had been blunted, was happy to appoint a set of commissioners of the kind that Sir Leonard had proposed. The chief commissioner was Sir Colin Campbell and the others were non-lawyers who were largely specialists in human resources. Alas, their judgement was not quite of the ringing kind that had perhaps been expected. The Commission for Judicial Appointments, so far from backing up Sir Leonard Peach's clean bill of health, revealed the need for technical improvements to the process of judicial appointment so that it meets adequate standards of human resources performance. The Commission announced in 2002 that, despite recent improvement, existing

---

19 As quoted in R. Abel, *English Lawyers between Market and State* (2003) 40.
20 Report of Joint Working Party, *Equal Opportunities in Judicial Appointments and Silk* (1999).
21 id., p. 6.
22 Covering letter, id.
23 Lord Chancellor's Department, *An Independent Scrutiny of the Appointment Processes of Judges and Queens Counsel in England and Wales* (1999).

procedures remained, at least in some aspects, 'opaque'; lacking in clear documentation and 'audit trails'; and subject to undue delay.[24] In its 2003 report, the Commission found failings of procedure but, more seriously, also of structure, identifying, for example:

> Apparent heavy reliance on automatic consultation, which may have disadvantaged suitable candidates who had less visibility to automatic consultees.[25]

The Commission, and Sir Colin in particular, became a vociferous advocate of further change and, in due course, argued for a particularly radical package of reform that included an independent commission with a lay chair and a majority of lay commissioners.[26] They undoubtedly gave a crucial dynamic force to the pressure for change.

Thus, although it came as an unexpected bombshell on the day, it was, at one level, no real surprise that the Blair government announced on the 12 June 2003 that the office of Lord Chancellor would be abolished, a Supreme Court established to take over from the appellate committee of the House of Lords, and the creation of a Judicial Appointments Commission. Out with the old went its defender, Lord Irvine, who had apparently expressed a reluctance at the last to fall on his sword with full equanimity. In came the more pliant Lord Falconer, former flatmate of the Prime Minister, veteran of the Dome, and champion of David Blunkett's Home Office policies. He immediately renounced any right to sit as a judge. It looked as if the office of Lord Chancellor was over.

THE WOOLF AT THE DOOR

The unexpectedness was not in the announcement of broad policy change but its timing, its manner, and its details. Lord Irvine was dismissed, apparently after a row with the Home Secretary as to the relative powers of the reformed ministry. The *Daily Telegraph* reported:

> He wanted criminal justice policy taken out of the hands of Mr Blunkett, with whom he had clashed over the independence of the judiciary.[27]

The reshuffle became mired in controversy because it was clear that a number of details had not properly been considered – not least the fact that legislation was required to abolish the office of Lord Chancellor. There then

---

24 id., paras 5.5–5.18.
25 id., para. 2.16.
26 H.M. Commissioners for Judicial Appointments, *Response to the Department of Constitutional Affairs Consultation Papers on Constitutional Reform* (2003) para. 3.4.
27 'Blair forced Irvine to resign in humiliating reshuffle row' *Daily Telegraph*, 15 June 2003.

followed a period of farce where the House of Lords, restive in any event over wider reform proposals for its membership, were uncooperative in releasing the Lord Chancellor from his role as its speaker. There was a background concern that Lord Falconer was considerably more compliant to the wishes of the executive than had been the prickly, and hitherto somewhat unappreciated, Lord Irvine.

Most significant in an appallingly handled announcement was the failure to consult the judiciary. From their corner emerged the Lord Chief Justice, a radical in his own right, respected within the world of the law almost to the level of saintliness. Lord Woolf knows a thing or two about public presentation and an elementary grasp of politics would have suggested that he was a man to be got on side for such a tricky set of reforms. It seems bizarre that this was not done. Certainly, the judiciary – unattracted by the substance of the proposals – built up a chorus of complaint. Lord Woolf's own hurt could still be felt as he announced, somewhat later, how he had managed to salvage something from what he saw as the mess that had been created:

> The question that needs to be asked is whether as part of the process of change we are paying sufficient attention to retaining or replacing the checks upon which, in the past, the delicate balance of our constitution has depended. Initially, the announcement may not have been seen as being of great significance.
> Certainly, the Government did not appreciate its significance because, if they had, it would have been announced in a different way. It was apparently seen by Government as a reform capable of being achieved by press release.[28]

Lord Woolf mobilized his considerable resources on behalf of the judiciary, swallowed his pride, and disappeared to negotiate with Lord Falconer. He emerged with a piece of paper, christened 'the concordat', in which the two made the best of a bad job. The details would be less relevant but for the fact that, to obtain peace with an outraged judiciary, Lord Falconer made concessions. He agreed that his powers as Secretary of State in relation to judicial appointment should be minimized; there should be a lay chairman and large group of lay members but not that they would be in the majority. He obtained agreement that judges of every level would be represented and that, expressly, the Lord Chief Justice would be consulted on appointments. Lord Woolf expressly assumed the mantle of the judiciary's advocate and made clear:

> I emphasise that what is announced is a package of proposals and I make it clear that the judiciary's endorsement is conditional on the proposals being implemented as a whole.[29]

---

28 Squire Centenary Lecture, 'The Rule of Law and a Change in the Constitution', 3 March 2004.
29 Lord Woolf, LCJ, 657 *H.L. Debs*. col. 22 (26 January 2004).

Lord Woolf was effectively announcing that debate was over. Thus it was that the continuing call from the Commission for Judicial Appointments for a majority of lay members looked vain in the face of the agreement that had been demanded by the judiciary and which Lord Falconer had little political room to deny. This may have been one of the casualties of the botched process of reform. It may also have been affected by a more widespread growth of distrust of government that was given momentum by issues around the Gulf War and the fulsome attacks on the judiciary indulged in by Labour's Home Secretary. The Commission's position is logical and its own work demonstrates how effective a lay body can be. In the current circumstances, however, there is the overwhelming problem that the appointment of a majority of lay members unavoidably gives enormous power to the executive. It is true that the composition of the existing commission shows how well the executive can demonstrate the worth of that trust. However, that trust does not currently exist over an appointing commission.

Lord Woolf postponed his retirement and got what he regarded as a reasonable settlement for the judiciary. A man of his word, he then backed the proposals and argued passionately that they should be implemented and not delayed by a recalcitrant House of Lords that yoked its annoyance at the government's hubris in relation to the Lord Chancellor with its anger at reform of its own membership. One of the consequences of this settlement is that the mantle of 'head of the judiciary' falls in practice on the Lord Chief Justice and will be recognized by a change of title that looks likely to become 'President of the Courts of England and Wales'. The President will have 'the statutory authority and, therefore, the authority to speak on behalf of the judiciary on matters that concern the judiciary'.[30] This, in its turn, may provoke difficulties. Lord Woolf expressly articulated the views of the judiciary, after consulting with them, on an issue on which it had a pretty consistent and widespread view. This will not always be the case. Further, we will see in due course whether subsequent holders of this somewhat politically exposed office will have the wisdom and presentational skills shown by the Lord Chief Justice as he fought to defuse this row. The judiciary may well throw up a succession of remarkable leaders of Lord Woolf's quality who will tread the difficult political path of expressing the views of an unelected judiciary to those that they would not accept were their democratic masters, popularly elected though they may be. The government might well have been better advised to have retained the Lord Chancellor role (whatever it was formally called) as a Minister within Government who saw the role as particularly orientated towards providing the appropriate hinge with the judiciary.

30 id., col. 24.

196

THE HUMAN RIGHTS ACT, THE RULE OF LAW, AND THE DEPARTMENT OF CONSTITUTIONAL AFFAIRS

Most advocates of a reformed Lord Chancellor's Department argued for a replacement body that would have been effectively a Ministry of Justice. In other words, a ministry would have been created very much in the mould of the Lord Chancellor's Department with its core responsibilities as the administration of justice, overseeing judicial appointment, the courts, and legal aid. Around the margins, there was debate about whether the new ministry would take responsibility for criminal procedure from the Home Office – the issue on which Lord Irvine was reported to have stuck.

The Prime Minister's decision was very different from this previous thinking. He created a Department of Constitutional Affairs whose remit included the Channel Islands, Freedom of Information, Human Rights, reform of the House of Lords, creating 'greater public trust', and elections – somewhat of a ragbag of responsibilities which formerly were the responsibility of the Home Office. Lord Falconer promoted a manifesto to celebrate the new department:

> The new Department represents a wholesale change from the work and priorities of the old [Lord Chancellor's Department]. The new Department is no longer built around the needs of a cabinet Minister who was head of the Judiciary and presided over the Lords. Now it is a mainstream public service delivery Department, delivering a court and justice system which provides people with security that the system will fight crime effectively ...[31]

Lord Woolf indicated that such a change of perspective was to be numbered among the reasons for his conversion to some version of the government's package of reform:

> The Department now has three Ministers in addition to the Lord Chancellor and two Permanent Secretaries. The junior ministers do not see themselves as mini-Lord Chancellors or as being subject to restraints that, by convention, apply to this role. They are, and see themselves as being, ministers having main-line departmental responsibilities.[32]

The new orientation of the department is confirmed by it statement of objectives and detailed 'performance targets' or 'public sector agreements', to which the Secretary of State announced his signature in July.[33] Given most prominence was to 'improve the delivery of justice by increasing the number of crimes for which an offender is brought to justice to 1.25 million by 2007–8.' None of the detailed objectives related to constitutional change or legal aid. This top goal is shared with the Home Office, indicating a problem foreshadowed in the DCA's manifesto. The DCA is the lead

---

31 DCA manifesto: <www.dca.gov.uk/dept/manifesto.htm>.
32 Squire lecture, op. cit., n. 28.
33 29 July 2004 see <www.dca.gov.uk>.

government department on human rights and on protection of an independent judiciary. Yet, it has selected one single indicator of improvements in the delivery of justice: an increase in findings of guilt. In doing so, it pays little attention to those of its responsibilities which are about guaranteeing the fair trial rights to due process set out in Article 6 of the Human Rights Act and which had led the government to such fundamental constitutional reform. This indicator is met by increase in the number of convictions. Actually, the DCA spends over £1 billion a year on funding criminal legal aid to ensure that Article 6 obligations are met. This is somewhat in conflict.

This fussiness of focus has practical effects. The department and its ministers have paid so little attention to human rights that it has been left to parliamentary Select Committees to identify its possible effect on proposed legislation advanced by the department. In relation to a draft Criminal Defence Service Bill, the Parliamentary Committee for Constitutional Affairs argued that the department had just ignored the implications of the Human Rights Act for its proposals. It was left to the chair of the Joint Parliamentary Committee on Human Rights to assert their relevance.[34] She identified three ways in which the department's proposals potentially broke Convention requirements to which the department had made no reference whatsoever – apparently oblivious to the relevance of human rights principles to its proposals.

The lack of any departmental objective on human rights raises issues as to the extent that the government, its ministers, and the DCA have institutionalized a human rights culture within the constitutional department charged with its responsibility. Its absence – and the presence of a rather bizarre choice of alternative objectives, such as time taken to complete certain types of case – might be seen as simply an ironic comment by the department on the value of such objective-setting exercises. The neutralizing of unworkable bureaucratic measures, such as nonsensical targets, is admittedly not without its value. The problem is that the DCA is manifestly not 'mainstreaming' human rights into its policies even though it has embarked on major and difficult constitutional reform, one stated objective of which was precisely to carry forward a human rights agenda. After all, the government cited the Human Rights Act as justification both for a judicial appointments commission, as '... [the existing] system ... is increasingly hard to reconcile with the demands of the Human Rights Act',[35] and the creation of a Supreme Court:

> The Human Rights Act 1998 ... has made people ... more aware of the anomaly of the position whereby the highest court of appeal is situated within one of the chambers of Parliament.[36]

---

34 id., appendix, p. 67.
35 Department of Constitutional Affairs (DCA), *Constitutional Reform: a new way of appointing judges* (2003).
36 DCA, *Constitutional Reform: a Supreme Court for the United Kingdom* (2003).

This is more than a point about the inconsistencies of government presentation. Another very practical example of not emphasizing human rights in the delivery of policies is provided by the latest annual report of the Legal Services Commission, responsible for the administration of the Criminal Defence and the Community Legal Services. This contains no mention of the Commission's commitment to human rights and conflates the role of the defence lawyer with taking 'a proactive role in tackling the causes of offending and re-offending behaviour'.[37] The Commission then proceeds to state:

> We aim to target available resources on highest priority clients and where legal aid interventions can add the greatest value and provide the most beneficial outcomes. An example of our work is the Reducing Offending through Advice Scheme ...[38]

This may be defended as loose language taken out of context. But, it is more an illustration of the potential problems of lack of clarity over objectives and how distortion within government filters down into other agencies. The overall purpose of the benefit formerly known as criminal legal aid is to ensure due process. Its available resources are actually targeted, entirely correctly, on ensuring that the innocent go free. That involves putting prosecution to proof. Convictions are correctly impeded. The danger of reductionism at this level is that, at its crudest, the best way to hit an increase in convictions would be to withdraw legal aid. That is not what the government, nor the Commission mean or probably even understand. It does, however, illustrate a severe potential distortion that develops from a confused statement of aims. At a very practical level, it must be dangerous for a body like the Legal Services Commission to be advancing its priorities in terms which are little short of nonsensical. Proper constitutional protections should be celebrated, not concealed. The Commission's statement only makes sense if words of qualification are inserted so that it reads 'any available resources in addition to those used to meet our core functions'.

Beyond this specific example is a wider problem. Lord Falconer asserts that the rule of law is safe with him and within his department's brief:

> As Ministerial Head of a significant Department of State, responsible not just for the administration of the courts and legal aid, but also for politically sensitive issues such as human rights, freedom of information, methods of election, devolution, and constitutional affairs, [the Secretary of State for Constitutional Affairs] should be free to concentrate on those very important roles. But just as significantly, there is no doubt he has a special obligation to put the values of justice, the independence of the judiciary, and the rule of law above partisan considerations ... The function – as voice of the rule of law within the Cabinet – is critical. I have identified it as a function, but it goes beyond that. It expresses the values for which the role stands. That voice is as

---

37 Legal Services Commission, *Annual Report 2003/4* (2004) 17.
38 id.

part of government, not separate from it. It ensures there is a counter-weight to the pressures which come from other departments and Ministers. The rule of law must apply everywhere. There cannot be any no-go areas.[39]

This raises pertinent questions. Just how reconcilable at a practical level are, first, a ministerial responsibility for human rights and, secondly, for the rule of law with the more conventional 'management' brief for which Lord Falconer hankers. We have the example of the DCA's objectives, its silence over human rights in relation to legal aid, and the lack of much appreciation by the Legal Services Commisison. There are indications of difficulty. The DCA's main objective is shared with the Home Office. But, most tellingly, Lord Falconer did not oppose publicly, nor – so far as has been revealed – privately, the outrageous intention to remove judicial review of asylum claims by the legislation that became the Asylum (Treatment of Claimants) Act 2004. The extent to which this went beyond justifiable proposals to speed up asylum hearings to an attack on the constitution do not appear to have been appreciated by the Secretary of State. Indeed, there is a feeling abroad among the judiciary and press that the Attorney-General has more understanding. For example, the influential Joshua Rosenberg reported in the *Daily Telegraph*:

> Although others in Government – including the Attorney General, Lord Goldsmith – wanted to toss out the ouster clause, Lord Falconer appeared to pay no attention to the growing dissent – until his hand was forced by Lord Irvine, his predecessor. A stronger minister would have stood up to Mr Blunkett, telling him earlier that his proposals were unacceptable.[40]

David Blunkett set himself up as lightning rod for the government's restiveness at the judiciary and the broader effects of the Human Rights Act. He was happy to tell the BBC:

> Frankly, I am personally fed up with having to deal with a situation where parliament debates issues and the judges then overturn them. We were aware of the circumstances, we did mean what we said and, on behalf of the British people, we are going to implement it.[41]

Mr Blunkett himself showed no sign of having understood the finer points of what Parliament itself decided in Section 3 of the Act, the first constitutional bombshell for which the government was responsible. The problem is, however, more widespread within government than just the expressions of a recalcitrant and populist Home Secretary. One of Lord Falconer's continuing refrains has been that a fundamental objective is the creation of a human rights culture and not human rights litigation. This has been a central concern in the development of ideas for a Commission for Equalities and Human Rights. He told the Human Rights Lawyers Association:

39 Lord Falconer, 'Advancing Global Citizenship: The protection of Human Rights and the rule of law in an insecure world', speech at RSA conference, 13 July 2004.
40 J. Rozenberg, *Daily Telegraph*, 6 May 2004.
41 *World at One*, 19 February 2003.

The type of culture we need was very well defined by the Parliamentary Joint Human Rights Committee. They said this: 'A culture of respect for human rights would exist when there was a widely-shared sense of:

- entitlement to these rights, of
- personal responsibility and of respect for the rights of others and when this
- influenced all our institutional policies and practices.'

This is about much more than legal cases. It is about the whole apparatus of how the State and public authorities operate.[42]

This government has some way further to go to demonstrate that a human rights culture has permeated the substance of government policy as well as the form of government. The danger of insufficiently incorporating human rights within the institutions of government is evident: the Conservative Party has committed itself to a review of its provisions. The practical possibility of repeal of the Act is probably, for a variety of reasons, low. However, the toying with its repeal by the largest party of opposition is an indication of the thinness of its constitutional acceptance.

The Human Rights Act was itself a bold constitutional reform for which the government should be praised. So too was the essence of its reforms of the constitution in relation to the judiciary and the Lord Chancellor. The government's commitment to diversity in the judiciary is exemplary. We will hopefully be able to agree with Lord Falconer in a final assessment of the Constitutional Reform Act as it will emerge from its long sojourn through Parliament:

These proposals will put the relationship between Parliament, the Government and judges on a modern footing. We will have a proper separation of powers and we will further strengthen the independence of judges.[43]

We need, however, one further step: the full internalization by government, led by the Department of Constitutional Affairs, of a practical commitment to human rights and the rule of law that will lead to a genuine human rights culture of which the government and its ministers can be seen as true champions. The Constitutional Reform Bill has focused us too much on form. We need more substance.

42 17 February 2004.
43 DCA press release, 14 July 2004.